State Politics in
Contemporary India

Westview Replica Editions

The concept of Westview Replica Editions is a response to the continuing crisis in academic and informational publishing. Library budgets for books have been severely curtailed. Ever larger portions of general library budgets are being diverted from the purchase of books and used for data banks, computers, micromedia, and other methods of information retrieval. Interlibrary loan structures further reduce the edition sizes required to satisfy the needs of the scholarly community. Economic pressures on the university presses and the few private scholarly publishing companies have severely limited the capacity of the industry to properly serve the academic and research communities. As a result, many manuscripts dealing with important subjects, often representing the highest level of scholarship, are no longer economically viable publishing projects—or, if accepted for publication, are typically subject to lead times ranging from one to three years.

Westview Replica Editions are our practical solution to the problem. We accept a manuscript in camera-ready form, typed according to our specifications, and move it immediately into the production process. As always, the selection criteria include the importance of the subject, the work's contribution to scholarship, and its insight, originality of thought, and excellence of exposition. The responsibility for editing and proofreading lies with the author or sponsoring institution. We prepare chapter headings and display pages, file for copyright, and obtain Library of Congress Cataloging in Publication Data. A detailed manual contains simple instructions for preparing the final typescript, and our editorial staff is always available to answer questions.

The end result is a book printed on acid-free paper and bound in sturdy library-quality soft covers. We manufacture these books ourselves using equipment that does not require a lengthy make-ready process and that allows us to publish first editions of 300 to 600 copies and to reprint even smaller quantities as needed. Thus, we can produce Replica Editions quickly and can keep even very specialized books in print as long as there is a demand for them.

About the Book and Editor

State Politics in Contemporary India: Crisis or Continuity?
edited by John R. Wood

Although the Congress Party has dominated Indian national politics in recent years, a more uncertain picture has emerged at the level of India's twenty-two states. Tensions resulting from modernization and increased popular participation in politics have aroused unprecedented factionalism in Congress-run states and brought opposition parties to power in others; in a few states, democratic government has been forced to a standstill. Prior to her assassination in October 1984, Prime Minister Indira Gandhi strove to control state politics, but her efforts brought charges of interference and manipulation and, in some states, triggered massive violence.

Does this unrest point to a profound crisis in the politics of the world's most populous democracy? The evidence from some of the states suggest a continuation of past trends while current developments in others seem more ominous. The articles in this book examine the politics of seven of India's major states during the Indira Gandhi years to assess the effects of central government's intervention and the intensification of political conflict. Among the themes covered are the political results of social and economic change, the rise of previously disadvantaged groups in politics, struggles over agrarian benefits, electoral strategies and performance, the fragmentation and "de-institutionalization" of political parties, and the changing nature of the relations between the states and the central government.

Dr. John R. Wood holds a Ph.D. in political science from Columbia University and is associate professor of political science at the University of British Columbia, Vancouver, Canada.

To our fellow social scientists
at the
Centre for the Study of Developing Societies, Delhi

State Politics in Contemporary India
Crisis or Continuity?

edited by John R. Wood

Westview Press / Boulder and London

A Westview Replica Edition

Copyright © 1984 by Westview Press, Inc.

Published in 1984 in the United States of America by Westview Press, Inc., 5500 Central Avenue, Boulder, Colorado 80301; Frederick A. Praeger, Publisher

Library of Congress Cataloging in Publication Data
Wood, John R.
   State politics in Contemporary India.
   (A Westview replica edition)
   Bibliography: p.
   Includes index.
   1. State governments—India—Addresses, essays,
lectures. 2. Political parties—India—States—
Addresses, essays, lectures. I. Title.
JQ298.8.W66   1984   320.2′0954   84-15243
ISBN 0-8133-7002-7

Composition for this book was provided by the editor
Printed and bound in the United States of America

10   9   8   7   6   5   4   3   2   1

Contents

Tables and Map

Preface

This volume grew out of a panel on Indian state politics presented at the thirty-sixth Annual Meeting of the Association for Asian Studies in Washington, D.C., on March 24, 1984. Brass, Kohli, Manor and Wood gave papers and Church served as discussant; subsequently, Blair, who chaired the panel, and Lele and Varkey generously offered to participate as well. All of the papers were revised and edited speedily in order to take advantage of Westview Press' rapid publication and distribution through the Replica Edition process.

Our wish to make these papers directly available to a wider audience is motivated by an awareness that 1985 will be an important year for Indian politics. In 1985 it is expected that the Indian electorate will, for the eighth time since Independence, go to the polls in a national election; as well, 1985 marks the centennial of the Indian National Congress, whose current incarnation governs India under Indira Gandhi's leadership. We believe this is an appropriate occasion for students of Indian public life to take stock of the Indira Gandhi years and to assess the performance of the party which has dominated Indian politics almost uninterruptedly since 1947. Our contribution to this enterprise is to examine politics in the Indian states, where Indira Gandhi and the Congress(I) face many challenges and challengers in a continual struggle for power.

Apart from a few memorable studies of individual states, the systematic analysis of Indian state politics was largely neglected until 1967 when two pioneering efforts, one by Iqbal Narain and the other by Myron Weiner and both entitled *State Politics in India*, emerged to set the standard for symposia on state political activity. While in this collection we have discussed recurring themes and patterns of political change in the states we have studied, we have not tried to emulate Narain's or Weiner's efforts to construct an overall comparative framework for the analysis of Indian state politics. Such a framework might now be too confining. This is because Indian politics, particularly at the state level, have become vastly more complicated in recent years. Not only has India created more states, but major developments, such as the Congress Party splits of 1969 and 1978, the de-linking of national and state elections, the proliferation of new parties and "fronts," the imposition of Emergency rule during 1975–77, and the trial of Janata Party government during 1977–79, have altered many landmarks in the Indian political scene. In addition, remarkable changes in Indian social and economic life have created new and divergent contexts for political behavior in each state. All of these changes, plus an unprecedented outpouring of literature by social scientists who have struggled to keep up with them, have made the task of understanding Indian state politics in the 1980s more daunting than it was in the 1960s.

The task of editing has been made less daunting by the assistance of many individuals and institutions. My thanks go to Barbara Ramusack of the 1984 Association for Asian Studies Program Committee, for her support in arranging the original panel; Robert L. Hardgrave, Jr., for proposing publication and Dean Birkenkamp for supporting it; H.B. Chamberlain of *Pacific Affairs* for editorial encouragement and permission to republish a section of Atul Kohli's article; Akhileshwar Jha of Chanakya Publications for permission to republish Paul Brass' article; Paul Marantz for his tireless sharing of wordprocessing wisdom; and Frank Flynn of Arts Computing, UBC for daring us to use TEXTFORM. The University of British Columbia provided support in the form of a Humanities and Social Sciences research grant and a British Columbia Department of Labour youth employment grant. The latter funded Michael Kirkwood, my student assistant, without whose mastery of wordprocessing and patient typing of innumerable drafts this project would never have been completed.

I wish to thank all of the participating authors for their willingness to produce and revise their contributions within a tight time schedule. Each of them is perforce responsible for his analysis of politics in his own state; I confess accountability for any editing errors that may remain.

Finally, to my family, for whom the summer of '84 was divided between a maternal dissertation and a paternal book, my fondest gratitude.

Vancouver   John R. Wood
September 1984

ADDENDUM TO THE PREFACE

Only hours before this book was to be printed, the news arrived: Indira Gandhi is dead, assassinated by gunmen seeking revenge for her government's intervention in Punjab in June 1984. Rajiv Gandhi, her son, has taken over as prime minister amidst great communal tension and political uncertainty. It is not known at the time of writing whether the expected general election will be held, delayed, or postponed indefinitely.

Indira Gandhi's India is now history, and the question in our subtitle seems to be answered: India *is* in crisis. On top of the numerous problems delineated in this book, one might now add that with Mrs. Gandhi gone, the authority of India's central political institutions is weakened; the apparatus for maintaining law and order is stretched dangerously thin; the security of a significant minority is in doubt and Indian secular norms are under great stress. Mrs. Gandhi's violent end is a stark reminder of the precariousness of civil society within a context of enormous social complexity, persistent economic scarcity, and growing political impatience.

The fact that Mrs. Gandhi's assassination arose directly out of a problem in center–state relations underlines this book's main theme: the growing importance of state politics in all–India governance. Here we have a continuity which will extend long after the current crisis. Indira Gandhi's dilemma, as I have described it in my Introduction, will also be Rajiv Gandhi's. In order to survive politically at the Center, he must exert influence in state politics; however, in attempting to do so he risks dissidence within his own party's ranks and alienation, or worse, outside them. Perhaps in the aftermath of his mother's tragic death Rajiv will be able to consolidate his party's power if Indian voters, fearing instability, decide to place their faith in Congress(I) governments as opposed to less predictable alternatives. Whatever the outcome, those charged with governing India in the post–Indira years will, more than ever before, have to understand and conciliate the divergent needs and demands of the Indian states.

November 1, 1984   J.R.W.

Contributors

HARRY W. BLAIR, Professor of Political Science at Bucknell University, Lewisburg, Pennsylvania, U.S.A.

PAUL R. BRASS, Professor of Political Science and South Asian Studies at the University of Washington, Seattle, Washington, U.S.A.

RODERICK CHURCH, Associate Professor of Politics at Brock University, St. Catherines, Ontario, Canada

ATUL KOHLI, Assistant Professor of Politics and the Woodrow Wilson School, Princeton University, Princeton, New Jersey, U.S.A.

JAYANT LELE, Professor of Sociology at Queen's University, Kingston, Ontario, Canada

JAMES MANOR, Lecturer in Politics at the University of Leicester, Leicester, England, and Editor of the *Journal of Commonwealth and Comparative Politics*

OUSEPH VARKEY, Associate Professor of Political Science at East Stroudsburg University, East Stroudsburg, Pennsylvania, U.S.A.

JOHN R. WOOD, Associate Professor of Political Science at the University of British Columbia, Vancouver, British Columbia, Canada

THE STATES OF INDIA

1

Introduction: Continuity and Crisis in Indian State Politics

John R. Wood

As India prepares for its eighth general election since Independence, there is much speculation about the ability of Indira Gandhi's Congress(I) Party to repeat its election victory of 1980. Myron Weiner has suggested that that election, in which Mrs. Gandhi rose from her 1977 defeat to trounce the remnants of the Janata Party coalition, brought India back to political normality.[1] According to Weiner, this meant "the combination of a popular prime minister, an institutionally weak governing party, a fragmented opposition, and a deteriorating economy."[2] Many observers would argue that these "business as usual" conditions – with all the variations and exceptions India inevitably produces – persist at mid-decade and indicate a continuation of Congress(I) government for the rest of the 1980s.

Others, including several authors in this volume, are more pessimistic.[3] They point out that although Congress(I) won convincingly in the 1980 national elections, it has been beset ever since by dissidence and factionalism from within and by regionalist parties and secessionist movements from without. According to these authors, Indira Gandhi's government – ordinarily characterized by strong personal and centralized rulership – appears unable to direct and control events. In many parts of India the struggle for scarce resources has so eroded political values and institutions that government has lost most of its integrity and authority.

These developments, which, in the pessimists' view, add up to a serious crisis for the Indian political system in the mid-1980s, are most dramatically revealed in the politics of the Union's twenty-two states.

The significance of the states, many as large and populous as the countries of Europe, is little understood outside of India. Whereas India's states were originally regarded as little more than subordinate components of a highly centralized governmental structure, it is now clear that the political relationship between the Center and the states is an interdependent one. While the states must recognize the Center's constitutional superiority and, in varying degrees, depend on New Delhi for financial support, they have also been evolving as powerful political arenas in their own right. Those who rule at the Center may try to influence the outcomes of the struggles in these arenas but, in the end, they must come to terms with the combatants. The combatants who lose may represent a growing political force that cannot, ultimately, be suppressed. The combatants who win, meanwhile, control political resources — organization, money, votes — that are of vital importance to the central rulers. Thus, especially in the bigger or more affluent states, the winners at the state level are able to assert their power against the power of the Center. Center–state relations in India used to be described as cooperative. Now they are conflictual, and they appear to be mutually weakening.

It has been a commonplace since Mughal times that India is too large and complex to be governed from a central capital. As Paul Brass has recently argued, despite periodic appearances to the contrary, the long–term tendency in India is towards pluralism, regionalism, and decentralization.[4] One of the fundamental reasons for this is that significant political change in India occurs first at the state level and subsequently shapes national political processes. State governments, in effect, are in the front line when it comes to coping with the tensions produced by socio–economic change. The struggles over land and agrarian benefits, the pressures produced by industrialization and urbanization, the demands for education, jobs, better health and living standards — all of these must be dealt with by state governments. New Delhi can produce national plans, but it is too far away from developmental realities to make them work; it is in the states where allocations are effectively decided and implemented.[5]

It is in the states, too, where many of India's most ambitious politicians concentrate their energies. They directly represent and serve the needs, not only of territorial constituencies, but frequently the more tangible ones of primordial groups.[6] Members of the Legislative Assembly (MLAs) in a given state may differ on ideological or programmatic grounds; class, sectoral or regional interests may also divide them. But over and above these interests, or interwoven among them, primordial interests and ties – usually expressed in caste or communal terms – continue to be powerful determinants of political activity at the state level. Moreover, three decades of democratic elections have brought more and more primordial groups to an awareness of the rewards to be had in politics. Primordial politics, social scientists are now well aware, not only imply that primordial ties influence political behavior; modern democratic politics in turn secularize the meaning of primordial relationships.[7] But as the essays in this collection and virtually all scholarship on Indian state politics demonstrate, struggles for power between castes or communal groups, however secularized, are intensifying.[8] While the struggles may occur at any site from the village upwards, they are usually focussed most significantly at the state level where the rewards for winning – or the penalties for losing – are greatest.

INDIRA GANDHI'S DILEMMA

Throughout her Prime Ministership, Mrs. Gandhi has felt continually challenged to intervene in state politics and her tendency to do so has increased in the 1980s. Many have viewed her involvement as a force for national unity and progressive action, but others have seen it as a disruptive interference which undermines the integrity of state government. The Prime Minister's dilemma is that her, and the Congress(I)'s, electoral and governmental success – some would say survival – depends on her ability to control politics in the states. Her attempts to exert control, however, often produce dissidence, alienation, and increasingly, violent opposition.

The most vivid illustrations of this dilemma have occurred recently in three border states: Punjab, Assam, and Jammu and Kashmir. A detailed analysis of the politics of these states is not presented in this volume; each day's newspaper headlines unfold new dimensions of complexity in them and they may be too controversial for dispassionate study.[9] But even a brief reference reveals the elements of continuity and crisis which in one way or another are inherent in the politics of all the states of India.

In Punjab, the struggle for power between the Akali Dal party and an incumbent Congress government dates back to Independence. The demand by Sikh separatists for an independent Khalistan originated in the trauma of Partition, which highlighted the Sikh minority's plight of being squeezed between Muslim and Hindu majorities in what were to become

Pakistani and Indian Punjab respectively.[10] In the aftermath, the Akali Dal
in India's Punjab developed its role as defender of Sikh interests against
Congress governments in the state and at the Center. Though it won a
major victory in agitating for a Sikh–dominated Punjabi Subah (province)
in 1966, the Akali Dal was always able to find and champion further Sikh
causes in the succeeding years — protection for Sikh religious rights, access
to inter–state river water and other developmental resources, and
exclusive possession of Chandigarh as Punjab's capital. The Akali Dal
rode these demands to victory in the 1977 election and formed a coalition
government. Indira Gandhi's return to national power in 1980, however,
brought in its wake the dismissal of the Akali Dal government, the
imposition of President's Rule and, after fresh state elections, the return of
a Congress(I) government in Chandigarh. In the turbulence that followed,
Sikh extremists under Sant Jarnail Singh Bhindranwale revived the
demand for Khalistan and fanned Sikh discontent with terrorist violence.
Moderate Sikhs projected their demands in the form of the Anandpur
Sahib resolution of 1973, which would give Punjab greater autonomy
within the Indian federation. With an eye to other states' autonomist
designs, the Center largely ignored these demands. Meanwhile, the
Congress(I) state government, thrust on the defensive amidst escalating
Sikh–Hindu   bloodshed,   became   increasingly   unable   to   govern.
President's Rule was again imposed, and then, on June 6, 1984, the central
government, to the world's amazement, sent in the army to militarily
defeat the terrorists and control the state. Whether its resolute action will
serve to extinguish the secessionist threat or create a new generation of
Khalistan sympathizers remains to be seen.

In Assam, geographically India's most peripheral and, many
Assamese would allege, India's most neglected state, regionalist sentiments
have similarly been in a state of ferment for many years.[11] Native
Assamese antagonism against in–migrants from other parts of India,
principally Bengalis, was longstanding but it increased greatly as a result of
the refugee influx from Bangladesh both before and after the secessionist
war of 1971. The Assamese, fearing the subordination of their language
and culture and protesting Bengali dominance in administrative and
economic activity, struck back in 1979 when it became known that illegal
aliens from Bangladesh had swollen the voters' lists. So violent was the
reaction that the January 1980 elections in Assam were postponed. The
All–Assam Students' Union staged demonstrations that were met by police
firing, and the crisis quickly escalated when extremists cut rail links to the
rest of India and interrupted Assam's oil production. Mrs. Gandhi and
the central government undertook negotiations with moderate agitators

and installed a Congress(I)–led coalition ministry in December 1980, but it lasted less than six months. When it became constitutionally imperative to hold an election in Assam in February 1983, the voters' list issue had still not been resolved — because, the agitators charged, the illegal aliens would vote for the Congress(I). Amidst unprecedented violence and an election boycott, the election produced an overwhelming Congress(I) majority on a voter turnout of less than 33 percent. Since 1983, New Delhi has strengthened the hand of Assam's state government with infusions of military and economic aid. Its response to the illegal immigration issue has been to begin building a half–billion dollar fence around the Bangladesh border. The Assamese attitude to these moves has been underlined by fresh AASU–led violence in June 1984. Assam remains, in the words of one observer, "an undetonated bomb that could go off at any moment."[12]

Political developments in Jammu and Kashmir did not attract much attention until after the Indian army crackdown in Punjab in June 1984. The link between the two states was obvious: the security of Jammu and Kashmir was threatened by instability in Punjab, which links it to the rest of India. Moreover, reports of Sikh extremists using the Jammu area as a staging ground for violence in Punjab heightened New Delhi's concern to tighten its grip on the northernmost state. Jammu and Kashmir, claimed by Pakistan in 1947, but with its most populous portion held by India after the Kashmir war ceasefire in 1948, has gradually been governed like other states.[13] The original post–Independence government of the National Conference party in the state was led by Sheikh Abdullah, the hero of the nationalist movement in Kashmir, but he was dismissed and jailed by the central government in 1953. He remained popular despite a succession of badly factionalized National Conference and Congress governments and eventually an accord reached between Abdullah and Mrs. Gandhi in 1975 resulted in his reinstatement as Chief Minister. Mrs. Gandhi wanted the Sheikh to join the Congress, but he continued as President of the National Conference and, before he died in September 1982, passed on its leadership to his son, Farooq Abdullah. Farooq's first major test came in June 1983 in a mid–term state election which the National Conference easily won. But Congress(I) victories in the Hindu–majority Jammu constituencies, resulting from an appeal to Hindu sentiment in which Mrs. Gandhi joined, drove Farooq into an anti–Center posture and an alliance with Muslim communalist and secessionist forces in the Kashmir valley. In May 1984 the National Conference split, and Farooq's estranged brother–in–law, Ghulam Mohammad Shah, organized a meeting of National Conference dissidents to "expel" Abdullah.[14] This set the stage, a month after the Indian army's entry into the Golden Temple in Amritsar, for a toppling of Abdullah's ministry in which Shah and eleven dissident National Conference MLAs defected and then were rapidly asked to form a ministry in coalition with the Congress(I). Abdullah protested that Jammu and Kashmir's anti-defection law disqualifies defecting MLAs from voting in the State Assembly, and he called for a legislative vote of confidence. The newly-appointed Governor refused, and dismissed him. In response to mass demonstrations and a *bandh* (work stoppage) launched by Abdullah's supporters, seventeen battalions of the Indian army were deployed in the Kashmir valley in July 1984.[15]

It may be argued that Punjab, Assam, and Jammu and Kashmir are "special cases" because of their unique geographical locations, their peculiar communal problems, and their critical roles in preserving India's military security. There is no doubt that their internal politics and center-state relationships are extraordinarily vexed at present. But in a very real sense *all* of the Indian states are "special cases," each possessing particular historical, geographic, cultural, or economic conditions which give rise to idiosyncratic problems of governance. Over half of the Indian states have sensitive international borders, and most have distinctive minorities, whether communal, linguistic, tribal, or regional. Virtually every state lays claim to a special cultural heritage and most can mount a case for being "neglected" or "maltreated" by New Delhi.[16]

The Punjab, Assam, and Jammu and Kashmir cases suggest a number of themes which are echoed in an increasing number of states. The first is that the stakes in Indian state politics are higher, far higher, than ever before. This is clearly indicated by the rapidity of the resort to extra-constitutional means and the use of violence both by opponents of government and government itself. Conflictual tactics, including preemptive ones, which even a decade ago would have seemed illegitimate or unnecessary are now readily used. Second, the battle lines are primordially drawn and involve deeper primordial passions the more the conflict intensifies. This is partly because developmental gains or losses are involved for primordial groups, but also because politicians are more willing to exploit primordial ambitions or fears in order to win. Third, the desperation of the central government to maintain control at any cost is evident, and also the increasing cost of its intervention. The main cost lies in the weakening of state political institutions where, previously, conflicts might have been worked out more peacefully. Thus New Delhi's intervention becomes self-defeating: as state governments become weaker more and more central intervention is required to control events.

This brings us back to Mrs. Gandhi's dilemma. To understand it we must grapple with several questions. Should the states as presently constituted and governed be allowed to develop as strong political arenas within the larger Indian Union? Or do their divergencies threaten Indian national integrity? Within the states, can there be a greater sharing of political and economic benefits through enhanced restratification and distribution? Or will such sharing only exacerbate primordial conflict and endanger political stability? And can this stability, along with that of the country as a whole, be maintained without increasing intervention in state politics by New Delhi?

There are no simple answers to these questions, as the contributions to this book will testify. During the years of Indira Gandhi's Prime Ministership, however, evidence has been accumulating which, *mutatis mutandis*, predicts a number of trends which generally apply in all the states.

STATE-BUILDING: INTERVENTION VERSUS AUTONOMY

Out of India's inheritance of fourteen jurisdictions of British India and five hundred and fifty-odd states of princely India emerged twenty-nine states in the Constitution of 1950.[17] Then followed the agitations for the linguistic reorganization of states, and, by 1956, after the major thrust of this reorganization was completed, India had fourteen states.[18] By the end of the Nehru era, the number of states had risen to sixteen; during Indira Gandhi's Prime Ministership another six have been added (see Table 1:1).

The process of state formation has, since Independence, involved intervention by the Center in state politics. Central intervention occurred in some cases for reasons of strategic security or administrative efficiency, but most frequently to accommodate a primordial demand. The Center in virtually every instance created states in response to pressure exerted by primordial groups that had the most to gain by acquiring statehood. In some instances, the decision appeared to be weakly reactive. But it was usually manipulative as the Center sought to outbid the primordialists and to ensure the installation of a state government that would support or at least not undermine national unity.

Table 1:1

The Indian States: Creation Dates, Area, Population

States	Creation Date	Area (*sq. km.*)	Population (1981)
Andhra Pradesh	1956*	276,814	53,403,619
Assam	1950**	78,523	19,902,826
Bihar	1950*	173,876	69,823,154
Gujarat	1960	195,984	33,960,905
Haryana	1966	44,222	12,850,902
Himachal Pradesh	1971	55,673	4,237,569
Jammu and Kashmir	1950	101,283	5,981,600
Karnataka	1956*	191,773	37,043,451
Kerala	1956	38,864	25,403,217
Madhya Pradesh	1956*	442,841	52,131,717
Maharashtra	1960	307,762	62,693,898
Manipur	1972	22,356	1,433,691
Meghalaya	1972	22,489	1,327,824
Nagaland	1963	16,527	773,281
Orissa	1950	155,782	26,272,054
Punjab	1966	50,362	16,669,755
Rajasthan	1956*	342,214	34,102,912
Sikkim	1975	7,299	315,682
Tamil Nadu	1956*	130,069	48,297,456
Tripura	1972	10,477	2,060,189
Uttar Pradesh	1950*	294,413	110,858,019
West Bengal	1950	87,853	54,485,560

Source: *Constitution of India* (Lucknow: Eastern Book Co., 1981), pp. 154–8, and *The Statesman's Year-Book* (London: Macmillan, 1983) pp. 609–610.

Note: Creation date refers to date of acquisition of statehood under the Constitution of 1950 or, apart from minor adjustments (*), of present boundaries. Assam's territory (**), was successively reduced in 1963 and in 1972 with the reorganization of the north-eastern areas. Figures for Jammu and Kashmir exclude Pakistan-occupied territory.

This meant a state-building process which, above all, served the electoral and governmental interests of the Congress Party. The risk of national fragmentation which might result from state-building in response to primordial demands was seen to be counterbalanced by the national reach and integrative strengths of the predominant party. The "Congress system" became renowned for its resilience and its ability to create consensus out of diversity.[19] Moreover, where state governments were captured by non-Congress parties or coalitions, the Center had a variety of options. The non-Congress government might be isolated, or tolerated if its leadership was willing to adjust to central Congress government interests. Where it represented a real threat, the constitutional provisions for President's Rule could be used until a state government more amenable to central control could be installed.

For the first two decades, in most of the states and most of the time, these interventionist measures were minimally employed and the states were able to develop as relatively autonomous political arenas. The image of strong states in a strong Union was encouraged by linguistic reorganization, by the effective use of the constitutional powers given to the states, and most of all, by the freedom of state units of the Congress Party to build mass bases. During the Nehru years, strong state leadership was allowed to grow; most of these leaders could be trusted by New Delhi as they had been socialized in the nationalist movement and were allied to the central leadership by shared values or personal ties.

Thus, in the 1960s the power of state leaders and the autonomy of their state polities appeared to increase, but with the general election of 1967 the Congress "system" received a major setback. The clamor for increased political participation exacerbated Congress factionalism and bolstered opposition parties. The Congress majority at the Center was severely reduced in 1967; at the state level, six non-Congress governments came to power and the Congress was forced to enter shaky coalitions in four more. Here was a turning point in Indian state politics: "one-party dominance" in its original form was gone.[20] Voters learned that their ballots could remove Congress governments. Non-Congress politicians began to taste the fruits of wielding ministerial power. In many states the years 1967–1971 were years of great uncertainty and instability. The "politics of defection," practised by Congress and non-Congress forces alike, turned the toppling of state governments into a game and introduced new lows of political morality.[21] Most significantly, the Congress Party split of 1969 shook the political system of each state to its foundations as state party factions sought desperately to ascertain or to influence which

Congress — Indira Gandhi's ruling Congress(R) or the opposition Congress(O) — would emerge victorious.

Eventually, as the results of the 1971 general and 1972 state elections showed, Indira Gandhi's Congress(R) won convincingly not only at the Center but in nearly every state. However, while Congress predominance appeared to have been reestablished throughout India, its organizational basis was not. In order to survive the Congress split, and since the old Congress organization remained largely in Congress(O) hands, Mrs. Gandhi had resorted to a populist electoral strategy. Congress(R) governments in the states came to power on the strength of her charisma and reformist appeal and, lacking a solid base, looked to her to appoint chief ministers and resolve intra–party disputes. These disputes multiplied rapidly, principally between old and new arrivistes on the Indira bandwagon. Mrs. Gandhi's interventions — particularly where she picked chief ministers whose primary qualification was personal loyalty to her — aroused antagonism among other contenders for power. Popular cynicism grew when bad monsoons and rising prices undermined the Congress(R) pledge to "abolish poverty."

Meanwhile, opposition parties, many of whose leaders had grasped state governmental power but had been submerged in the Indira wave, became less inhibited in their efforts to recover their position. During 1974–75 they, along with frustrated Congress dissidents, helped to instigate populist agitations in Gujarat and Bihar. The Center's repression of these agitations led to Mrs. Gandhi's declaration of an all–India Emergency in 1975. During the Emergency, central attempts to suppress opposition and control state politics created the conditions for the formation of the Janata Front coalition of opposition forces which won power in New Delhi in 1977. The Janata government, in order to consolidate its victory and ensure election of its Presidential candidate — despite protests regarding the constitutional legitimacy of the move — dissolved state assemblies and staged fresh elections in eleven states. It won decisively in seven; West Bengal returned a solid Communist Party (Marxist) majority and regional parties prevailed in three others (Punjab, Jammu and Kashmir, and Tamil Nadu). By the end of 1978, only two states in all of India had Congress governments. Here was another turning point, then: India experienced its first non–Congress government in New Delhi and an unprecedented proliferation of non–Congress governments in the states. The result was another Congress split, creation of the Congress (Indira) Party and the redoubling of its leader's and followers' determination to regain power.

A detailed analysis of what happened to state politics in India during the brief and eventually chaotic rule of the Janata coalition in New Delhi would be far too lengthy and complicated for a brief introduction. This is because with less intervention by New Delhi in state politics than ever before what James Manor calls "the natural heterogeneity" of the Indian states reasserted itself.[22] Not only were nine of the states eventually ruled by parties or fronts with no base beyond their own state, but those under Janata governments were ruled by amalgams of local interests, for the most part consisting of locally dominant middle–peasant castes. The Janata government in New Delhi, because it was preoccupied with its own fragmentation and was dependent for its survival on the support of state Janata units, left the state governments to go their separate ways. In some states this allowed energetic governments to pursue progressive action; in others, the results were drift and corruption. Overall, however, until the political revival of Indira Gandhi's fortunes and the collapse of the Janata coalition in July 1979, politics in the states remained relatively free of New Delhi's influence.

STATE POLITICS IN INDIRA GANDHI'S INDIA: THEN AND NOW

The first period of Indira Gandhi's Prime Ministership spanned eleven years (1966–76); since her return to power in 1980 she has ruled another five years, and if she continues after the anticipated election of 1985 she is likely to be Prime Minister longer than her father, Jawaharlal Nehru, who ruled for eighteen years (1946–64). "Indira Gandhi's India" is a valid phrase: she has put her stamp on a generation of Indian politics. What have been the consequences for the politics of the Indian states?

As already indicated, many of the developments in Indian state politics which are associated with Indira Gandhi's political performance since 1980 were already underway in the first period of her rule. They include her efforts after 1969 to centralize and personalize decision–making within the ruling party and in the country as a whole. Her interventions in state politics took the form of choosing or dismissing chief ministers, deciding state ministerial allocations, and influencing the outcomes of factional struggles in state Congress party units. Her opponents continually accused her of more sinister manipulations: the extraction of money from one state to fund elections in another, the engineering of MLA defections and the overthrow of non–Congress governments, the partisan direction of state governors, and the use of central intelligence and surveillance to control ministers. During Mrs.

Gandhi's Prime Ministership, President's Rule was increasingly invoked, or threatened, to bring states into line.[23] The use of these methods culminated, of course, in the declaration of Emergency in 1975; under its provisions opposition was repressed not only at the national but at the state level (albeit mostly in north India) and non-Congress governments were unseated in a number of states.

While the use of many of these interventionist measures has continued, and even increased, since 1980, it is their consequences which have brought a new context to state politics in India. The first consequence is that central intervention no longer has shock value; in fact, state politicians have learned to manipulate central intervention to their advantage. The overuse of central authority undermines its credibility and the legitimacy of those who benefit by it at the state level. A pervasive side effect is cynicism and distrust where all who are involved in a state-level conflict expect the worst of each other, and act accordingly. Of perhaps greater long-range concern is the public alienation that is a corollary to the cynical behavior of public representatives.

A second consequence of increasing central intervention is the precariousness of state governments. This condition was already prevalent in states like Bihar in the 1960s, but has since become widespread. This is not only because the Center has been more ready to unseat state governments, but because of the fragility of the link between state politicians and their constituencies. State ministers and MLAs see the authority for their continuation in office coming down from above, rather than up from below, from the people who elected them. As a result, while MLAs are as anxious as ever to win favor in their constituencies through the adroit use of whatever patronage they may acquire, they have become less assiduous in building and maintaining a mass base. The state politicians who won office after years of self-sacrifice in the nationalist movement and through social service of the kinds promoted by Mahatma Gandhi are fast disappearing. In their places have risen politicians chosen because of their primordial ties or their access to the increasing amounts of money needed to fight elections.

Much of what I am describing has been characterized as the "de-institutionalization" of Indian politics: the reversal of the process whereby the Congress and other parties built political, social and economic organizations which would channel popular participation into constructive and lasting developmental activity.[24] Many of these institutions — youth, women's, agriculturalists', trade union, and businessmen's organizations;

rural cooperative and lending societies; movements aimed at spreading literacy, increasing Harijan and tribal welfare, or promoting health and family planning — continue to be at least marginally effective. But the more expressly political institutions — *panchayati raj* and other forms of local government, and especially party organization below the state level — have generally languished. The only cadre–type parties functioning effectively in Indian state politics are the Communist Parties and the Bharatiya Janata Party (formerly the Jana Sangh), whose territorial and social bases are quite limited. The Congress Party, meanwhile, during Indira Gandhi's rulership has lapsed into inactivity between elections in most of the states; at the district and *taluka* levels there may be Congress organizations but their role as animators and channels of popular participation is either non–existent or restricted in its benefits to a limited clientele.

State politics in contemporary India may, according to this description, seem stagnant and futile, but that is not at all the case. There is more to gain, or lose, than ever before. Developmental change, while undermined by population increases, is highly visible in many states. Statistics showing impressive if relative rates of growth among the states are plentiful,[25] but they hide the real source of political tension within states: the real (or perceived) disparities, between social groups, between rural dwellers and urbanites, and between regions within states. As Robert Hardgrave has recently noted:

> It is not in the most backward regions and among the most depressed classes that discontent is most likely to manifest itself. Rather, the sources of social unrest are most likely to be found in those regions and among those classes experiencing more rapid change . . . [C]onflict occurs along social fault lines, between groups in competition for the scarce goods of prosperity and power. It occurs most sharply between those groups who are rising and those who feel themselves threatened.[26]

The discontent and conflict Hardgrave writes about have become increasingly virulent in many states during the Indira Gandhi years. They are a reflection of socio–economic gains and losses which are, or are seen to be, politically derived. Mrs. Gandhi's populist rhetoric of *garibi hatao* ("abolish poverty") and her 20–Point Programme have been aimed at those who are most socially deprived and who, not incidentally, possess great voting potential. Her strategy for regaining national power as well as for Congress(I) success at the state level has been to extend her appeal to the disadvantaged: the Harijans (ex–untouchables), the tribals, the minorities (especially the Muslims), and the "other backward classes." The strategy worked well in the 1971 and 1980 elections. But to go on winning their support she has had to deliver more than rhetoric and, where the disadvantaged are both numerous and mobilized, the results can be explosive. First, the well of discontent which she has tried to tap is enormous and, once tapped, hard to control. Second, gains by the previously deprived are viewed as immensely threatening by those above them in the social hierarchy. Particularly in the four–fifths of India which is rural, the middle–peasant castes, many of whom threw their support to Janata and non–Congress parties in the 1970s, regard the rise of their social "inferiors" as a direct challenge to their economic and political position.

And thus an irony in contemporary Indian state politics: although Mrs. Gandhi's populist appeal is universalistic and humanitarian, the reality in most states is a politics which is more frankly particularistic and brutally self–interested than ever before. In order to attract the votes of "the disadvantaged" the Congress(I) must deal with increasing numbers of leaders of groups as primordially organized and self–conscious as they are "deprived." I use quotation marks because their deprivation is relative; as Hardgrave suggests, often these deprived groups are on the rise in socio–economic terms. Their leaders, in particular, are usually beneficiaries of developmental change who, eager to capitalize on the Congress(I)'s promises to raise living standards, are quick to mobilize their groups for political action.

As a direct consequence, higher castes, especially those whose members have hitherto been the socio–economic patrons of the disadvantaged, have mobilized all the more intensively to protect their advantaged positions. How they have done this varies from state to state. In some (Bihar, Gujarat, Uttar Pradesh), they have used violence to intimidate and repress lower caste, Harijan, or tribal "upstarts." In others, as witnessed recently in Bombay and Hyderabad, communal, that is, Hindu–Muslim, violence has erupted from the same general cause. Where the advantaged have hitherto controlled Congress organizations, they struggle to maintain their control; where they have abandoned the Congress and supported opposition parties, their struggle is no less intense. Since the breakup of the Janata coalition in 1979, supporting opposition parties has, in many states, seemed frustratingly futile for the higher castes. In some states, however, such as West Bengal, there has been reconciliation between a non–Congress ruling party and higher caste interests. In others, such as Punjab and Andhra Pradesh, regionalist parties have become the vehicles for discontent.

In the face of this complex and turbulent picture it is extremely difficult to determine whether current political developments at the state level in India represent continuity or crisis. They may be interpreted as a projection of past trends if one analyses them as consequences of a continuing democratization of Indian politics and as tolerable if one believes the accompanying tension to be manageable within the existing institutional framework. Indeed, a great deal of the current ferment in Indian state politics may be seen as healthy, as proof that democratic change is taking hold.

Alternatively, "crisis" may be read into the same developments, but if so, the term needs careful definition. If it is "crisis" in the ominous sense where events are interpreted as leading to a disastrous climax, then analysts would do well to remember that such predictions have proved false in India many times in the past. If, however, "crisis" is understood in the dramatic sense, as a turning point where old norms cease to apply and new ones are created, then the Indira Gandhi years, particularly the post–1980 ones, may be seen as particularly significant for state politics. But here the analyst must again be wary. First, what is an old and what a new norm must be defined and the means of transition explained. Second, the diversity of the Indian states predicts that the norms and the transition will be expressed differently in each case. Some of the states may have passed the turning point, others are at it, still others have yet to reach it. And it is altogether possible that, as with many other Indian paradoxes, the politics of each Indian state may contain elements of *both* continuity and crisis.

Not all of the authors who have contributed to this volume have addressed this issue directly. This is partly because of the way the collection came together, with each author left free to interpret the politics of his state as he saw most fit. To make a familiar virtue of necessity, however, the result represents a sampling not only of the heterogeneity of the states and their politics, but also of analysts' approaches and emphases which are as fruitful as they are diverse.

The articles that follow are presented in a geographically clockwise progression around India, beginning with Uttar Pradesh and Bihar in the north, moving on to West Bengal in the east, Kerala and

Karnataka in the south, and thence to Maharashtra and Gujarat in the west. Paul Brass focusses on Uttar Pradesh politics during the first period of Mrs. Gandhi's rule. He shows how conflicts over agricultural policy were interrelated with caste and factional struggles within the U.P. Congress and how all these conflicts were translated into and affected by the larger Congress–Janata competition at the all–India level. Harry Blair investigates the slow transformation of Bihar's agriculture and the rise of backward caste farmers both in agricultural enterprise and in politics. He explains how a politics of "venality and violence" has developed as the higher castes cling to their established positions. In West Bengal, Atul Kohli presents a different picture: the Communist Party (Marxist) government has consolidated its grip on state government through the combination of a reformist program which has so far not alienated the landholding peasantry, and a careful "strained coexistence" approach to relations with Mrs. Gandhi.

In Kerala, the case of the Left and Democratic Front (LDF) government illustrates the vulnerability of a Marxist–led coalition government which is perceived as too radical. Ouseph Varkey analyses how extreme fragmentation in Kerala's party system and the Center's influence resulted in the defeat of the LDF in 1982. In Karnataka, James Manor investigates the momentous defeat of the Congress(I) in 1983 at the hands of the Janata–Kranti Ranga alliance. Here is a clear case where central intervention, by installing an inept chief minister, proved counterproductive, not only because it precipitated the Congress(I) electoral defeat, but because it disrupted Karnataka's politics by blurring the lines between parties and their social bases.

Jayant Lele examines the chaotic state of Congress(I) politics in Maharashtra, where there have been four chief ministers since 1980. He analyses the state's stagnating economy and the continuation of Congress(I) rule in terms of enduring elite Maratha domination, which although factionalized, is largely impervious to Mrs. Gandhi's influence. In Gujarat, my own study focusses on restratification in the Congress via a strategy which has given greater emphasis to lower caste, Harijan, tribal, and Muslim recruitment. The result has been a departure from the Congress "catch–all" norm and a violent backlash among higher castes in a previously stable state.

In the Conclusion, Roderick Church performs the unenviable task of comparative analysis amidst divergent evidence. He focusses on the crises in political participation and in the party system which, in his words, "have given rise to instability and confusion." On the basis of the case study evidence, Church analyses patterns of political mobilization among lower castes and of their accommodation by higher castes in the different states. He relates these in turn to Mrs. Gandhi's and the Congress(I)'s dilemma of trying to win power electorally and also promote reformist government at the state level.

NOTES

1. Myron Weiner, "Congress Restored: Continuities and Discontinuities in Indian Politics," *Asian Survey* 12:4 (April 1982), p. 347.

2. Myron Weiner, *India at the Polls, 1980: A Study of the Parliamentary Elections* (Washington: American Enterprise Institute, 1983), p. 141.

3. James Manor, "Party Decay and Political Crisis in India," *The Washington Quarterly* 4:3 (Summer 1981), pp. 25–40; Paul Wallace, "Centralization and Depoliticization in South Asia," *Journal of Commonwealth and Comparative Politics* 16 (March 1978), pp. 3–21.

4. Paul R. Brass, "Pluralism, Regionalism and Decentralizing Tendencies in Contemporary Indian Politics," in *The State of South Asia: Problems of National Intergration*, eds. A. Jeyaratnam Wilson and Dennis Dalton (Honolulu: The University Press of Hawaii, 1982), pp. 223–264.

5. Francine R. Frankel, *India's Political Economy, 1947–1977: The Gradual Revolution* (Princeton, N.J.: Princeton University Press, 1978), pp. 293–340 and 548–582.

6. Clifford Geertz has defined primordial attachments as those which stem from the "givens" of social existence — "immediate contiguity and kin connection mainly, but beyond them the givenness that stems from being born into a particular religious community, speaking a particular language, or even a dialect of a language, and following particular social practices." See "The Integrative Revolution: Primordial Sentiments and Civil Politics in the New States," in *Old Societies and New States: The Quest for Modernity in Asia and Africa*, ed. Clifford Geertz (New York: The Free Press, 1963), p. 109.

7. Rajni Kothari, ed., *Caste in Indian Politics* (New Delhi: Orient Longman Ltd, 1970), pp. 3–25; Lloyd I. Rudolph and Susanne Hoeber Rudolph, *The Modernity of Tradition: Political Development in India* (Chicago: The University of Chicago Press, 1967), pp. 29–87.

8. See, for example, three recently published studies by Indian scholars: Babulal Fadia, *State Politics in India*, Vols. I and II (New Delhi: Radiant, 1984); Jawaharlal Pandey, *State Politics in India (A Study*

18 *Wood*

in Coalition Politics in an Indian State) (New Delhi: Uppal, 1982); and Balbir Singh, *State Politics in India: Explorations in Political Process in Jammu and Kashmir* (Delhi: Macmillan, 1982).

9. Just as this volume goes to press yet another crisis appears to have arisen in the state of Andhra Pradesh, where N.T. Rama Rao's Telegu Desam government was toppled on 16 August 1984. Reports of widespread violence, the A.P. Governor's resignation and an opposition party-sponsored all-India general strike suggest that Mrs. Gandhi's dilemma is intensifying as the 1985 elections approach.

10. For background on Punjab politics, see Baldev Raj Nayar, *Minority Politics in the Punjab* (Princeton, N.J.: Princeton University Press, 1966); Dalip Singh, *Dynamics of Punjab Politics* (New Delhi: Macmillan, 1981); and Paul Wallace and Surendra Chopra, eds., *Political Dynamics of Punjab* (Amritsar: Guru Nanak Dev University, 1981).

11. For background on Assam politics, see Myron Weiner, *Sons of the Soil: Migration and Ethnic Conflict in India* (Princeton, N.J.: Princeton University Press, 1978), chapter 3; for the wider northeast Indian context, see V.I.K. Sarin, *India's North-East in Flames* (New Delhi: Vikas, 1980).

12. Robert L. Hardgrave, Jr., "India in 1983: New Challenges, Lost Opportunities," *Asian Survey* 24:2 (February 1984), p. 210.

13. For background on Jammu and Kashmir politics, see Balraj Puri, "Jammu and Kashmir," in *State Politics in India*, ed. Myron Weiner (Princeton, N.J.: Princeton University Press, 1968), pp. 215-243, and Balbir Singh, *State Politics in India*.

14. *Times of India*, May 24, 1984.

15. *Times of India*, July 3-4, 1984.

16. For a comparative account of the general process of regionalization, see Robert L. Hardgrave, Jr., "The Northeast, the Punjab, and the Regionalization of Indian Politics," *Asian Survey* 23:11 (November 1983), pp. 1171-81.

17. The twenty-nine included nine Part A states, mostly composed of ex-British territory, nine Part B states, mostly ex-princely states or amalgams, and eleven Part C and D states, centrally governed like today's territories. See Shriram Maheshwari, *State Governments in India* (Delhi: Macmillan, 1979), p. 7.

18. In Table 1:1 and this volume generally we have ignored India's centrally-governed territories, which have increased in number from six in 1956 to nine today. For the evolution of the states, see Maheshwari, *State Governments in India*, pp.6-32; Fadia, *State Politics in India*, 1, pp. 43-61. See also Jyotirindra Das Gupta, *Language Conflict and National Development: Politics and National Language Policy in*

India (Berkeley: University of California Press, 1970).

19. Rajni Kothari, "The Congress 'System' in India," in Centre for the Study of Developing Societies, *Party System and Election Studies* (Bombay, Allied Published, 1967).

20. Paul R. Brass, "Political Participation, Institutionalization, and Stability in India," in *Asian Political Processes: Essays and Readings,* ed. Henry S. Albinski (Boston: Allyn and Bacon, 1971), p. 194.

21. Subhash C. Kashyap, *The Politics of Defection: A Study of State Politics in India* (Delhi: National Publishing House, 1969).

22. See his article, chapter 6 in this volume.

23. Bhagwan D. Dua, *Presidential Rule in India, 1950–1974: A Study in Crisis Politics* (New Delhi: S. Chand, 1979).

24. James Manor, "Party Decay and Political Crisis in India."

25. See, for example, Harry W. Blair's article in this volume, chapter 3.

26. Robert L. Hardgrave, Jr., *India Under Pressure: Prospects For Political Stability* (Boulder: Westview Press, 1984), p. 25.

2
Division in the Congress and the Rise of Agrarian Interests and Issues in Uttar Pradesh Politics, 1952 to 1977

Paul R. Brass

The years 1967 to 1969 form a major divide in the post–Independence history of the Congress in U.P., which turned out to have even broader implications in the developing struggle for power in the country.[1] Not only did the Congress lose power in the state for the first time, but the party split three ways, the Congress base in the countryside was severely damaged, and a new party was formed, the Bharatiya Kranti Dal (BKD) of Charan Singh, that later formed the core of the Janata coalition that defeated the Congress in the 1977 parliamentary elections. The political struggles of the years after 1967 also brought more clearly to the fore than previously some basic issues of economic development strategy and of the role of agriculture and agrarian interests in the economic development of the country.

The manner in which these striking changes emerged out of the factional conflicts that had dominated the Congress in U.P. during the preceding two decades also provides insights concerning the relationship between power struggles and policy issues in Indian politics and in politics generally. The struggle of personalities and factions that became articulated also into a struggle of policies and principles developed in two stages in the two years between 1967 and 1969. In the first stage, Charan Singh outwitted and outmaneuvered C.B. Gupta, the dominant leader in the state Congress at the time, to become the first non–Congress chief minister of the state on April 3, 1967. Gupta, the man of organization and of patronage, who built a formidable Congress political machine in this huge state through close attention to and cultivation of personal relationships was defeated by Charan Singh, who stood forth as a symbol of personal integrity, with a clear economic policy and a distinctive support base among the middle peasantry and backward castes in the state. The second stage began in 1969, when the Congress split and C.B. Gupta formed the Congress(O) and Charan Singh the BKD, leaving the Congress(I) in U.P. in the hands of Kamalapati Tripathi. In this stage it became clear that only one of the three former Congress factional leaders, Charan Singh, had a mass base and that his challenge to the Congress in this critical state was so formidable as to require the strong and repeated intervention of Mrs. Gandhi and the development of new Congress programs and policies to counter the appeal of the BKD in the countryside. Clear evidence of the mass base of the new political party of Charan Singh was provided in the mid–term election of 1969 when the BKD won 89 seats with more than 21 percent of the vote, a larger share of both seats and votes than that won by any other non–Congress party in the state in any election since Independence. As a consequence of the new challenge posed by the BKD to a Congress weakened in the electorate and reduced in strength in the legislature from its days of dominance in the 1950s and 1960s, agrarian issues and interests became more central than they had been during the Nehru period and it became necessary for competing political forces to pay closer attention to the distinctive interests of different social classes and castes in the north Indian countryside. Agrarian issues and interests also acquired increased importance during these years, which were the early years in the spread of the high yielding varieties of wheat and rice that came to be called the "Green Revolution."

In politics, it is normally the case that policy issues provide a cover behind which struggles for power take place that do not always follow the same lines as the issue struggles. In U.P. for two decades after Independence, there were two lines of conflict within the Congress: a persistent struggle for control over the party organization by rival factional groups and a policy question concerning the role of the peasantry in the economic development of the state. What is remarkable about Congress politics in those days is the extent to which social and policy conflicts were kept hidden under a cover of struggle for power that cut across the social and policy differences separating the main contenders.

Throughout the first twenty years of Congress dominance in U.P. politics, Charan Singh spoke consistently in internal conflicts within the party on behalf of the values of village life, peasant economy, backward castes, and rural democracy. However, he did so mostly in private memoranda and letters, through anonymous press releases, and through books not meant for a mass audience. Only after his defection from the Congress and the formation of the BKD did he present his ideas in public manifestoes and policy statements. In Charan Singh, therefore, we have the case of a man who held a consistent and coherent ideological view, but did not break from a party with whose policies he was in fundamental disagreement until such a break could bring him into power directly. However, when he did make the break, his move led to a transformation of the terms of political debate, of conflict in the countryside, and of the struggle for power in U.P. and at the Center.

FACTIONAL GROUPS IN THE U.P. CONGRESS, 1952 TO 1969

Between 1952 and 1969, Congress politics in party and in government in U.P. were characterized by persistent internal group factionalism which focused around the activities of three leading personalities — C.B. Gupta, Charan Singh, and Kamalapati Tripathi. The three principal groups differed considerably in their leadership styles and composition, in the competence and effectiveness of their leadership, in their regional support bases, and in the social forces supporting them. The core leadership of the Gupta group came principally from urban groups, most notably from the Bania caste category. However, through skillful forging of alliances with powerful rural leaders from the leading rural castes and through the liberal distribution of party and government patronage, a state-wide network was established for this group which remained the strongest in the Congress until the split in 1969. Once deprived of access to both party and government patronage, however, the social base of the group proved to be narrow and the Gupta group did not emerge as a powerful force in its reincarnation as the Congress(O).

In contrast to the Gupta group, Charan Singh and his closest allies and followers were identified with rural peasant interests and values. Although Charan Singh in the Congress never developed a political machine based on patronage ties comparable to that of C.B. Gupta, he did develop a network of relationships in the districts, particularly among the middle caste groups in the state — Jats and Yadavs especially. He also developed for himself a reputation as a man of integrity, action and clear direction in favor of peasant-based agricultural development, especially in the Jat and middle peasant-dominated districts of western U.P. His network of relationships and his personal reputation stood him far better than C.B. Gupta's political skills when Charan Singh left the Congress to form his own party. In contrast to the Gupta group's fate in opposition, Charan Singh's BKD, formed in 1969, emerged in two successive elections as the second strongest party in the state with a strong rural base and with considerable urban support as well.

It is somewhat of an irony that the least cohesive group with the least skillful leadership emerged ultimately in control of the U.P. Congress organization. Tripathi rode to power as chief minister in 1971 only after both Gupta and Charan Singh had departed from the Congress and only on the back of Mrs. Gandhi. He remained in power for more than two years, but he left office in discomfort after a mutiny of the state police forces in 1973 that had to be suppressed by the Indian Army. He was replaced by one of his erstwhile, but none too faithful followers, H.N. Bahuguna, who remained in power until February 1976, when his own ineffectiveness as a leader and his egocentric behavior led Mrs. Gandhi to remove him also. Bahuguna was the last "political" Congress chief minister of the state before the Emergency. He was replaced by an "Emergency-type" figure, Narayan Dutt Tiwari, a policy-oriented but totally non-political man who lacked any political base of his own.

Under the control of Mrs. Gandhi and the amorphous Tripathi-group forces, the composition of the leadership became much less diverse than it had ever before been. Although Mrs. Gandhi in U.P. and elsewhere attempted with some success to identify the Congress with the interests of the poor and the low castes, the state and district leadership of the Congress in U.P. became much more of a Brahmin affair than ever before. Tripathi, Bahuguna, and Tiwari were all Brahmins. Five of the fifteen cabinet ministers in Tripathi's government (including Tripathi) were Brahmins. Thirty-eight of the 75 District Congress Committee (DCC) and City Congress Committee presidents in 1973 also were Brahmins. The most notable underrepresentation was of the middle proprietary castes. There were no Jat presidents, only two Yadavs, and only two Kurmis.[2]

AGRARIAN INTERESTS AND THE
U.P. GOVERNMENT IN THE 1950s

During the long period of Congress dominance, agrarian interests in the U.P. government were represented most strongly by Charan Singh and his allies and followers. In the first post-Independence government of Pandit Pant, Charan Singh was Minister for Revenue. In that capacity, he became the principal architect of that government's major piece of legislation, the famous Zamindari Abolition Act, which abolished the system of intermediaries in the collection of land revenue in U.P. and attempted to establish in place of the old and complicated system of land tenures a uniform pattern of land ownership based on an ideal of peasant proprietorship on personally–cultivated landholdings of moderate but economic size. While his colleagues in the Pant ministry were establishing bases in the party organization through the use of government patronage, Charan Singh was following a somewhat different course. He did not hold portfolios that controlled important sources of patronage. He did, however, differ from his colleagues in having a strong policy orientation, with an emphasis on protection of the middle peasantry, with whose interests he became identified increasingly over time.

Although it was not publicized at the time and it did not divide the government significantly, Charan Singh differed with Pandit Pant and the rest of his cabinet on an issue affecting the interests of the peasantry in February, 1953 when the cabinet voted to increase irrigation rates by 50 percent. Charan Singh, in a note to the Chief Minister dated February 7, 1953, pressed for reconsideration of this decision and used arguments which identified him clearly as a spokesman for three interests – rural interests over urban, western region peasants over eastern region peasants, and peasants who took up full proprietory rights under the Zamindari Abolition Act (*bhumidhars*) against those who did not (*sirdars*).[3] On the first point, he argued against the assumptions of his colleagues that rural areas were undertaxed in relation to urban areas. On the second point, he argued against excessive burdens of taxation on irrigated lands, which were more numerous in his own western region than in the poorer eastern region of the state. On the third point, he proposed that, instead of increasing irrigation rates by 50 percent, they be increased by only one–third, but that the land revenue of the *sirdars* also be increased by one–third. In making this third proposal, Charan Singh was also indicating his pique against the majority of the tenantry who had refused to take advantage of the provision in the Zamindari Abolition Act to establish themselves as *bhumidhars* by making a one–time payment equivalent to ten times their land revenue, in exchange for which they received a 50 percent reduction in land revenue and permanent, heritable, and transferable right to their lands. Although Charan Singh's proposal was not accepted, his behavior on this issue was characteristic of him and indicative of the role that he would continue to play in the politics of the state. That role was one as an independent and cantankerous gadfly, standing forth alone against his colleagues in defence of the interests of the peasant proprietors of the state, particularly those of his own western region.

By the time Pandit Pant left for the central government in 1955, two lines of conflict were developing in the Congress. One involved a non–ideological struggle for control over the party organization among the second rank of Congressmen who were coming to prominence in the post–independence period. The second involved the broad policy question of the role of the peasantry in the economy of the state and the extent to which the peasantry should be taxed to provide resources for economic development. Neither of these problems affected the stability of Pant's government, but they were to figure in the stability of every government that followed.

Pandit Pant was replaced as chief minister of the state by Dr. Sampurnanand who, though a Kayastha, led a group that was solidly based upon the rural support of elite castes in the countryside, particularly the Brahmins, who predominated in the leadership of the group in the districts as well as in the state government. Sampurnanand himself was quite explicit in private in his wish to appeal to the rich and well–born. In a secret note presented by Sampurnanand during Pandit Pant's tenure as chief minister at a meeting of ministers held to discuss the defeats of Congress candidates in by–elections in 1953, Sampurnanand complained that Congress policies had antagonized the zamindars, middle class tenants who feared the loss of their lands, village patwaris, and primary school teachers whose demands had not been accepted.[4] He remarked,

> It comes to this that we have antagonized every class which has so far possessed education, wealth, social status and, consequently, influence . . . .
> The classes to which I have referred above belong, in general, to the Brahmin, Rajput, Bhumihar, Kayastha and Vaishya communities, namely the . . . "higher castes." The measures which we have adopted, and apparently intend soon to adopt, have had the definite tendency of affecting adversely the interests of the higher castes who, it must be remembered have, in general, been the people from whom the Congress has derived the greatest measure of support in the past. They have been culturally affiliated to our leadership and we have come to office literally on their shoulders.

Sampurnanand went on to argue that Congress policies had benefited mainly the landless and very small landholders who belong to backward classes and whose frustration "keeps them apart from others." These groups, he insisted, "instinctively distrust the great mass of Congress leadership" and, therefore, were not likely to support the Congress no matter what benefits the Congress government allocated to them.

Standing apart from both the urban–financed organizational machine of C.B. Gupta and the rural elite–based forces of Sampurnanand and his followers was Charan Singh. Although it is clear that the initial source of Charan Singh's discontent with Dr. Sampurnanand arose from the fact that he was denied the important Agriculture portfolio that he ultimately held under the Pant government, Charan Singh articulated his opposition to Sampurnanand in specific policy terms. He rejected the portfolios of Transport and Cooperation that were offered to him in January, 1955, but kept the important portfolio of Revenue because he wished to use that department to complete "the picture of rural democracy that has been established in our countryside,"[5] to extend land reforms to the few areas still untouched by the Zamindari Abolition Act, and to begin the work of consolidation of landholdings. He also argued that the state was heading towards bankruptcy under Sampurnanand's government, that the government was providing favors to big industrialists at the expense of the general public, that the bureaucracy had expanded and bureaucratic corruption had increased, that food production had declined, and that consolidation of landholdings had been stopped. During this period also, Charan Singh placed himself on record in opposition to the Congress policy of encouraging joint cultivation in agriculture. In a statement prepared in connection with his resignation on April 21, 1959, but never delivered, Charan Singh summed up part of the reasons for his opposition to Sampurnanand as follows:

> We have all to accept one fundamental truth. In the conditions of our State or country no man can truly serve the people unless he knows the villages and understands the problems of the villages. Towns will go into ruins if the villages do not prosper. But, unfortunately, for Uttar Pradesh, the villages are a sealed book to its Chief Minister.[6]

Clearly, in his criticisms of the Sampurnanand government Charan Singh was putting himself forth as the defender of rural society, "rural democracy," and peasant proprietorship against both the interests of industrialists and business groups and misguided reformers who proposed joint farming and had no genuine understanding of village life. He also established for himself in the party organization a reputation for defending the interests of the backward castes against the dominance of the elite caste groups favored by Sampurnanand. In the disputes over selection of Congress candidates to contest the 1957 elections, Charan Singh supported the claims of backward caste persons, especially the Yadavs, but all the backward castes in general. Thus, in his policy positions and in his political actions, Charan Singh continued to carve out a unique position for himself as the defender of rural values, of peasant proprietorship, and of the backward cultivating castes.

Charan Singh continued to play the same role in the first government of C.B. Gupta, which came to power in 1960. The major policy issue that arose during the Gupta government concerned a proposal, introduced in response to demands from the Planning Commission to the state governments to increase revenue from agriculture, to impose a surcharge of 50 percent on the land revenue in U.P.[7] Charan Singh opposed this proposal in the cabinet meetings held to discuss the issue, in an extensive and increasingly bitter confidential correspondence with the chief minister after the decision was taken, and in a forty–page note prepared by him that placed the specific taxation issue in the context of the entire rural and urban economy of U.P. In these letters and statements, Charan Singh argued: 1) that the tax was an unjustifiable burden on the peasantry who, he insisted — against the prevailing notions — were already paying their full share of taxes in relation to urban classes and groups; 2) that, even if it were true, as proponents of the measure argued, that rural per capita income had increased, this did not justify a 50 percent increase in the land revenue; 3) even if the increase in rural incomes had been substantial, it was not wise to absorb it through taxation and, thereby, reduce the purchasing power of the peasantry, which would harm the entire economy; 4) the necessary resources could be acquired by other means than the proposed tax, such as through government economy or through an increased tax on urban incomes; and 5) an increase in the land revenue would be a political liability for the Congress.[8]

In place of the proposed 50 percent surcharge on the land revenue of all landholders, Charan Singh suggested a plan that he had for long wished to implement, namely, a new campaign to persuade *sirdars* (tenants of the state) to acquire *bhumidhari* (full proprietary) rights in their lands by paying in advance a single payment of ten times their land revenue. As for those *sirdars* who still refused to acquire *bhumidhari* rights, Charan

Singh proposed that their land revenue be increased by one–third. In an exchange of confidential correspondence with C.B. Gupta on this proposal, Gupta responded: 1) that Charan Singh's own proposal contradicted his claim that the peasants had no taxable capacity since he was himself proposing that the poorer peasants pay an increased land revenue; 2) that arguments against the tax based on low rural per capita income figures were irrelevant since the new tax was to be levied only on landholders; 3) that rural people were paying far less than their fair share of taxes compared to urban residents; and 4) that the current incidence of land revenue was only two percent of the state agricultural income and the proposed tax would increase that proportion by only one percent. Moreover, Gupta argued that Charan Singh's proposals were designed to protect the interest of a privileged rural class, the *bhumidhars*, and to discriminate against urban classes.[9]

As the correspondence between Charan Singh and Gupta extended over the months between March and October, 1962, increasing emphasis was placed on the distinctions between rural and urban classes and on their incomes and taxable capacities. Charan Singh continued to argue that urban classes, even if they were paying higher taxes, could afford to do so because their incomes were much higher than rural incomes and that manufacturing, commercial, transport, and service sectors produced much larger surpluses than the agricultural sectors. Moreover, he pointed out that urban people received many amenities provided by the state that rural people did not, such as electricity, roads, railways, post and telegraph services, and the like. In the course of the correspondence, Charan Singh also revealed that his counter–proposal for saving state revenue through economy in government expenditure was directed in part at urban groups for he complained that, since Independence, the numbers of government servants had increased by three times and of gazetted officers by four times and he noted that "our official machinery, at least, in the higher reaches is overwhelmingly drawn from the cities." Gupta in reply again disagreed that urban people had a greater ability than rural people to absorb new taxes and pointed out that central government taxes also hit urban people more than rural people. Charan Singh's relentless opposition to the tax measure, however, and his symbolic framing of the issue as one involving a defence of rural life and rural economy persisted to the end, even after a compromise measure was introduced reducing the surcharge to 25 percent and exempting dwarf landholders and even after the Chinese attack of October 20, 1962, which put an end to the controversy for most politicians. However, Charan Singh wrote his last letter on the land tax issue to the then Home Minister of the Government of India, Lal Bahadur Shastri, on October 25, 1962, five days after the opening of the Sino–Indian war. In this last letter, Charan Singh regretted that he had to disturb the Home Minister at a time of national danger, but he appealed to him nevertheless to use his influence to have the land tax withdrawn and noted that the young fighting men of the country were mostly from the agricultural classes!

The dispute between Charan Singh and C.B. Gupta over the land tax issue revealed the presence in the Congress government of the state of two entirely distinct ideological perspectives on economic planning and development, which in turn presumed two different images of the future ideal society. Charan Singh stood forth on this issue, as always, as a person devoted to the ideal of developing a society based on a prosperous agricultural economy, in which the *bhumidhars* or peasant proprietors would be the leading class. Resources were not to be taken from the agricultural sector for the sake of projects that would benefit the urban sectors primarily, but rather the development of the urban–industrial sectors would depend upon increasing the prosperity of the peasantry and, hence, the purchasing power of the peasants. In contrast, C.B. Gupta defended the predominant view of Indian planning efforts and of the desirable future social order, which involved the goal of creating a modern industrial society and which was based on the presumption that it was necessary to extract resources from agriculture to support industrial development.

CHARAN SINGH AND THE IDEOLOGY
OF PEASANT PROPRIETORSHIP

By this time, Charan Singh's views on Indian economic development and the place of agriculture in it were not only well–formed, but had been published in book form. In 1959, in response to the Nagpur Resolution of the Indian National Congress, which proclaimed as one of the principal goals of the Congress the establishment of large–scale cooperative farms in India as a means of solving India's agricultural problems, Charan Singh published his *Joint Farming X–Rayed: The Problem and Its Solution.*[10] Although the book takes off from the issue of cooperative farming and is an attack upon it, it is far more interesting as a positive statement and proposal for an economic development strategy for India based upon agricultural rather than industrial growth and as a defence of the system of peasant proprietorship as the most suitable form of social organization to achieve both the economic goals of development and the political goals of democracy. It is also interesting for its criticism of every form of large–scale mechanized farming as completely unsuited for Indian conditions. The book was published at the height of the Nehru–era emphasis on an economic development model based upon rapid industrialization, with the agricultural sector providing food for the cities and revenue for plan projects.

Charan Singh's book is based upon three premises, which are defended and elaborated at length. The first premise is that capital–intensive industrialization is an inappropriate strategy for India. India's physical resources, he argued, were insufficient to sustain such a process in the manner of earlier developing countries, whereas its high population density required the creation of employment opportunities in both industry and agriculture through small–scale, low capital–intensive industrial development combined with a land–augmenting agricultural strategy calling for the investment of capital in agriculture, that is, for a capital–intensive strategy for agriculture in India, but without "large machinery."[11] Industrialization in India must not and cannot be based on the exploitation of existing agricultural resources but must be preceded by "a revolution in agricultural production – a technological revolution which will ensure far greater production per acre than to–day."[12] In order to achieve such an agricultural revolution, however, the priority given to industrialization in the first two plans would have to be reversed.[13]

Charan Singh's second premise is implicit in his first, namely, that land, being India's most valuable resource and also being scarce, must be used in such a way as to bring the greatest return possible and to provide "a living to a maximum number of people."[14] Capital also being scarce and labor abundant, what is required for India is an approach to agricultural development calling for capital investments that are both land–augmenting and labor–intensive in their impact, with the emphasis on increasing production per acre of land. In this strategy, it is the use of and return from the land that takes priority so that the approach is not simply capital–intensive and not merely labor–intensive either.

The bulk of the book then focuses upon elaborating the third premise, namely, that the most effective use of India's land and the solution of its economic problems lies in "an economy of small farms operated by animal, or . . . manual power."[15] Charan Singh's defence of this premise was based upon evidence he found from various sources that "an increase in the size of the farm does not lead to greater production per acre."[16] Rather, he argued that available evidence demonstrated that maximum productivity per acre on family farms using manual and animal labor was achieved on farms of a size between 2.5 and 27.5 acres. Charan Singh insisted that a system of peasant cooperatives would provide the peasantry "all the benefits and technical advantages of a large-scale undertaking" while still retaining the "freedom or advantages of private property." The aim of agricultural policy in India should be not institutional reform through joint farming, but the provision to the farmer of technical and technological improvements, namely, "water, manure, improved seeds, pesticides and better farming practices in general."[17] Noticeably left out of this list were chemical fertilizers, which Charan Singh considered a poor substitute for organic manure because of their tendency to "give rise . . . to a number of plant maladies" which cannot be adequately controlled even with the use of insecticides and pesticides.[18] Also left off the list were tractors and other large-scale machinery which, Charan Singh argued, increase output per worker but not per acre and which also cause erosion of the soil and depletion of soil nutrients. Although Charan Singh has modified his opposition to the use of chemical fertilizers in recent years, he has continued to argue for maximal use of organic manure in preference to fertilizers and he has maintained unequivocally his opposition to mechanized farming in India.[19] Charan Singh opposed mechanization because, he thought, it did not increase productivity per acre, because it would displace labor when there was already a serious problem of rural unemployment and under-employment, because there was "no work in the sphere of agriculture that human or animal labour cannot perform," and because the necessary labor "to complete any farm operation in the quickest possible time" can easily be procured in Indian villages.[20] Charan Singh was not arguing against the "use of all machines by the peasant farmers." Any machine which lightened the peasant's "drudgery" and increased his "efficiency and productivity" without displacing human or animal labor was to be welcomed, but "the all-purpose tractor" clearly did not fit this description.[21] Moreover, in a telling remark made long before the spiraling increases in petroleum prices, Charan Singh argued that it would be sheer "lunacy" to plan for an agricultural economy dependent on external fuel and foreign exchange resources.[22]

What the Indian peasantry required was a knowlege of "improved techniques" of agriculture relevant to Indian conditions, credit, and capital inputs into irrigation. However, Charan Singh argued against the emphasis on large-scale dams and irrigation systems and on tubewells and insisted instead that capital should be invested in masonry wells "fitted with Persian wheels, and other small irrigation works." The larger irrigation works tied up large amounts of capital for too long and either were not accessible to the small cultivator, as in the case of tubewells, or took so long to complete that, by the time they were ready to provide water to farmers' fields, "the wealth they will produce, distributed evenly among the people, would leave them no better off than they were before."[23]

Charan Singh's defence of peasant agriculture in India was based not only on economic and ecological grounds, but also on ideological and political grounds. In an agricultural society, he insisted, democracy was dependent upon the existence of small farms. Large farms, whether capitalist or collectivist, were inimical to democracy. In large capitalist farms, the few give orders to the many. In collective farms, bureaucratic control, compulsion, and political propaganda restrict the liberty of the cultivators and are used to extract capital from them for large-scale industrialization.[24] Both types of big farms inevitably involve concentration of power and the direction of farm operations by a few, offering to the peasantry the prospect of a countryside "turned into huge barracks or gigantic agricultural factories."[25] In contrast, peasants and peasant agriculture offer the greatest support for democracy for "where the worker himself is the owner of the land under his plough," the people will be independent in "outlook and action," conservative but not reactionary, non-exploitative, giving orders to none and taking orders from none. A "system of family-size farms" offers stability also "because the . . . peasant has a stake in his farm and would lose by instability."[26]

It should also be noted, of course, that Charan Singh's proposals favor a particular social class or group of classes, namely, the locally dominant landed proprietors in the countryside who, according to the 1971 agricultural census, constitute approximately one-third of the landholding classes and control approximately 70 percent of the land.[27] Moreover, Charan Singh's policies have never offered much hope for the marginal farmers with less than a hectare of land or for the landless. Although he has argued for placing a maximum limit of 27.5 to 30 acres of land on the permissible holding of a farm family, he has never advocated large-scale redistribution of surplus land either to the marginal farmers or to the landless. Instead, he advocated and, as Revenue Minister, implemented abolition of landlordism and granting of rights in the land to the actual cultivators, the taking away of land from families holding more than 30 acres per worker,[28] and the placing of restrictions on the acquisition and sale of lands to prevent large landholders from acquiring holdings above

27.5 acres. However, he did not argue for rigorous land ceiling legislation and redistribution of land. The BKD party manifesto in 1969 did call for a land ceiling of 27.5 acres and for redistribution of land to the landless and those holding less than 2.5 acres of land, but Charan Singh has never favored giving everybody "a patch of land to cultivate" and thereby increasing the number of poor peasants in the country. Rather, he has favored the development of small–scale industry to draw off the surplus labor force from the countryside and the maintenance of a stable, self–sufficient body of peasant proprietors cultivating economically viable holdings and free from the threat of "class conflict" aroused by "land hunger" among the poor and landless villagers.[29]

Despite his political disaffection from and his ideological disagreement with the Congress leadership and its policies in U.P. and in New Delhi, expressed so forcefully and coherently in *Joint Farming X- Rayed*, Charan Singh remained in the Congress and in the state government for several years more, serving as Minister of Agriculture until 1965 in the government of Sucheta Kripalani, which replaced that of C.B. Gupta, and as Minister for Animal Husbandry, Fisheries, Forests, and Local Self–government until 1967. During this period, Charan Singh continued to disagree with the party leadership on matters of agricultural policy. His principal complaint during his tenure as Minister of Agriculture was that the division of responsibility at the ministerial level for various aspects of agricultural development, with such matters as credit, irrigation, and fertilizers each handled by different departments of government and not under the overall coordination of the agriculture ministry, made it impossible to develop a coherent agriculture policy to increase production.[30] As a result of his disagreements with the chief minister on this and other matters, the Agriculture portfolio was taken away from Charan Singh in 1965.

AGRARIAN INTERESTS AND U.P. GOVERNMENTS
IN THE POST-GREEN REVOLUTION PERIOD

It was not until after the 1967 elections and the formation of the second government of C.B. Gupta in a precariously balanced legislature that Charan Singh found the decisive political moment to break from the Congress. On April 1, 1967, Charan Singh and seventeen followers defected from the government and formed a coalition with nearly all the non–Congress parties in the legislature. On April 3, the first non-Congress government in the state was formed with Charan Singh as chief minister. Between 1967 and 1971, Congress and non-Congress governments alternated in power, each successive government being either a coalition or minority government (see Table 2:1). During this period also, Charan Singh formed the BKD, a party with a specific appeal to the interests of the self-sufficient cultivating peasantry and with a manifesto that drew its leading ideas from Charan Singh's *Joint Farming X-Rayed.*

Opportunities for innovative agricultural policies were, however rather limited in this period because of the instability of governments. Moreover, although Charan Singh led two of the governments in the years between 1967 and 1971, the nature of the political issues affecting agriculture within the U.P. government changed substantially. Whereas in the Congress governments issues could often be framed in terms of the interests of the peasanty in general against urban, industrial, commercial, and bureaucratic interests, some of the issues that arose between 1967 and 1971 in the coalition governments that often included parties of both the Right and the Left had the potential for dividing the poor peasantry from the middle and rich peasants and the landless from the landowning peasantry. For example, two agriculture-related issues that divided the first government of Charan Singh concerned foodgrains procurement and abolition of land revenue. On the first issue, Charan Singh found himself faced with opposition from a big farmer lobby that demanded a reduction in the foodgrains procurement target. On the second issue, the Chief Minister was faced with a demand from the Left parties that would benefit principally the poorest peasants, would affect the middle peasantry only marginally, but would withdraw substantial revenue from the state exchequer. On the latter issue, Charan Singh, who had opposed any increase in land revenue by the C.B. Gupta government, now opposed also any reduction in it. Although he was compelled finally to compromise on both issues, his stands on both of them defined his position in relation to the various rural social classes more precisely. He favored a graduated procurement policy that drew most heavily from the biggest farmers. While he did not support any increases in land revenue, he saw no reason why the middle peasantry should not continue to pay the traditional, and very modest, land revenue charges that also provided the principal basis for maintaining the peasants' records of title to their lands. However, he did agree to abolition of the land revenue payment on small holdings.

During his second government, between February and October, 1970, Charan Singh promised that "all measures shall be taken to increase agricultural production." In his government, he said, "the interests of big

Table 2:1

Governments of Uttar Pradesh, 1952 to 1976

Chief Minister	Date of Formation	Date of Termination	Governing Party or Coalition
1. Govind Ballabh Pant	May 20, 1952	Dec. 28, 1954	Congress
2. Dr. Sampurnanand	Dec. 28, 1954	Dec. 6, 1960	Congress
3. C.B. Gupta	Dec. 12, 1960	Oct. 1, 1963	Congress
4. Sucheta Kripalani	Oct. 2, 1963	Mar. 13, 1967	Congress
5. C.B. Gupta	Mar. 14, 1967	Apr. 1, 1967	Congress
6. Charan Singh	Apr. 3, 1967	Feb. 17, 1968	Coalition: Jana Congress, Jana Sangh, Swatantra, SSP, CPI, RPI, Independents
7. C.B. Gupta	Feb. 26, 1969	Feb. 10, 1970	Congress
8. Charan Singh	Feb. 17, 1970	Oct. 2, 1970	Coalition: BKD, Congress
9. T.N. Singh	Oct. 18, 1970	Mar. 30, 1971	Coalition: BKD, SSP, Congress(O), Jana Sangh, Swatantra
10. Kamalapati Tripathi	Apr. 4, 1971	June 12, 1973	Congress
11. H.N. Bahuguna	Nov. 8, 1973	Jan. 21, 1976	Congress

traders or businessmen and big industrialists or financiers shall be given a second place."[31] However, it was not possible for Charan Singh to frame the issues that arose during this period as exclusively between agriculture and big industry and big business. He adopted, partly by choice and partly because of pressure from other parties, positions that identified him with the interests of the middle peasantry as opposed to those of the big peasantry, on the one side, and the landless, on the other side. True to the position taken in the BKD party *Manifesto* for the 1969 elections, Charan Singh's government moved to reduce land ceilings from 40 acres to 30 acres. At the same time, however, he dealt very firmly with the "land grab" movement of the CPI and SSP, which sought by forcible action against the allegedly illegal holders of large estates to symbolize the plight of the landless and to grab lands for them. Nor, of course, did he move for a more radical reduction in land ceilings and for a major redistribution of land to the landless.

Charan Singh's second government was a coalition government with the Congress(I). It was marked by conflict, tension, and persistent maneuvering for advantage by the two parties throughout. During the eight months in which the government was in power, Mrs. Gandhi played an active role, directly and indirectly, in decisions concerning the fate of the U.P. government, which affected critically the fate of her rule and that of the Congress at the Center, which at that time was functioning with a precarious majority in Parliament. In fact, it was clear throughout that Kamalapati Tripathi, the state Congress leader, could take no initiative without consulting the Center. The fate of the U.P. government became, in effect, a contest between the political skills of Mrs. Gandhi and Charan Singh that presaged a similar contest in 1979 when Charan Singh became Prime Minister with the support of the Congress(I).

It is clear that the breakup of the coalition in U.P. related primarily to matters of power in Lucknow and Delhi, and especially to Mrs. Gandhi's anger over the unwillingness of the BKD members of parliament in the Rajya Sabha to support her attempt to abolish the privy purses of the princes. After its passage on September 2, 1970 in the Lok Sabha, the Twenty-Fourth Constitutional Amendment Bill, whose object was removal of the privy purses, failed by three votes to acquire the necessary two-thirds majority in the Rajya Sabha. Those three votes were in the hands of the BKD, whose three members in the upper house voted against the Amendment. It was this failure of support to Mrs. Gandhi in September, 1970 that brought the Charan Singh government down.

At the same time, several issues were also outlined during Charan Singh's government concerning agrarian and urban industrial interests in which the BKD and the Congress(I) leaders attempted to demarcate their own and their rivals' positions. Thus, the Congress insisted and Charan Singh agreed, "much against my better judgment . . . to abolition of land revenue on holdings of a size of 5 bighas or less simply in order to meet New Congress half–way."[32] Charges were traded concerning the postponement of nationalization of the sugar factories in the state, whether the postponement was the fault of the state or the central government, and whether or not such postponement indicated that the other side was captured by the millowners and, thereby, was deluding the peasantry.[33] On the issue of the privy purses, the Congress sought to portray the BKD as on the side of the former princes, whereas Charan Singh argued that the Congress stand was only a political stunt, that it represented a "breach of faith" of the original agreement, whose abrogation might ultimately threaten the right of "private ownership of property" in the country.[34] In fact, Charan Singh argued, the Congress was falsely putting itself forth as hostile to the former rulers when there were several ex–rulers in its ranks. Moreover, its attack on the privy purses diverted attention from its partiality to the "big capitalists and industrialists," whose income tax arrears alone were "equivalent to 180 times the amount of the privy purses."[35] Finally, Charan Singh pointed out that he had only recently proposed to Mrs. Gandhi that a law should be passed "demarcating the sphere of small and big industries" such that big industries in such sectors as textiles would be confined to export markets only while the supply of the internal market would be left to small–scale, labor–intensive industry, thereby solving the problems of rural unemployment. However, the Prime Minister's secretariat dismissed the proposal as impractical, which Charan Singh used as a basis for supporting his charge that "the old policy of laying emphasis on big or heavy industries and thus favouring the rich as compared with small enterprises . . . still continues."[36] Finally, to the charge made by the Congress that the BKD's opposition to abolition of the privy purses reflected its attachment to the "landed interests" generally, Charan Singh pointed with pride to his role in the enactment of the Zamindari Abolition Act in U.P. and his insistence that no loopholes be allowed in it that would permit ejectment of tenants, as had happened in other parts of the country.[37]

Even if most of the charges and counter–charges are dismissed as political rhetoric, the two sides were taking quite different positions on major issues of agrarian and industrial policy. Charan Singh and the BKD adhered to the policy of promoting the interests of the self-sufficient peasantry who, it was insisted, could afford to pay the modest traditional land revenue and who did not require and should not be permitted to hold more than 30 acres of land. The Congress, in contrast, succeeded in placing itself in the position of beneficiary of the marginal peasantry by compelling Charan Singh to accept elimination of land revenue payments on the smallest holdings. It also used the privy purses abolition issue symbolically against Charan Singh and the BKD to identify them with the big landed interests, which the Congress has continued to do ever since.[38]

The two sides also revealed fundamentally different positions on industry, employment, and property. The Congress did, in fact, adhere to its traditional position that large-scale industry was vital to the development of the country. It also revealed, in its willingness to abolish the privy purses of the princes through amendment of the provisions in the Constitution protecting private property, that it was not committed to private property as such. Charan Singh and the BKD, in contrast, presented themselves as in favor of protection of private property and small-scale industry.

Finally, there was also a somewhat subterranean issue that bobbed to the surface less prominently at this time, but has become increasingly important since then. Congressmen accused Charan Singh of favoring his own and other backward caste persons in administrative postings. He replied that, in fact, persons from these castes were hardly represented in the senior postings in "the entire administration" in U.P.[39] During the next decade, this issue of elite and backward caste representation recurred on several occasions and also linked naturally with the broader question of the support bases of the Congress and the BKD among elite and backward caste groups, respectively, in the U.P. countryside.

Charan Singh's second government was followed by another short-lived coalition government led by T.N. Singh, in which the BKD was the principal coalition partner in alliance with the Congress(O), Swatantra, the Jana Sangh, and the SSP. In this government, as in previous coalitions, the BKD and the SSP differed again on the land revenue issue. In his own government, a compromise had been worked out that exempted land holdings of less than 3 1/8 acres from payment of land revenue, but the T.N. Singh government under pressure from the SSP agreed to raise the exemption to 6 1/4 acres.

The T.N. Singh government was defeated in the U.P. Legislative Assembly on March 30, 1971 and was followed by a succession of Congress governments. During the restoration of Congress rule between 1971 and 1977, the U.P. and the central governments passed several measures and adopted positions that identified the party more with the poorer peasantry and the landless than with the middle peasantry. For example, the Congress in this period passed new land ceiling legislation that reduced land ceilings to 18 acres of irrigated land per family and reduced the range of the ceiling for non-irrigated or otherwise less productive land from 17 to 60 hectares per family. During the Emergency, the enforcement of land ceilings was one of the 20 points. The U.P. government moved more vigorously in the implementation of the ceiling laws during the Emergency, especially against former big zamindars and talukdars, than previous governments in this state.

It was during this period of restored Congress rule that the government of U.P., along with other states, took over the wholesale trade in wheat, a move which antagonized not only the traders but all peasants with a marketable surplus. On the other hand, the Congress government made specific efforts to provide benefits to the rural poor, the landless and the small farmers. Funds were provided for rural public works projects. Housing sites were allotted to Scheduled Caste persons. Greater efforts were made to provide government jobs for Scheduled Caste persons. The implementation of land ceiling legislation was directed largely to providing surplus land to the landless, especially from the Scheduled Castes. Wells were dug in Scheduled Caste villages to ensure adequate supplies of drinking water. Small and marginal farmers also became special objects of attention by the Congress governments in this period as the Small Farmers Development Agency and the Marginal Farmer and Agricultural Labour Agency came into operation to provide subsidies to the small and marginal farmers for agricultural loans, to spread knowledge of the new agricultural technology among them, and to provide them with help in developing new sources of income through such activities as "dairy-farming, poultry, piggery, sheep and goat rearing."[40]

During this period, the BKD was the principal opposition party and Charan Singh the Leader of the Opposition in the U.P. Legislative Assembly. In several debates in the assembly during the chief ministership of Kamalapati Tripathi, the differences between the Congress and the BKD on agrarian issues were made clear. In his speeches in the assembly, Charan Singh pursued the general themes raised in his *Joint Farming X-Rayed*.[41] He insisted that economic development in the country, especially in U.P., had been unsatisfactory because too much emphasis had been placed on the development of heavy industries and too little on agriculture. This emphasis had been "inspired," Charan Singh charged, "by Soviet or socialist ideology." Whereas Nehru himself had "realised his mistake" at the end of his life, his daughter, Mrs. Gandhi, continued to pursue "the old policies."[42] While some large–scale industries were no doubt necessary, the government was misguided in permitting new textile factories to be set up that deprived handloom operators from the possibility of a livelihood. Urban residents had benefited more from such economic development as there had been, leading to disparities in the incomes of the rural and urban populations to the disadvantage of the former. Among the greatest beneficiaries of "economic development" had been the government employees, who were continually being given excessive pay increases that were eating up a huge portion of the state budget.

The government should reverse its policies, Charan Singh argued, and provide non–agricultural, non–governmental employment by promoting the production of mass consumption goods through cottage industries. Big factories should not be permitted to compete with the small–scale sector in such production for the domestic market. The salaries of government employees should be frozen.

Charan Singh also criticized some of the specific policy measures adopted by the Congress in these years on behalf of Scheduled Castes and the landless. The BKD did not oppose the reduced land ceilings introduced by the Congress, but Charan Singh criticized several features of the new legislation. He argued against introducing the legislation with "retrospective effect" because that would "undo genuine transfers also [in addition to bogus transactions] and unsettle people's mind in regard to their property rights." Insofar as redistribution of any land made surplus was concerned, he supported preference for Scheduled Castes, but proposed that beneficiaries should be persons holding less than a hectare, who should be given a full hectare of land, that is, enough for a viable holding.[43] Moreover, he argued that reducing the land ceiling and distributing surplus land was an inadequate substitute for a policy of promoting rural industries that would provide employment to the poor because there was not sufficient land to distribute. He also castigated a government proposal to bring about a "White Revolution" by giving every landless and Scheduled Caste person a milch animal as based upon pure ignorance.

Charan Singh also opposed the takeover of the wholesale trade in wheat, which he predicted would hurt the grower and would lead to administrative corruption. He also argued that the procurement prices for wheat of Rs. 72 to 74 per quintal to be offered to the growers were too low and should be a minimum of Rs. 90. Higher prices to the grower were necessary because the cost of inputs for irrigation, power, and fertilizer had gone up. For the same reasons, he argued, it was improper for the government to impose a "development levy on the farmers in Uttar Pradesh."[44] He criticized especially the imposition by government of a tax on fertilizer and contrasted this unheard-of policy with central government policies to promote television production and purchase by giving a subsidy to buyers of television sets.

Caste issues also continued to be raised during this period. As Charan Singh had been accused during his chief ministership of being partial to the backward castes and of doing nothing for Harijans, so he accused the Tripathi government of pursuing casteist policies that favored Brahmins in appointments while atrocities against Harijans were being committed in increasing numbers in the countryside. The latter, Charan Singh argued, were directly attributable to the chief minister's "attitude towards castes which he considers lower than his own caste and his inefficiency."[45]

Two features of the debates in this period are especially worth noting. The first is the linkage between state and central government policies. Just as the politics of U.P. and the stability of the state government were a matter of the utmost concern for the central leadership and the intervention of the central leadership in state politics a matter critical to the political future of the state, so were the government's policies seen as interlinked. Pay increases given by the central government to its employees were criticized by Charan Singh as inevitably precipitating demands by state government employees for similar increases. State government neglect of agriculture and support for heavy industries were attributed to the central government and the leadership of the Nehru family, even though agriculture is primarily a state subject.

Second, economic and caste issues were also linked by both sides, directly and indirectly. The direct link focused around the status of the Scheduled Castes. Many Congress policies were specifically directed to the benefit of these castes in this period or to the poor and landless generally, the largest percentage of whom were from these castes. Charan Singh's argument that a reorientation of government policies and resources to agriculture and rural employment would serve them better could only be seen as "pie in the sky" whatever its merits on economic grounds. In this respect, the Congress acquired an advantage in this period that has persisted to the present.

The indirect linkage of economic and caste issues arose out of the charges and counter-charges of casteism, that Charan Singh favored Jats and other backward castes while the Congress government favored Brahmin and other elite castes. Over the next decade, the linkage gradually became one of identifying Charan Singh's policies for the benefit of agriculture, high farm prices, and the backward castes as a policy to favor *kulaks*, whereas the Congress, which depended even more heavily on rich peasants and ex-landlord support, downplayed its reliance on these social forces while emphasizing its policies for the poor, the landless, and the Scheduled Castes.

It was during the period from 1967 to 1977, when both the representation of agrarian interests in the U.P. government and the type of agrarian issues that were articulated changed in the ways indicated above, that new resources were being put into agricultural development activities and demands were being made for even greater investments in agriculture as a consequence of the spread of the Green Revolution technology. For example, between the First Five Year Plan and the Fourth Plan, allocations for agricultural production programs increased from 2,663 lakhs of Rupees in the First Plan to 9,202 lakhs of Rupees in the Third Plan, doubling to 18,041 in the Fourth Plan. The bulk of this increased allocation went for minor irrigation projects, for which funding increased by a multiple of 18 from 580 lakhs in the First Plan to 5,749 in the Third Plan and 10,629 in the Fourth Plan. Dramatic increases also occurred in the allocations for irrigation and power development, which rose from 5,622 lakhs in the First Plan to 55,500 in the Fourth Plan, with those for power development alone going from 2,331 lakhs in the First Plan to 40,828 in the Fourth Plan.[46]

Although the absolute level of expenditures for agricultural production and irrigation and power increased greatly, only the allocations for irrigation and power showed a relative increase in relation to other plan sectors (as indicated in Table 2:2). It deserves to be especially noted, however, that the relative increases in the allocations for irrigation and power occurred at the expense not of industry, but of non-production-oriented aspects of rural development and social services. During the Fifth Plan, however, which began in 1973-74, during the

Table 2:2

Percentage Distribution of Expenditure by Broad Sectors,
First Through Fifth Plan Periods, Uttar Pradesh

Sectors	First Plan	Second Plan	Third Plan	Three Annual Plans	Fourth Plan	Fifth Plan
Agricultural production and allied programmes	19.14	17.05	19.14	25.57	19.23	18.40
Co-operation and Community Development	6.40	13.62	10.13	3.16	2.59	1.80
Irrigation and Power	36.66	35.21	39.01	50.34	52.13	43.10
Industry and Mining	4.16	5.54	3.72	3.94	4.18	4.50
Road and Road Transport	4.47	6.59	5.02	3.79	5.87	12.60
Social Services	29.17	19.47	18.32	11.04	13.69	19.30
Miscellaneous	–	2.52	4.66	2.16	2.31	0.50
	100.00	100.00	100.00	100.00	100.00	100.00*

*Figures adjusted and rounded off to equal 100.00
Source: Government of Uttar Pradesh, Planning Department, *Draft Fifth Five Year Plan, 1974–79*. Vol. I (Allahabad: Superintendent, Printing and Stationery, 1973), pp. 73 & 291.

period of restored Congress rule, the allocation for social services, which provides most of the benefits for the rural poor, was increased once again to 19.3 percent of the total plan outlay while that for irrigation and power was reduced to 43.1 percent.

From the perspective of the government of U.P., therefore, the role of agrarian interests has changed over the past three decades in two important respects. During the long period of Congress dominance from 1947 to 1967, the Congress in U.P. followed the lead of the Center and emphasized in principle, if not in practice, economic development policies oriented towards large–scale industrialization and mechanized agriculture, to be financed by extraction of resources from the peasantry. These policies, however, were effectively blocked in U.P. even during the period of Congress dominance. Large–scale industrial development has been very limited in U.P. since Independence, the state government has been unable to tax the peasantry, and economic policies have increasingly been oriented toward providing agricultural inputs to the peasantry. The Green Revolution has been spreading since 1967 in this state, particularly in the wheat–producing regions. Allocations for agricultural development, particularly for minor and major irrigation projects and for power, have increased substantially.

The second important change has concerned the character of the agricultural issues that have divided the government. During the first period of Congress dominance, the principal issues affecting agriculture that arose within the government concerned the relative attention to be paid to rural and urban interests and to agriculture and industry. This period was also marked by the displacement of the former zamindars and talukdars by the middle and rich peasantry as the principal rural social force. Increasingly since 1967, however, as the non–Congress parties entered the government, issues arose within the government that concerned the relative attention to be paid to the needs and interests of different rural categories — particularly the interests of the middle and rich peasants who benefit most from the new agricultural technology as against the interests of the small and marginal farmers, on the one hand, and the interests of all the landed proprietors who employ agricultural labor against the landless and dwarf landholders, on the other hand.

CONCLUSION

The conflicts and issues concerning the place of agriculture and the peasantry in Indian economic development that arose after the first displacement of the Congress from power in U.P. in 1967 and the rise of the BKD in 1969 have not only persisted but have become central issues in the struggle for power at the Center since 1977. The struggle for power in the north Indian countryside between the Congress on one side and the BKD, the Janata party, and the Lok Dal on the other side, has also continued. In the course of these struggles, which have become increasingly critical as the parliamentary election results have come to depend upon huge swings in the north, the Congress has pursued a political strategy of squeezing the middle peasantry between the former landlords and rich peasants, on the one hand, and the rural poor, on the other hand. The Congress has increasingly mobilized the support of the dominant castes of Brahmins, Rajputs, and Bhumihars, who continue to be the most powerful landed castes in the north Indian countryside, while providing ameliorative measures to the rural poor and landless, of which the latest in a long series of such measures is the Integrated Rural Development (IRD) program. Under the IRD programs, grants, subsidies, and loans are provided to the poor and landless for purchase of buffaloes, establishment of piggeries, purchase of carts, and the like.

Part of the strategy of the Congress, to which the press and many Indian intellectuals have contributed, is to brand Charan Singh and the Lok Dal as *kulaks* and to attempt to associate the backward castes and by inference the Lok Dal with various atrocities committed against the poor and landless in the countryside. In fact, if *kulaks* are defined as labor–employing rich peasants and farmers, hostile to the "rural proletariat" below them, such a class is far more powerful in the Congress than in the Lok Dal.[47] Close scrutiny of incidents of alleged atrocities against the low castes, the poor, and the landless in U.P. also does not indicate any clear pattern of association of such incidents with the middle castes or the Lok Dal. Such incidents tend to be more complex and diverse in origin and are not even necessarily tied to class struggles in the countryside.

It is to be expected, of course, in a competitive political system, that competing parties will attempt to blur the genuine differences in their social bases, which often also become blurred in practice as politicians themselves attempt to make inroads into their opponents' social bases and as they sacrifice principle for power at critical moments of .opportunity.

There has, nevertheless, been a fairly persistent set of social divisions in the north Indian countryside that is reflected also in the bases of party support and that, in U.P. at least, can be traced back to the events of 1967 to 1969.[48] Those divisions take two forms: conflict among the dominant landed castes in the countryside for political control of available economic resources and the struggle for survival of the low castes, the poor, and the landless in relation to all the landed castes above them. In the struggle among the landed castes, the Congress and the BKD/Lok Dal have been fairly evenly divided, which means that the low castes hold the balance electorally. In these struggles, the Congress, with its dual base among the elite landed castes and former landlords and the rural poor has continued to hold the edge against the BKD/Lok Dal, with its base primarily among the middle peasant castes. The Congress lost its edge only in 1977 when the Janata coalition was able to reverse the Congress advantage by capturing some of the Congress' own support among the poor.

Finally, it should be noted that the continuities in political conflicts and issues discussed in this chapter between U.P. politics and politics at the Center exist largely because of a major discontinuity that occurred in the early 1970s between politics in U.P. at that time and in the previous decades. In 1970 and 1971, state politics in U.P. became much less autonomous than they had been in the 1950s and 1960s and central and state politics more closely linked than ever before. The decisive watershed in this transition occurred during the second government of Chaudhuri Charan Singh when, for the first time in the history of the state, both the formation and termination of a government were considered critical for the future of the Union government, which played a determining role in both outcomes. Since then, the state of U.P. has not been considered a separate arena in which political forces acted relatively autonomously, but a base of power for the stability of the Union government that must be maintained at all costs. The closer interlinking, therefore, of political conflicts and policy issues in Lucknow and Delhi is related also to transformations in the dynamics of the federal system itself.

NOTES

1. The first draft of this paper was written several years ago, but was never published. It was revised in 1984 for publication in a collection of my essays under the title, *Caste, Faction, and Party in Indian Politics*, Vol. 1: *Faction and Party* (New Delhi: Chanakya Press, 1984). Permission of Chanakya Press to reprint the article in this volume is gratefully acknowledged.

The original draft was prepared during the tenure of grants from the program in Ethical and Human Values in Science and Technology of the National Science Foundation and the program of Grants for Research on South Asia of the Social Science Research Council (U.S.A.). Neither agency is responsible for the accuracy of facts and statements presented herein or for the opinions expressed.

2. Figures provided to the author by the UPCC office, Lucknow.

3. Personal papers of Chaudhuri Charan Singh, hereafter referred to as *CCS Papers.*

4. *Ibid.*

5. *Ibid.*

6. *Ibid.*

7. For a more detailed discussion of this issue, its relationship to factional conflicts in the Congress, and the role of opposition parties at the time, see Paul R. Brass, "Uttar Pradesh," in *State Politics in India*, ed. Myron Weiner (Princeton, N.J.: Princeton University Press, 1968), pp. 100–109.

8. *Ibid.*

9. *Ibid.*

10. Charan Singh, *Joint Farming X-Rayed: The Problem and Its Solution* (Bombay: Bharatiya Vidya Bhavan, 1959). A second revised edition was published under the title, *India's Poverty and Its Solution* (Bombay: Asia Publishing House, 1964). All citations are from the earlier edition.

11. *Ibid.*, p. 257.

12. *Ibid.*, p. 229.

13. *Ibid.*, pp. 250–251.

14. *Ibid.*, p. 20.

15. *Ibid.*, p. 19.

16. *Ibid.*, p. 62.

17. *Ibid.*, p. 63.

18. *Ibid.*, p. 54.

19. Bharatiya Kranti Dal, *Aims & Principles* (Lucknow: BKD, 1971), pp. 10 and 14.

20. Charan Singh, *Joint Farming X-Rayed*, p. 79.

21. *Ibid.*, p. 84.

22. *Ibid.*, p. 126.

23. *Ibid.*, p. 260.

24. *Ibid.*, pp. 94–96.

25. *Ibid.*, p. 103.

26. *Ibid.*, p. 104.

27. Government of Uttar Pradesh, Board of Revenue, *Agricultural*

Census in Uttar Pradesh, 1970–71 (1973, no other publication details).

28. Charan Singh, *Joint Farming X- Rayed*, p. 91.

29. *Ibid.*, p. 137.

30. *Statesman*, 25 March 1966.

31. Press release, 16 February 1970: *CCS Papers.*

32. Chowdhary Charan Singh, *The Story of New Congress- BKD Relations: How New Congress Broke the U.P. Coalition* (Lucknow: BKD, 1970), p. 9. The *bigha* is a land measure that varies considerably in different parts of north India. The exclusion of "5 bighas" here translates to 3 1/8 acres.

33. Charan Singh, *The Story*, p. 11. Characteristic of the exchanges at the time in which the opposing sides attempted to tar each other with the same brush is this excerpt from a letter of Charan Singh to Mrs. Gandhi, dated 2 September, 1970 (*CCS Papers*):

> As you must be aware, a mendacious campaign has been launched against me particularly by Congressmen both here and in Delhi that I have accepted huge funds from sugar factory owners in consideration of postponement of nationalization of these factories by one year. I am said to have accepted these funds as the sinews for the next election . . . .
>
> I want to state categorically, once again, that, perhaps it is BKD alone which has not accepted donations from capitalists while almost every other political party has done so and continues to do so. It is fantastic, indeed, to find that those who themselves are guilty of this practice should accuse others who are absolutely innocent of it.

34. Charan Singh, *The Story*, pp. 17–18.

35. *Ibid.*, p. 19.

36. *Ibid.*, p. 20.

37. *Ibid.*, p. 22.

38. A letter from K.D. Malaviya to Charan Singh, dated 8 September 1970, is illustrative, as the following excerpts indicate (*CCS Papers*):

> The decision of the B.K.D. to oppose the Constitution (24th) Amendment Bill abolishing Princes' Purses and Privileges and the consequential opposition by you of this epoch-making measure has indeed given the final blow to all our hopes of any Congress coalition government to continue in U.P. . . . The whole country has learned with shock and sorrow that your leadership

and that of the B.K.D. Party stood to maintain the unjust
and anti-social rights enjoyed by a group of privileged
people . . . .

　　　Why have you sided with the Princes? . . . I was
especially pained at the fact that with your eyes open you
chose to remain on the side of this super-class obviously
with the plan that in future you would be able to mobilise
the caste and sectarian emotions of considerable section of
our society with the help of rajas and maharajas to win
elections . . . . As history records at this critical moment
of your Party going against wishes and interests of people,
we of the Congress in U.P. must dissociate ourselves with
your conservative, die-hard and sectarian policies.

39. Press release of 19 September 1970 and *National Herald*, 20
September 1970. From *CCS Papers*.

40. Biplab Dasgupta, *Agrarian Change and the New Technology
in India* (Geneva: United Nations Research Institute for Social
Development, 1977), p. 308.

41. The arguments by Charan Singh referred to below were made
in debates on demands for grants in the U.P. Assembly in July, 1971, in a
motion of no-confidence in the Tripathi government in August, 1972, and
in a speech on the budget in August, 1973. References to these speeches
in the text below come from the *CCS Papers*.

42. From "Points for Budget Speech," dated March 14, 1973, p. 1,
in *CCS Papers*.

43. Comment on the Imposition of Ceilings on Land Holdings
(Amendment) Bill, 1972, by Charan Singh, Chairman, B.K.D., 13 May
1972; *CCS Papers*.

44. Press release, 19 June 1972; *CCS Papers*.

45. From "Points for Budget Speech," p. 5.

46. Government of Uttar Pradesh, Planning Department, *Draft
Fifth Five Year Plan, 1974-79*, Vol. I (Allahabad: Superintendent,
Printing and Stationery, 1973), pp. 89-90.

47. Lenin himself used the term "peasant bourgeoisie" rather than
kulaks to refer to "well-to-do peasants," who controlled "no less than
half of all the implements of production and all the property owned by the
peasants," who cannot exist without employing seasonal and day
labourers," and who are "certainly hostile to serfdom, to the landlords,
and to the bureaucracy." However, he argued, "still more certain is its
hostility to the rural proletariat." V.I. Lenin, "The Proletariat and the
Peasantry," in *Collected Works*. Vol. 8, January-July, 1905 (Moscow:
Progress Publishers, 2nd. rev. ed. 1965), p. 234.

48. The social divisions themselves were reflected in patterns of voting even before 1967, but were not articulated clearly until after the defection of Charan Singh from the Congress and the formation of the BKD. See Paul R. Brass, "The Politicization of the Peasantry in a North Indian State: 1 & 2," *Journal of Peasant Studies*, 7:4 (July 1980), pp. 395–426 and 8:1 (October 1980), pp. 3–36.

3
Structural Change, the Agricultural Sector, and Politics in Bihar

Harry W. Blair

Was the decade of the 1970s at long last a time of economic transformation in Bihar? Did India's most backward state finally join the onward march from precapitalism to capitalism that had reached full flower in states like Punjab and Haryana in the previous decade? Or is Bihar, now on the eve of the eighth general elections, still locked in the embrace of a semi–feudal agricultural structure that has thus far been able to thwart any real change, whether initiated from above through reform and five–year plans or pushed from below through the efforts of an embryonic "progressive farmer" stratum? This essay will endeavor to address these issues in several steps. First, the agricultural sector will be examined with a view to detecting any evidence of a shift to capitalism. Second, the political and social aspects of rigidity and change in Bihar will be taken up, particularly the relationship between caste and politics. Third, connecting links between structural change, caste and politics will be touched upon. And finally an effort will be made to fit all these considerations together as aspects of the fundamental difference between the India of Jawaharlal Nehru and that of Indira Gandhi.

AGRICULTURAL CHANGE IN BIHAR

Bihar's overall position among the Indian states is scarcely in doubt.[1] The most readily available and understandable indicator of economic development is probably the per capita state domestic product (SDP), which is roughly analogous to per capita gross national product in making comparisons between countries. In 1970–71, Bihar's per capita

SDP at current prices was Rs 402, lowest among the major states in India (the all-India figure was Rs 638; Orissa was next-to-lowest at Rs 428). By 1977-78, Bihar had climbed to Rs 735, but continued to hold last place among the Indian states as the all-India figure rose to Rs 1214 (and even Orissa to Rs 799). The Punjab, in contrast, enjoyed a per capita SDP of Rs 1962, more than 2 1/2 times that of Bihar.[2] Looked at another way, in 1970-71, Bihar's per capita SDP was 63 percent of the all-India net domestic product per capita in 1970-71. By 1977-78 the state had declined to 61 percent of the national figure.

In terms of productivity Bihar has done equally poorly. The net domestic product (NDP) per worker in Bihar in 1977-78 was Rs 622 at 1960-61 prices, as against an all-India datum of Rs 1148. By comparison, the Punjab's NDP per worker that year was Rs 2128, almost 3 1/2 times the Bihar figure. Nor was Bihar showing any signs of catching up. The growth rate in NDP per worker had grown by 20.5 percent over the period from 1960-61 to 1977-78 in Bihar (again at constant prices), but it had grown by 57 percent for India as a whole and by 82 percent for the Punjab. Only Uttar Pradesh and Madhya Pradesh had lower growth rates than Bihar.[3]

And as for catching up in the future, things did not look any better. The ratio of bank credits to deposits in Bihar at the beginning of the 1980s was .49 (the lowest in India), indicating that less than half of the money deposited in Bihar banks was being issued in the form of loans within the state.[4] In other words, not only was Bihar's economy stagnant, but the state was subsidizing development elsewhere by making its savings available to other areas.[5] Nor can future help be expected from the national level. The Congress(I) government's Sixth Five Year Plan (for 1980-85) allotted some 7.4 percent of its outlays to Bihar, which had about 10.9 percent of the 1981 population.[6] Finally it might be noted that little can be anticipated in the way of human capital development, for here too Bihar has made small headway. The percentage of 11-14 year olds enrolled in 1979-80, for example, was 27.8, lowest among the major states except for Andhra Pradesh.[7] Such a record does not augur well for the future.

It is on the agricultural sector that this essay will focus, however, for Bihar continues to be an overwhelmingly rural state. Even in 1981 when the census showed the country as a whole to be almost one-fourth urbanized (23.7 percent), Bihar had just one-eighth (12.5 percent) of its population living in cities (followed only by Orissa among the major states, with 11.8 percent urbanization). The labor force included only 20.2 percent of its workers outside agriculture in 1981, lowest in India (even Orissa had more than 25 percent off-farm).[8] The generation of income follows this pattern, with over 50 percent of the state domestic product generated within agriculture, as opposed to something under 40 percent for the whole country.

Given that agriculture is the place to look if one wishes to understand Bihar, then, what is happening in that sector? As Alice Thorner and Gail Omvedt have shown in their recent surveys of the literature on the "mode of production" debate about Indian agriculture, there cannot be much doubt that the "great transformation" to capitalist agriculture is well underway in rural India generally.[9] Agricultural production accelerated rapidly in the late 1960s and throughout the 1970s, as investment in inputs had increased, particularly in irrigation and fertilizers. Along with these developments has come a decline in tenancy, as feudal landlords managing sharecroppers have turned into (or sell out to) "progressive farmers" working their own land. Sharecroppers have turned into day laborers and clients locked into lifelong feudal relations with their patrons have become proletarianized as "free" laborers. Diminishing tenancy, decreasing indentured or bonded labor and declining indebtedness to employers are all evidence of the transition to capitalism, as well as the more immediately obvious increases in ˙input use and production.

How has Bihar fared amid all this evidence of agrarian change? In the most direct sense we could merely note that cereal production over the "Green Revolution" period (1964–65 to 1979–80) grew in India as a whole at a 1.8 percent compound annual rate, whereas in Bihar the rate was 0.1 percent. The Punjab by comparison raised its cereal production by an 8.7 compound annual growth rate over the same period, Haryana by 6.9, Maharashtra by 3.1, Uttar Pradesh by 1.6 and even West Bengal, scarcely a focal point of the Green Revolution, by 0.8 percent, in this case eight times the rate of growth in Bihar over this 16-year period.[10]

The reasons behind this extraordinarily low growth rate are naturally complex, but examination of virtually any measure of agricultural change reveals much the same pattern of stagnation. Among the various inputs to agriculture that can be measured reasonably easily,[11] fertilizer use is arguably the most immediately indicative index of development, for farmers can begin to use it immediately after deciding to do so, assuming of course that both the material and the funding for it are available. With minor irrigation, even when tubewells and funding are available, application is more difficult, installation delays are inevitable, and so on. And these constraints are greatly exaggerated with major irrigation work or electrical power, which takes years to be put on line, even after construction has begun.

Bihar, which contained some 11.3 million cropped hectares in 1970–71,[12] or about 7.1 percent of the all–India total, consumed in that same year some 97,000 metric tons of fertilizer, or about 4.5 percent of the all–India total. Bihar thus used about 63 percent of its "share" (i.e., what it would have used if all states had consumed fertilizer at the same rate in proportion to their total gross cropped areas). By 1978–79 fertilizer use in Bihar had slightly more than doubled, to 195,000 tons, a definite sign of agricultural development, it might seem.[13] India as a whole, however, went up by 135 percent over the same period, so that by 1978–79 Bihar's consumption was only 3.8 percent of the all–India total, or about 53 percent of its "share" on a gross cropped area basis.[14]

A better way to understand the situation in Bihar might be to note that in 1970–71 fertilizer use in the state was about 9 kilograms per hectare, against 39 in the Punjab, 37 in Tamil Nadu and 19 even in Uttar Pradesh. By 1977–78 use in Bihar had grown to 16 kg/ha but over the same period had grown to 77 in the Punjab, 64 in Tamil Nadu and 38 in Uttar Pradesh. Use in Bihar was growing, but at the same time it was growing so much faster elsewhere that Bihar was being left behind.

Perhaps, it might be argued, the low overall use in Bihar is masking very intensive use among a relatively small group of farmers. That is, maybe there is in fact an elite of "progressive farmers" applying large quantities of modern inputs to their holdings and acting as a vanguard of technological change. It would only be a matter of time, such an argument might go, and quite likely a short time at that, before other farmers, particularly the *kisans* of the middle castes, begin to imitate them, thereby bringing a real agricultural revolution to Bihar. Data on this question are harder to come by, for surveys are required, but fortunately there is a good one at hand in the form of a study by the National Council of Applied Economic Research.[15] This NCAER survey found that for some states such a case might well be made. In Orissa, for example, only 21 percent of the surveyed cultivating households used fertilizers, as opposed to 92 percent in the Punjab. But Orissa's 21 percent used their fertilizer at the same rate (91 kg/ha) as the Punjab's 92 percent of users. It could be argued, then, that there was such a "vanguard" in Orissa. For

Bihar, though, there was no such pattern. Some 42 percent of cultivating households used fertilizer in Bihar (as against around 45 percent all–India), and the users applied it at a rate of 50 kg/ha, as against 128 in Tamil Nadu and 65 in Uttar Pradesh, to follow through with the examples above (the all–India average was 78). A breakthrough for capitalist agriculture, then, did not appear to be in the offing for Bihar in the 1970s, at least on the fertilizer front, although there clearly was some progess.

In terms of irrigation, Bihar was somewhat better situated than several states. India overall by 1979–80 had realized about 40 percent of its major and medium irrigation (i.e., large–scale works with heavy construction, like the Sone or Kosi systems) potential. Behind as always, Bihar had reached 26 percent of potential, far behind Tamil Nadu at 78 percent and the Punjab at 77, but somewhat ahead of Maharashtra (15), Madhya Pradesh (17) and Gujarat (19). In the minor irrigation (essentially wells) field, Bihar had realized 40 percent of its potential in 1979–80, as against 56 percent of India's altogether. Again Tamil Nadu (79 percent) and the Punjab (82) among others were ahead, while Kerala (28) and Orissa(29) were behind. It is when major/medium and minor are put together that things fall into perspective, for then it develops that Bihar had by 1979–80 managed to exploit just 33 percent of its total irrigation potential, the lowest in India save for Maharashtra (31) and Madhya Pradesh (25). The all–India figure was 48 percent, with leading states like the Punjab (80), Tamil Nadu (78) and Haryana (64) doing quite well. In irrigation, then, as in fertilizers, there is some movement in Bihar, but nothing like the scale experienced by other states. Again, even Uttar Pradesh (54 percent of all potential utilized) and West Bengal (46) were significantly ahead of Bihar's 33 percent.[16]

Electric power generation is a bit more tricky to relate to agriculture as an input, since farming is only one of many uses to which electricity is put. Still, a momentary glance at the data reveals Bihar's position. Even at the end of the Sixth Plan, Bihar's installed capacity is expected to amount to some 42 percent of the all–India figure, a serious underrepresentation when compared with the state's 10.9 percent of the population. It is instructive to compare Haryana and the Punjab, both of which will have about twice as large a share of the power capacity as of population.[17]

The composition and behavior of landholders and the rural labor force should be another rich area of inquiry in any effort to acertain a movement toward capitalist agriculture, especially in view of the wealth of census and survey data available. The main things that should be appearing here, if a capitalist transformation is occurring, are a decrease in marginal landholdings, a decrease in tenancy and an increase in landless laborers. These processes are a function of production becoming concentrated in the hands of a market–oriented "progressive farmer" stratum and the rural labor force becoming "proletarianized," as traditional clients in *jajmani*–type relationships with their patrons are thrown off the land to become "free" laborers.

   Patterns in labor force composition are arguably less difficult to deal with than tenancy or landholdings, so that would be the best place to begin. The Rural Labour Enquiry (RLE) of 1974–75 did indeed report an increase in rural labor[18] for Bihar since the previous survey of a decade before, from 32 to 36 percent of the state's rural households, a growth of 4 percent that might hint of some proletarianization. For other states, though, increases were a good deal higher, as in Maharashtra (34 to 45 percent), Tamil Nadu (31 to 44) or West Bengal and Andhra Pradesh (both 34 to 39). The Punjab, our bellwether of capitalist development wich might be assumed to show a large increase, in fact registered a gain from 17 to 26 percent, at 9 points twice as large as Bihar's 4 percent gain, but at the end of the period, the Punjab was still only 26 percent "proletarianized," as against 36 percent in Bihar.

   Still, the difference in growth rates of rural labor maybe an important one. The census of 1981 actually shows a *drop* of 1.7 percent in agricultural laborers as a proportion of the rural labor force in the major Indian states over the 1971–81 period, with Bihar (–3.5 percent) and Uttar Pradesh (–3.7 percent) registering the largest decreases. Most of the decrease here (and one would assume all of it for states like Bihar) was due to changes in occupational definitions over the two decades, in that a stricter definition was imposed on the "agricultural laborer" category for 1981.[19] But what is interesting here is the relative decreases and increases between the states. For the Punjab, even with the more rigorous definition employed in 1981, agricultural laborers *increased* by some 2.7 percent, thereby showing a similar pattern to that observed in the RLE. Interestingly, the change in agricultural laborers that the census measured registers a correlation (Pearson's r) of .59 with the annual compound growth rate in cereal production in the 1964–65 to 1979–80 period[20] among the 14 major Indian states,[21] indicating that there is quite a strong (though far from perfect) connection ($r^2 = .35$) between "proletarianization" and agricultural growth.[22]

In terms of tenancy we would expect the incidences of sharecropping or *bataidari* to decrease as landowners, lured by the prospect of profits, reclaim their holdings, discharge their tenants and implement high–yielding technologies themselves. But whether this has happened or is happening and if so to what extent is notoriously difficult to ascertain in the Indian case. Landowners do not want to admit to letting out their land on share, for fear that land ceiling laws or tenancy rights laws will be enforced, and perhaps nowhere has this been more true than in Bihar, with its long and acrimonious history of struggle over land reform.[23]

It is perhaps understandable, then, that the agricultural census of 1970–71 showed less than one percent of operated farm area was recorded as being "taken on rent."[24] I.J. Singh has assembled data derived from the National Sample Surveys showing the level of tenancy to be a good deal higher than that evidenced in the census, almost 15 percent of Bihar's cultivated area in 1970–71 (as against an all–India figure of 10.6 percent).[25] Other estimates are substantially higher. A government study in the late 1960's found about 23 percent of cultivated land in the Kosi area of northeast Bihar to be sharecropped,[26] though the survey and settlement operations conducted in the district somewhat earlier found only around 12 percent of the cultivated land under *bataidari*.[27] Over on the other side of the state in Shahabad District Wolf Ladejinsky estimated in the early 1960s that about 25 to 30 percent of the land was sharecropped,[28] and that continues to be the figure generally accepted for Bihar as a whole, though no one really knows how accurate it is. It is also unclear what is happening to sharecropping over time. The case for or against an agricultural transformation will have to be made largely independently of hard data on *bataidari* relations.[29]

Presumably more accurate but still very puzzling are the latest figures on landholding. The agricultural census conducted in 1976–77 found that over the period since the previous agricultural census in 1970–71, a surge towards miniholdings had taken place in Bihar. For the country as a whole there was a drop of 12 percent in the number of operational holdings over 10 hectares and a drop of 15 percent in the area occupied by such holdings, and a concomitant increase of 23 percent in the number of holdings of less than one hectare, along with a 20 percent growth in their total area.[30] A good part of the shift could be explained through generational change and fragmentation of landholdings, though some of it was doubtless due to concern over the land ceiling enforcement and surplus land acquisition drives mounted during the 1975–77

Emergency period, as larger landowners partitioned their holdings through transfers both real and *benami*.[31]

Bihar showed a striking exaggeration of this trend. There the number of over-10-hectare holdings decreased by 38 percent (area also by 38 percent) and those under one hectare grew by 48 percent in number, 40 percent in area. None of the other major states even approached this level. Holdings under one hectare did increase by 40 percent in Rajasthan, but area by only 27 percent, while in West Bengal the numerical growth was 39 percent and areal increase was 30 percent.[32] The real growth in Bihar was in the under 0.5 hectare category, where the number went up by 54 percent and area by 56 percent.[33]

How to account for this huge increase? Was Bihar becoming an economy of *minifundistas* in the 1970s? A shift to capitalist agriculture presumably would entail the elimination of smallholdings, as the larger farmers drive smaller ones off the land. Clearly this was not happening, for even in Punjab and Haryana holdings under one hectare grew by over 20 percent in number and over 15 percent in area; in none of the major states was there a reduction. But the Bihar case would appear to be a retrogression.[34] Perhaps, it might be thought, the much touted land reform policy pursued by the Jagannath Mishra ministry during the 1975–77 Emergency could account for the fervor with which the large holders split up or sold their land. A full analysis of this possibility will have to await the publication of the complete 1976–77 agricultural census data, but in the meantime, it can be said that any connection seems unlikely. Despite the self-adulatory rhetoric proliferated during the Emergency,[35] the government had taken over only some 90,000 hectares through the end of March 1977, just a bit less than 0.8 percent of all operational holdings in the state at the time of the 1970–71 agricultural census. This would seem scarcely enough to start a stampede of unloading land that people held in excess of the official ceilings.

In fact, the relationship between surplus acquired during the Emergency and land transfers between the two agricultural censuses is quite low. A Pearsonian correlation between the percentage of total agricultural holdings in each district acquired as surplus by the state during the Emergency[36] and the rate of increase in the number of holdings between the 1970–71 and 1976–77 censuses comes out to only .183, giving a statistical "explanation" of just over three percent ($r^2 = .033$). The great rise in miniholdings, then, would appear to be unrelated to the Emergency land reform enterprise.

Another aspect of the rural economy that should be related to any agricultural transformation is the pattern of indebtedness. Presumably the traditional mode of patron–client debt changes as labor becomes "free," and new debts are contracted with moneylenders, shopkeepers and the like, rather than with employers as previously.[37] Here the RLE can again be mustered into service. For rural laborers in Bihar, debt to employers decreased from 31 to 21 percent to total household indebtedness over the decade between 1964–65 and 1974–75. The gap was taken up by greater indebtedness to moneylenders and "others" (which meant mainly friends and relatives). Such a pattern would seem to indicate some movement towards a "free" labor force, but some questions are raised by data on the Punjab from the RLE, which show debt among rural laborers to employers *increasing* (from 20 to 27 percent of the total) while that to moneylenders and "others" is decreasing. Obviously, the matter is not a simple one.

To sum up the evidence thus far, there appears little reason — on the basis of admittedly rather gross state–level data — to think that any rapid agricultural changes were underway in Bihar during the 1970s. In its overall economy Bihar expanded, but at a significantly slower rate than the country as a whole. Further, the very low credit/deposit ratio demonstrated by the state's banking system meant that future economic growth into the 1980s would be low as well, for little investment was being made. And government investment followed the same pattern, with the state getting less than 7 1/2 percent of Indira Gandhi's Sixth Plan outlay for its 11 percent of the country's population.

In the agricultural sector the story was if anything even less promising. The production of cereal crops, the dietary staple of the state, grew by an annual rate of just one–eighteenth the national rate and one eighty–seventh the rate evidenced by the Punjab. This sad performance is reflected in the very modest growth in the use of agricultural inputs in Bihar. Fertilizers and irrigation have both been much less a part of the Bihar scene than the national one, and the same holds true for electricity. Trends in labor force composition were a bit more mixed, with the Rural Labour Enquiry study[38] showing an increase in unskilled rural laborers, while the 1981 census[39] showed a slight decrease in agricultural laborers. But both studies found any "proletarianization" tendency in rural Bihar to be far behind what was going on in the more advanced agricultural areas.

Tenancy and landholding data are even more puzzling, perhaps not surprisingly in a region where concerted resistance to attempts at tenancy reform has been the rule for a century and more. There probably is some tendency in the direction of expelling tenants and "resuming" cultivation, which would be expected in any agricultural transformation and is what Ladejinsky found in Purnea District in the late 1960s.[40] On the other hand, such a "modernization" of the rural economy does not fit in at all with the virtual explosion of miniholdings that appeared in the agricultural census of 1976-77, for if there were a structural transformation underway these holdings should be decreasing as their owners became proletarianized. Still, the overall picture seems to be one of a slow and uncertain groping toward a capitalist agriculture. Neither as rapid nor as impressive as what was happening elsewhere in rural India, to be sure, but the outlines of gradual change appeared nonetheless there.

CASTE AND POLITICS

Since the turn of the century, the connection between caste and politics in Bihar has been a close one, so close in fact that to mention one has been almost automatically to speak of the other. The story is a well known and often told one,[41] beginning with Sachhidanand Sinha's agitation at the century's beginning demanding a Bihar for the Biharis, a separate Bihar to be carved out of the Bengal Presidency. What he meant in reality was a Bihar for his fellow Kayastha Biharis, whom he was organizing into a political base, and when the agitation resulted in the creation of the province of Bihar and Orissa in 1912, Kayasthas were the main beneficiaries. These traditional scribes were able to get the lion's share of the higher level government jobs that the new province offered and, as the swaraj movement of the Congress slowly gathered steam, this now mobilized and politically conscious caste deftly assumed a commanding role there as well. It was no surprise that Rajendra Prasad, a Kayastha, should become the first Bihari Congressman of national prominence.

Over the years, then, the Kayasthas found their caste interests as scribes and account keepers in accord with their class interests as a "babu" stratum of bureaucrats. And in relatively short order the more articulate and ambitious leaders in the caste found that political involvement fit in as well.

In succeeding decades the other "twice-born" castes gradually entered the political arena, first the Bhumihars, then the Rajputs and finally the Brahmins. These groups, too, found that caste and class interests intertwined and that political involvement related very directly to both. Granted, there was much struggle and competition as the twice-born castes and their champions jostled and jousted for position and power. Sri Krishna Sinha, the Bhumihar stalwart, and Anugrah Narayan Sinha, the Rajput tribune, were the main contenders in the first Congress government in the late 1930s, and then again in the 1940s and 1950s after Independence. In the later years the Kayasthas had their man in Krishna Ballabh Sahay, and the Brahmins theirs in Pandit Binodanand Jha.

Caste solidarity was by no means complete even then, as leaders split and defected, and various freebooters like Kamakhya Narain Singh, the Raja of Ramgarh and a contender for Rajput supremacy, entered the fray. There were even some substantive issues dividing the leadership, like *zamindari* abolition, supported by S.K. Sinha and much more strongly by K.B. Sahay, but resisted vigorously by Rajendra Prasad and A.N. Sinha.[42] These squabbles, though, did not have any short-term effects on the dominance of the twice-born. By the early 1960s, *zamindari* abolition had substantially taken place in that there was no longer a class of *zamindar* intermediaries. But the inserting of loopholes in the legislature and the foot-dragging in its implementation were such that those owning the land were by and large the same twice-born castes as before and in many cases the same people as before, even if in somewhat reduced circumstances,[43] and even if a good many of the *ryots* who succeeded to ownership were not twice-borns but members of the lower castes. If not a feudal economy, Bihar certainly appeared to be a "semi-feudal" economy, as Prasad has shown in his analyses of the state's rural economy.[44]

As might be expected in such a state of affairs, the twice-born leadership was concerned primarily with the circulation of elites and keeping the economy keyed to the status quo. Who would succeed S.K. Sinha as chief minister? Would Pandit Jha be able to convince the Congress High Command in New Delhi to reverse his having been "Kamarajed" in 1963? (No, he was not.) Would the Raja of Ramgarh succeed in his scheme to bring his bloc of former Swatantra MLAs into the Congress (yes, he did) and realize his ambition to displace Satyendra Narayan Sinha (A.N. Sinha's son) as the Rajput Congress leader? (No, he did not.) These were the sort of questions that preoccupied Bihar politics in the 1950s and 1960s. These rivalries between and among the twice-born castes, however, did not prevent a basic understanding during the period of Congress hegemony through 1967 that their position of dominance in the rural political economy should remain in place. Quarreling among themselves was permissible, but the lower orders were not to be permitted to join the fray; their part was to be controlled by the twice-born. Accordingly, the purpose of such development programs as were encompassed by the five-year plans was not to develop the rural economy, for that might bring real change, but rather to develop patronage networks among elites, linking caste alliances between villages and the state capital.

But the system was not watertight, even at the beginning. Leakages in upper caste control began right from the granting of universal suffrage. The twice-borns, who amounted collectively at most to perhaps one-eighth of the population,[45] found themselves faced with the need to reach out for lower caste allies. Thus B.N. Jha promoted Birchand Patel, the Kurmi leader, while K.B. Sahay patronized Ram Lakhan Singh Yadav of the Yadav community, and so on.

In the forefront among the lower castes were the three great Sudra communities of Bihar, the Yadavs, Kurmis and Koiris, who together amounted to almost one-fifth of the state's people. Their rise to prominence, however, was a slow one. Some among them had tried to organize the three castes politically in the 1930s as the Triveni Sangh in competition with the high caste Congress,[46] but the effort failed in the election of 1936. In reality, it had to fail in a situation where the franchise entailed a property holding requirement that few outside the upper castes could meet, at least in 1936.

After the establishment of the universal franchise in independent India, all could vote, but participation of the lower castes was at the beginning essentially under the patronage and direction of the twice-borns. Over the course of the 1950s and 1960s, though, caste consciousness gradually turned into political consciousness, as was inevitable, given the example of the pathological fixation that the twice-borns had for caste competition among themselves.

This lower caste consciousness first manifested itself in panchayat elections in the 1950s and 1960s and quickly percolated upwards to elections for the State Assembly, particularly in areas where individual Sudra castes held numerical dominance. In some thanas of Saharsa District, for example, Yadavs alone are more than 30 percent of the population, and in some parts of Nalanda District Kurmis are equally predominant. Within individual villages and gram panchayat delimitations,[47] numerical dominance was often even greater than that, and it was relatively easy for these lower caste people to win election.

Similar developments occurred within State Assembly constituencies; MLAs from Saharsa and Nalanda have been overwhelmingly Yadavs and Kurmis repectively for more than two decades.[48]

The leaders of these three groups, particularly the Yadavs and Kurmis among them, came to see themselves as representatives of the "Backwards" in Bihar, that is, of all the Sudra communities taken together, as opposed to the twice–born "Forwards" on one side and the Harijans, Adivasis and Muslims on the other.[49] Altogether, the Sudra castes in Bihar amounted to perhaps half the total population of the state, so this was a very large constituency indeed.

The fact that more than three–fifths of this Backward constituency consisted of small and scattered caste groups[50] made the claim of representing them as a unified entity somewhat more difficult for any self–appointed leadership to make, but at the same time made it easier for those leaders to assert the claim without contradiction from those on whose behalf the claim was being made. For just as Sachhidanand Sinha asserted himself as the tribune of Biharis generally in his petitioning for a separate province back at the turn of the century while in fact representing primarily the interests of his Kayastha brethern, so too Backward caste leaders could claim to represent all Sudras while actually advancing the interests of relatively few. The ploy is an old one, after all, in India as well as elsewhere, and there is no reason why Backward politicians in Bihar should not have picked it up.

To be credible, though, the claim had to have at least some connection to a perceptible semblance of reality, so it was natural that the Samyukta Socialist Party in the 1967 election included in its manifesto a proposal to reserve an allotment of government posts for the Backwards. That election turned out to be the first one the Congress lost in Bihar, and the SSP actually emerged as the largest element in the United Front ministry that took power in Patna. Moreover, the Deputy Chief Minister in the new government was Karpoori Thakur, the main advocate of a pro–Backward posture within the SSP. Demands for a governmental Backward policy were thus put forward from within the government itself, but little was done at the time, as the United Front ministry quickly became consumed with the struggle to preserve itself against a Congress comeback.

During the decade between 1967 and 1977 power shifted back and forth between Congress and non–Congress ministries, and saw the JP

Movement of Jayaprakash Narayan, the Emergency and finally the Janata victory of 1977, which brought Karpoori Thakur to the chief ministership on the crest of the national anti–Congress wave. What was a suggestion in 1967 became state policy in 1978 as Chief Minister Thakur promulgated a plan whereby 20 percent of all state posts would go henceforth to the Backwards. In so doing he served notice on the Forwards that a new order had come to power in Bihar, one in which the Backward castes would have the leading role.

As expected, the Forwards reacted to this challenge with rage and violence. Against a background of campus disruption, government office pillaging and train seizures, the Forwards set about to undermine the Thakur ministry, and within a few months had toppled it.[51] An interim ministry headed by Ram Sundar Das, a Harijan, but dominated by Forwards ran things until the 1980 election when Bihar went the same way as the country as a whole, reinstalling the Congress(I) and the Brahmin Jagannath Mishra in Patna in the state elections just as it helped reinstate Indira Gandhi in New Delhi in the national elections.[52] In the end, Karpoori Thakur was unable to forge a Backward coalition that could capitalize on its demographic dominance to win and hold power.[53] Claims of any permanent change in the political economy of Bihar were premature.[54] The Forwards were simply too strongly entrenched.

CASTE, POLITICS AND STRUCTURAL CHANGE

The years since 1967 have seen the emergence of two struggles in rural Bihar. The first one represented a coalescence of the slow unfolding agricultural transformation that we have looked at earlier and the rather more rapidly growing momentum of the Backwards as a politically conscious force in Bihar. The Backwards appeared to be becoming a self–aware *kulak* stratum that was challenging the Forwards for dominance in the state.

This last assertion raises a crucial issue. It is clear that over the first three decades of independent India a Backward political movement developed in Bihar, culminating in Karpoori Thakur's chief ministership of 1977–79. It also appears to be the case, though less clearly so, that an agricultural transformation from feudalism or semi–feudalism to capitalism had begun to take place, however slowly, in the countryside. But how do we know that the same people have been at the center of both movements?

The answer to the question, of course, is that without detailed survey analysis of a sort that has not yet emerged into print, we cannot know for sure. Bihar's progressive farmers could after all be a *junker* stratum of the Forward caste ex–*zamindari* class rather than *kulak* upstarts from the Backward communities. Circumstantial evidence, however, makes a reasonably strong case that, while there are doubtless a number of *junkers* on the scene, the great preponderance of progressive farmers are Backwards.

There are at least three aspects to this evidence. First, there has been the behavior of the principal protagonists themselves. Karpoori Thakur at the state level and his patron at the national level, Charan Singh, certainly believed there was an overlapping constituency of progressive farmers and Backward castes. Both built their political strategies around a combination of increasing agricultural production by raising foodgrain prices, furnishing agricultural credit, providing inputs, and so on, along with advancing the cause of the Backward castes. For Charan Singh, to say progressive farmer was to say Jat *kisan* and vice versa, and while Karpoori Thakur did not speak quite so often of his own caste origins[55] or the need to build state policy around increasing agricultural production, he frequently and vocally pressed both causes.[56]

Second, there are the analyses of the scholars, in particular those who have done detailed field work, like Pradhan Prasad and Arvind Das.[57] And their analyses find support in observations made by virtually all the politicans and journalists with whom I talked while in Bihar during 1978 and 1980. It had by then become conventional wisdom that prospering middle farmers and rising middle castes were the same people. And like most conventional wisdom, while it may not always serve well for specific tasks like predicting elections (e.g., the 1980 elections, when the Lok Dal of Karpoori Thakur and Charan Singh did so much more poorly than had been expected), it can be expected to be generally fairly sound.

The last and somewhat less solid piece of evidence is the traditional taboo among twice–born *maliks* against taking up the plough, an inhibition absent among the Backwards, particularly the Yadavs, Kurmis and Koiris, whose hereditary caste occupations involve agricultural work. In contrast, the closest a *pukka* cultivator from the Forward community can come to actually cultivating is to manage or direct the work from a distance, preferably at least as far away as his own compound. Well, just so, it might be argued, here is a recipe for an agricultural transformation from above, as feudal landlords become *junker* capitalists, turning their lands previously let out on share into well-managed, profitable and labor-exploiting businesses. But such a move should go along with increasing concentrations of land in the middle and upper size ranges as the new capitalists squeeze out the small fry. And this is contrary to what was in fact going on in the 1970s when, as we have seen, the larger holdings decreased in area while the smaller ones increased — scarcely evidence supporting a *junker* capitalist tendency.[58]

As things worked out, the Backward challenge did not end in success in the 1977-79 chief ministership of Karpoori Thakur. The Forwards regained their dominance in the ministry that succeeded Thakur's and have held on since. And the election of 1980 did not shake the Forward hold, but rather if anything strengthened it.[59] Nonetheless it was clear that the hegemony of the Forwards was under threat and that the Backwards had become a real part of the game of politics in Bihar.

The second struggle, and one that developed almost simultaneously with the first one between Backwards and Forwards, pitted Harijans and landless laborers (two groups which also overlap in the main) against both Backwards and Forwards. This outcome was almost inevitable given the first struggle and its proximate causes. The same universal suffrage that made Backward votes a prize for Forward politicians to fight over also made Harijan votes a prize worth soliciting,[60] and the same eventual raising of Backward consciousness that slowly occurred in consequence also took place among Harijans. Their class demands were somewhat different — for enforcement of minimum wage laws, help in dealing with illegal land seizures, and recognition of sharecropper rights, rather than for higher foodgrain prices or more agricultural credit — but the connection between political mobilization and economic policy demands was quite similar.

The reception accorded to this agitation from below, however, was quite different from the experience of the Backwards. Rather than university politics (and even campus gang warfare), booth capturing at election time, reservation schemes with list-making commissions and toppling maneuvers in the State Assembly — all relatively genteel tactics by Bihar standards — direct and vicious repression at the local level was the rule in dealing with the lowest strata. Sometimes Forward communities appeared to be to blame, and sometimes Backward groups, in the "Harijan atrocities" (looting, arson, rape and often outright murder in assaults on Harijan *tolas* or neighborhoods in rural communities) that swept the state in the 1970s and have continued to the present. In no small number of cases the police were employed in the repression, too, as if a tacit agreement had been drawn up between landowners and government such that whenever the usual village–level machineries of control — employment at the *malik's* will, debts and the evergrowing interest on them, *goondas* and *lathials* for enforcing village norms — did not suffice to keep the lower orders in their place, the constabulary would be on call to protect "law and order."[61]

In some parts of the state the agitation from below apparently has been Naxalite in its inspiration, as in Bhojpur District, where there has been a long connection with the Naxalite movement.[62] In other areas landless laborer demands seem innocent of any such connection, as in the continuing pocket of unrest in the Masaurhi area of Patna District.[63] But nothing has prevented government from aligning with landowners to suppress all assertions from the bottom of the rural hierarchy with firm and violent resolve in the name of controlling insurrection and subversion.[64] Despite these efforts at repression, however, representations for redress from below and a predictable response from above have become a regular part of the rural scene in Bihar.

It should be noted that not all the responses from above have been negative. Despite the possibilities for booth capturing in a few areas of local strength, all parties still need votes and none have enough votes on a narrow caste or class basis to win more than a handful of constituencies. So they find themselves competing for Harijan[65] votes and courting Harijan favor by promising, for instance, to enforce minimum wage laws while at the same time aiding and abetting local landowners to suppress any local demands for enforcement of those laws.

CONCLUSION

The players are all in place for a long and likely bitter struggle on several levels, with the outcome very much in doubt. As the eighth general election approaches, it is clear that a number of dynamics are unfolding in terms of social change, but nothing decisive appears to be emerging in the short term. An agricultural transformation does seem to be very slowly moving the rural economy toward capitalism, and a rising class of middle caste progressive farmers is spearheading the transformation. This middle group of Backwards, mobilized politically partly as a consequence of the universal franchise and the erection of the panchayat system of representative governance at, local level, partly also as part of a strategy by Backward leaders seeking to combine caste and class interests, are bidding to displace the upper castes as the dominant element in state politics.

But thus far the Forwards have been able to contain the threat. They are still fixated on the same sort of internecine jostling among themselves that has characterized their rule in the past,[66] but because the Backwards have thus far been unable to organize their potential half of the population into a unified front, the Forwards despite their own divisions have managed to hang on. Meanwhile the landless Harijan laborers have begun to assert themselves as well, drawing some encouragement but mostly savage repression from both Forwards and Backwards.

The outcome that would obviously be most beneficial in the longer term would be some sort of consociational arrangement,[67] whereby elites would bargain and negotiate solutions that would provide minimally (and eventually one would hope maximally) acceptable situations for all concerned, even though their constituencies may remain hostile and unreconciled. Yugoslavia may be taken as a model case, where leadership at the central level has worked things out so that the many feuding ethnic nationalities have felt reasonably well looked after.

But any consociational solution is at best a long way off. In the meantime Bihar must contend with a political reality characterized by tension, violence and corruption. Paul Brass has observed of India as a whole that over the period covered by the present essay the basic political structure linking locality to the national level has changed.[68] Twenty-five years ago Jawaharlal Nehru's approach centered on linkage through institution-building: the careful putting together of patronage networks tying in local, state and national levels. Today Indira Gandhi's approach focuses on attempts to bypass all the intermediate levels by aiming rhetoric and grandstanding policy ploys directly at the voters. The Community Development program was characteristic of the Nehru style, while the elimination of princely privy purses symbolizes Mrs. Gandhi's orientation. The overall system, Brass concludes,

> shifts back and forth between jobbery and demagoguery and fails to confront effectively major issues concerning the economic future of India and the spread of lawlessness and violence in the countryside.[69]

From the Bihar perspective there has been an analogous change, from the stately and gentlemanly (though certainly competitive) politics of S.K. Sinha and A.N. Sinha to the venality and violence that have come to typify the era of Jagannath Mishra and Karpoori Thakur. But it should be also noted that the style of that earlier time was well suited to a system in which a few established upper castes dominated and disposed the lower orders. Now that those erstwhile lower groups have gotten into the act, it has all become more crude and unstructured. The rules that were observed when politics was restricted to an aristocratic few will no longer suffice now that the unruly many are in the game. In time new rules and customs will emerge to accommodate all the players, but the process of devising those new rules is going to take some time.

NOTES

1. Comparisons of Bihar with other states will refer in this paper only to the 15 major states; the peripheral hill states (including Himachal Pradesh and Kashmir) will be omitted, as will the various union territories. In some cases Assam will be omitted, too, for lack of data as in the 1981 census figures. Figures for "All-India" will then include only the 15 (or 14 when Assam is excluded) major states. Most of the statistical data used in this essay run through 1978 or in some cases 1981, owing to the unusual delays in publishing such information; conclusions drawn from these data should still be valid as of 1984, however. Change is taking place in Bihar, as it will be argued in the essay, but not so quickly that the figures here will be seriously dated.

2. Reserve Bank of India (RBI), "Estimate of State Domestic Product, 1970–71 to 1978–79," *RBI Bulletin* 35:9 (September 1981), p. 821.

3. V.K.R.V. Rao, *India's National Income, 1950–1980: An Analysis of Economic Growth and Change* (New Delhi: Sage Publications, 1983), p. 174.

4. RBI, *Report on Trend and Progress of Banking in India, 1981–82*, Supplement to *RBI Bulletin* (June 1982), p. 32.

5. A complaint noted earlier in the Janata government's draft five year plan for Bihar; see Government of Bihar (GOB) Planning Department, *Draft Five Year Plan, 1978–83* (Patna: Bihar Secretariat Press, 1978), p. v. See also, RBI Agricultural Credit Department, *Report of the Study Team on Agriculture Credit Institutions in Bihar* (Bombay: RBI, 1977), which is a comprehensive report on agricultural credit in Bihar.

6. Government of India (GOI) Planning Commission, *Sixth Five*

Year Plan, 1980–85 (New Delhi: GOI Press, 1981), p. 56, and GOI, *Census of India 1981*, Series 1, *India*, Paper 3 of 1981. *Provisional Population Totals: Workers and Non–workers*, by P. Padmanabha (Nasik: GOI Press, 1981), pp. 5–6. Again, as mentioned in note 1, the data base used throughout this essay is the 15 major Indian states (sometimes 14, when Assam figures are unavailable). Bihar's small share of national development expenditures is often noted within the state, e.g. Saumitra Banerjee, "Jagannath: Laughter in the Dark," *Sunday*, (Calcutta weekly) 11:5 (21–27 August, 1983), pp. 16–17, writing of a tirade against central stinginess on the part of Bihar Chief Minister Jagannath Mishra, shortly before his ouster from the job by Mrs. Gandhi.

      7. GOI, Planning Commission, *Sixth Five Year Plan, 1980–85*, p. 364.

      8. And much of that 20.8 percent non–farm labor in Bihar was concentrated in the small industrialized Chotanagpur area (where Dhanbad District had 75 percent of its work force off–farm, Singhbhum had 34 percent, Hazaribagh 33 percent, etc.) By contrast, the districts in the Gangetic plain area typically had 11 to 18 percent outside agriculture; See GOI, *Census of India, 1981*, cited in note 6 above.

      9. Alice Thorner, "Semi–Feudalism or Capitalism? Contemporary Debate on Classes and Modes of Production in India," *Economic and Political Weekly* 17:49 (4 December, 1982), pp. 1961–1968; 17:50 (11 December, 1982), pp. 1993–1999; 17:51 (18 December, 1982), pp. 2061–2066; and Gail Omvedt, "Capitalist Agriculture and Rural Classes in India," *Bulletin of Concerned Asian Scholars* 15:3 (July–Agust 1983), pp. 30–54.

      10. World Bank, "Economic Situation and Prospects of India," Report No. 3401–IN (Washington: World Bank, 1981), p. 274.

      11. That is, by a central office which can count things as they leave their distribution points, as with material inputs or cooperative credit, as opposed to inputs like labor time, which can only be measured by surveys, and not very accurately at that.

      12. GOI, Ministry of Agriculture and Irrigation, Depatrment of Agriculture, *All India Report on Agricultural Census, 1970–71*, by I.J. Naidu (Delhi: Controller of Publications, 1975)

      13. In this discussion the three main types of fertilizer — nitrogenous, phosphatic and potassic — are aggregated together. In Bihar, as in India as a whole, nitrogenous fertilizer (primarily urea) is by far the largest component. Fertilizer data used in this essay are from Balu Bung, *A Survey of the Fertilizer Sector in India*, Staff Working Paper No. 331 (Washington: World Bank, 1979) and A. Nageswara Rao, "Disparities in Fertilizer Consumption," *Agricultural Situation in India* 37 (3 June, 1982),

pp. 139–142. The 195,000 ton figure may have been something of an exaggeration, given the widespread corruption that has been known to characterize fertilizer distribution in Bihar. See Farzand Ahmed, "Cooperative Capers," *India Today* 8:14 (16–31 July, 1983), pp. 22–23.

14. A. Nageswara Rao, "Disparities in Fertilizer Consumption," pp. 139–142.

15. Balu Bung, *A Survey of the Fertilizer Sector in India*, p. A28.

16. Irrigation data from GOI, Planning Commission, *Sixth Five Year Plan, 1980–85*, pp. 162–163. Things may get better for Bihar on the irrigation front; Bihar's share of the Sixth Plan outlays are about 11 percent for major/medium and minor irrigation, a figure which compares favorably with its seven percent gross cropped area.

17. Data in this paragraph are from GOI, Planning Commission, *Sixth Five Year Plan, 1980–85*, pp. 250–251.

18. The RLE used two classifications — "agricultural labor," which meant deriving the major portion of household income from working on land for others, and "rural labor," which referred to manual wage labor generally. Agricultural labor households constituted 91 percent of those in the rural labor category in Bihar and 84 percent in India as a whole. Given the rather hazy line delineating what exactly is "agricultural," the wider category has been used in this essay. GOI, Ministry of Labour, Labour Bureau, *Rural Labour Enquiry, 1974–75: Final Report on Employment and Unemployment of Rural Labour Households*, 2 parts (Delhi: Controller of Publications, 1981). The patterns are generally the same for both groups.

19. From an interview with an official in the Office of the Census Commission for India in New Delhi, April 1982.

20. That is, the same agricultural growth statistic used earlier in this essay.

21. The growth in agricultural labor reported by the census over 1971–81 correlates only .54 with the growth of rural labor households shown by the RLE during the 1964–65 to 1974–75 period, perhaps because the time periods are different, as well as the measuring instruments (complete enumeration versus a sample) and the units observed (individual versus households).

22. Actually, the growth of the agricultural labor force employed in the Punjab and Haryana may be underestimated by both the census and the RLE, in view of the large number of people that migrate seasonally for work there, often reported as high as a million (e.g. Gail Omvedt, "Capitalist Agriculture and Rural Classes in India," p. 49; see also Umesh Sinha, "Travails of Migrant Labor," *Economic and Political Weekly* 17:43 (23 October, 1982), p. 1728). They are usually reported to be Biharis,

though this latter may be yet another canard against this much abused state.

23. See for example, F. Tomasson Jannuzi, *Agrarian Crisis in India: The Case of Bihar* (Austin: University of Texas Press, 1974).

24. Cited in note 12 above p. 137.

25. Inderjit Singh, *Small Farmers and the Landless in South Asia*, draft manuscript (Washington: World Bank, 1980), pp. ii, 101–104.

26. Government of Bihar (GOB), *Problems of Small Farmers of Kosi Area (Purnea and Saharsa Districts)* (Patna: Secretariat Press, 1969), p. 7.

27. S.K. Chakrabortty, *Final Report on the Revisional Survey and Settlement Operations in the District of Purnea (1952–1970)* (Patna: Textbook Press, 1972), pp. 116–121.

28. Wolf Ladejinsky, *A Study on Tenurial Conditions in Package Districts*, GOI, Planning Commmission (Delhi: Manager of Publications, 1965), p. 27ff.

29. From the available data it does appear that the incidence of reported sharecropping is not related to agricultural growth. Punjab and Haryana, for example, had much higher rates of tenancy in 1970–71 than Bihar (Inderjit Singh, *Small Farmers and the Landless in South Asia*, pp. ii, 101ff.), perhaps because "progressive farmers" found it profitable to cultivate land leased from others.

30. "Provisional Data on Number and Area of Operational Holdings in 1976–77 — Bihar," *Agricultural Situation in India* 35:9 (December 1980), pp. 681–683.

31. Transfers in name only. This practice of *benami* transfer was widespread at the time of *zamindari* abolition, when large holders would pretend to deed excess land to relatives, servants, bonded laborers, etc., while in fact retaining possession.

32. All data from the essay cited in note 30 above.

33. The references here are to the provisional results of the agricultural census, which appeared in the *Agricultural Situation in India.* The Bihar data listed 12 categories of landholdings, including holdings of less than 0.5 hectares and those of 0.5 < 1.0 hectares, while the all India figures included only holdings of less than one hectare. See "Provisional Data on Number and Area of Operational Holdings, 1976–77 — All–India," *Agricultural Situation in India* 36:7 (October 1981), pp. 561–570; also the essay cited in note 30 above.

34. Though not to any precapitalist egalitarianism. The gini coefficient of inequality decreased over the period only from .866 (on a scale where 1.0 is complete inequality) to .847. There were fewer big landowners but the large number of miniholders dragged out the lower

end of the lorenz curve, making the overall inequality about the same.

35. See, for instance, GOB, Directorate of Information and Public Relations, *Bihar Makes Phenomenal Progess* (Patna: Bihar Secretariat Press, 1976).

36. From data generously supplied by the Revenue Department, Government of Bihar. The data are for land acquired through 31 March 1977, just after the Janata government had replaced the Congress(I) at the Center and just before the analogous replacement of the Congress(I) at the state level.

37. Evidence of such change will of course be clouded by the extent to which patrons use their surplus to become moneylenders.

38. GOI, Ministry of Labour, Labour Bureau, *Rural Labour Enquiry, 1974-75.*

39. See GOI, *Census of India 1981*, cited in note 6 above.

40. Wolf Ladejinsky, "Green Revolution in Bihar, the Kosi Area: A Field Trip," *Economic and Political Weekly* 4:39 (27 September, 1969), pp. A147-A162; also see Pradhan H. Prasad, "Caste and Class in Bihar," *Economic and Political Weekly* 14:7-8 (February Annual Number, 1979), pp. 481-484, and Prasad, "Rising Middle Peasantry in North India," *Economic and Political Weekly* 15:5-7 (February Annual Number, 1980), pp. 215-219.

41. Though generally told only in parts and phases. Frankel's analysis is the first comprehensive account of the relation between caste and politics over the course of the 20th century. Francine R. Frankel, "Caste, Land and Dominance in Bihar: Changing Patterns of Socio-Political Conflicts Between Forward Castes and the Backward Castes," draft ms., University of Pennsylvania, 1983.

42. See Arvind N. Das, *Agrarian Unrest and Socio-economic Change in Bihar, 1900-1980* (New Delhi: Manohar, 1983), whose account and analysis are by far the best to date relating caste, class and the realm of political economy in Bihar.

43. F. Tomasson Jannuzi, *Agrarian Crisis in India.*

44. Pradhan H. Prasad, "Poverty and Bondage," *Economic and Political Weekly* 11:31-33 (August Special Number, 1976), pp. 1269-1272, and "Semi-Feudalism: The Basic Constraint of Indian Agriculture," in Arvind N. Das and V. Nilakant, eds., *Agrarian Relations in India* (New Delhi: Manohar, 1979), pp. 33-49.

45. See Harry W. Blair, "Rising Kulaks and Backward Classes in Bihar: Social Change in the Late 1970s," *Economic and Political Weekly* 15:2 (12 January, 1980), pp. 64-74. All data in the present essay on caste population are taken from this assessment or from Harry W. Blair, "The 1980 Election in Bihar: Disintegration or Emerging Party Stability?" in

Walter Hauser and James Manor, eds., *Two Faces of India: Social and Political Change in Bihar and Karnataka* (Delhi: Oxford University Press, 1984, forthcoming).

46. See Kalyan Mukherjee and Rajendra Singh Yadav, *Bhojpur: Naxalism on the Plains of Bihar* (New Delhi: Radha Krishna Prakashan, 1980), for an account.

47. Bihar has an average of one gram panchayat for every six revenue villages.

48. Almost all the Backward caste MLA and MP candidates I interviewed in Bihar in 1967 had gotten their start in politics in gram panchayat elections, whereas there was a much greater tendency for upper caste contestants to have come into political life through other routes, such as district party committees, university politics, professional activity and the like. This pattern of Backward caste participation in panchayat life was surely noted in Patna, and it may have been for this reason that Bihar was so slow to constitute the Panchayati Raj system of representative government at the block (thana) and district levels. Taken up by most of the other states in the 1960s, the block and district bodies were set up in only a few districts in Bihar. See also the Asoka Mehta Report on Panchayati Raj institutions, which found Bihar to have made the least progress in this area: GOI, Ministry of Agriculture and Irrigation, Department of Rural Development, *Report of the Committee on Panchayati Raj Institutions* (New Delhi: GOI Press, 1978). As late as 1978 only 210 of 575 blocks were covered and 8 of 31 districts. In that year the Karpoori Thakur ministry held gram panchayat elections in an effort to increase its hold at that level and in 1979 the Janata government expanded the system to full coverage at the block level, presumably in the hope that its supporters would win control at that level. But district panchayats remained only 8 in number. See, GOI, Ministry of Rural Reconstruction, *Report: 1980–81* (previously the annual report of the Department of Community Development) (New Delhi: GOI Press, 1981), pp. 89–92.

49. This process of Backward consciousness–raising was greatly helped by the Bihar government itself in composing lists of Backward Classes in 1951. See Harry W. Blair, "Rising Kulaks and Backward Classes in Bihar." For reasons that have always been somewhat murky, Banias (about 0.6 percent of the total population) have generally been included as Backwards, despite their position in the Vaishya varna.

50. After the Yadavs (roughly 11 percent of the population), Kurmis and Koiris (about 4 percent each), the next largest Sudra community are the Telis (3 percent), with nine others between 1 and 2 percent, and all the rest less than one percent.

51. For an account of these developments, see Harry W. Blair, "Rising Kulaks and Backward Classes in Bihar." Also see Francine R. Frankel, "Caste, Land and Dominance in Bihar." It is important to note that Thakur did not win the 1977 poll solely or even mostly on the basis of his Backward leadership; rather it was the same anti-Congress sentiment that swept the Indira Gandhi government out of New Delhi. But the fact of getting elected largely on the basis of one issue did not prevent him from interpreting his victory as a mandate to pursue an entirely unrelated policy initiative, any more than Ronald Reagan's anti-Carter victory in the 1980 American elections prevented him from perceiving his win as support for reducing taxes, escalating the Cold War, etc.

52. An analysis of the 1980 elections in Bihar will be found in Harry W. Blair, "The 1980 Election in Bihar."

53. Francine R. Frankel, "Caste, Land and Dominance in Bihar."

54. Including my own; see Harry W. Blair, "Rising Kulaks and Backward Classes in Bihar." See also James Manor, "Pragmatic Progressives in Regional Politics: The Case of Devaraj Urs," *Economic and Political Weekly* 15:5-7 (February Annual Number, 1980), pp. 201-213, who contrasts Thakur with his more successful counterpart in Karnataka, Devaraj Urs.

55. Perhaps in part because he is a Hajjam or Nai by caste, a relatively small (about 1.5 percent) community, as opposed to Charan Singh, whose Jat caste is the numerically dominant one in much of his western Uttar Pradesh stronghold. Thakur's belonging to such a small group, however, lent credibility to his claim to speak for all Backwards, whereas a Yadav or Kurmi would always have difficulty with people too ready to believe him to be only representing his own community under the guise of standing for the cause of all Backwards.

56. His devotion to the Backward cause should now be clear; for evidence of his solicitude for the progressive farmer, see *Statesman Weekly,* "Five States Demand Farmers' Budget," (10 February, 1979) and *Searchlight* (Patna daily), "Agricultural Income Tax Abolished," (10 February, 1979), two accounts from February 1979, just before the end of his chief ministership.

57. Pradhan H. Prasad, "Caste and Class in Bihar." Also see Arvind N. Das, *Agrarian Unrest and Socio-economic Change in Bihar, 1900-1980.*

58. In fact, all size categories from 3 hectares to over 50 hectares decreased in area, while all those up to 3 hectares increased, with the largest decreases coming in the ranges over 10 hectares and the largest increases coming in those under one hectare. See "Provisional Data on Number and Area of Operational Holdings in 1976-77 — All-India."

59. One measure of the reaction against the Thakur thrust was that in the 1980 poll for the Lok Sabha and the Legislative Assembly, correlations between vote for his party and landholding between one and 10 hectares were quite strongly negative, indicating that where the middle farmer constituency at which he aimed his appeal was strongest, the reception to that appeal (presumably among those above and below the middle farmer stratum) was most hostile. See Harry W. Blair, "The 1980 Election in Bihar."

60. The fact of reserved constituencies in a way made Harijan connections even more valuable, for it was foreordained that a certain number of Scheduled Caste MLAs and MPs would be elected, whereas Backwards might or might not get elected to the general seats.

61. For evidence, see the continuing stream of related articles in *Economic and Political Weekly* from the mid–1970s through the present, particularly those by Arun Sinha.

62. See Kalyan Mukherjee and Rajendra Singh Yadav, *Bhojpur: Naxalism on the Plains of Bihar*, and Arvind N. Das, *Agrarian Unrest and Socio–economic Change in Bihar, 1900–1980.*

63. See Anand Chakravarti, et al., "Agrarian Unrest in Patna: An Investigation into Recent Repression," (New Delhi: People's Union for Democratic Rights, 1981); "Landlord–Police Collusion in Lahsuna," *Economic and Political Weekly* 16:48 (28 November, 1981), pp. 1941–1942; Arvind N. Das, *Agrarian Unrest and Socio–economic Change in Bihar, 1900–1980.*

64. See, e.g., Arun Sinha, "Kill Them and Call Them Naxalites," *Economic and Political Weekly* 10 (7 June 1975).

65. *Mutatis mutandis* the same argument could be made concerning Muslims and Adivasis, the two major groups not taken up in this essay. They have political agendas of their own (declaration of Urdu as an official language for the Muslims, creation of a Jharkhand state for the Tribals, protection from discrimination and communal harassment for both) as well as votes to deliver, but they are not major actors on the political scene in Bihar at the moment.

66. The various caste maneuvers and intrigues that have typified the regimes of Jagannath Mishra and his successor Chandra Sekhar Singh during the 1980–84 period could have taken place just as well during the early 1960s. For insightful but typical accounts, see Arun Sinha, "Part of the Same Ploy," *Economic and Political Weekly* 18:43 (22 October, 1983), pp. 1823–1824; Sumit Mitra and Farzand Ahmed, "Wielding the Axe," *India Today* 8:16 (16–31 August, 1983), pp. 18–20; Seema Mustafa, "Jagannath's Broken Chariot," *Sunday* (Calcutta weekly) 11:5 (21–27 August, 1983), pp. 18–19; and Farzand Ahmed, "The Double Edged

Sword," *India Today* 8:5 (1–15 March, 1983), pp. 24–25; Ahmed, "Cooperative Capers," *India Today* 8:14 (16–31 July, 1983), pp. 22–23; Ahmed, "War Cries," *India Today* 8:18 (16–30 September, 1983), p. 19; Ahmed, "Expansion Backlash," *India Today* 8:22 (16–30 November, 1983), p. 20. The ministerial self-congratulation of the Emergency period also continues. See, for example, GOB, Planning and Development Department (Institutional Finance), *The Twenty Point Programme in Bihar: Progress up to the 31st March 1982* (Patna: Secretariat Press, 1982).

67. For a good summation of the consociational approach and literature, see Arend Lijphart, "Consociational Democracy," *World Politics* 21:2 (January 1969), pp. 207–225; and Hans Daalder, "The Consociational Democracy Theme," *World Politics* 26:4 (July 1974), pp. 604–621.

68. Paul Brass, "National Power and Local Politics in India: A Twenty-year Perspective," *Modern Asian Studies* 18: 1 (February 1984), pp. 89–118.

69. Paul Brass, *Ibid.*, p. 118.

4
Communist Reformers in West Bengal: Origins, Features, and Relations with New Delhi

Atul Kohli

Recent political trends in West Bengal have been at variance both with trends in other parts of India and with past political patterns within Bengal. Several of these distinctive trends are noteworthy at the outset:

1. If the dominant political tendency in Indian politics — at the Center and within the states — has been towards institutional fragmentation, West Bengal politics has moved towards the consolidation of rule by a well organized political party.

2. If power struggles and policy issues have become relatively divorced in much of Indian politics, a coherent policy is integral to the political strategy of West Bengal communists.

3. If ideological commitments to reformism have even lost their rhetorical and legitimizing function in much of Indian politics, West Bengal communists have taken small but important steps towards implementing redistributive reforms.

4. And if the "spread" of politics in India has created the problem of accommodating the middle groups (commercial peasantry, "backward" castes, and the urban educated unemployed) within the framework of elite caste and class politics, the challenge in West Bengal is deeper, involving the accommodation of the lower social classes.

The contemporary political situation in West Bengal is thus best characterized as one dominated by a relatively stable party regime with democratic–centralist organization, a reformist ideology, and a lower–middle and lower–class social base. In an attempt to explain the emergence and discuss the significance of such a parliamentary–communist rule in West Bengal, I will address three specific questions: (1) How has this distinctive political situation emerged within West Bengal? (2) What are the specific features of this reformist regime? and (3) What are the implications of such a parliamentary–communist rule both for the future of West Bengal poliics and for the relations of the communist rulers with New Delhi?

WHY IS WEST BENGAL RULED BY COMMUNISTS?

While the communists have only recently consolidated their electoral position within West Bengal, radical politics has a long history in Bengal. The contemporary political situation is thus best understood as a culmination of historically rooted Bengali radicalism, moderated by the imperatives of democracy and capitalism. In order to understand the emergence and the rise of communism in West Bengal, therefore, the first major issue requiring explanation is the radical political inclination in this region of India.

The historical roots of Bengal's radical politics can be delineated by addressing three important issues. There is first the need to focus on and explain the early rise of a critical intelligenstia within Bengal – the Bengali *bhadralok*. An understanding of this social group is critical because (1) Bengali radicalism has had elite origins and (2) many of the twentieth century Bengali radical political elite have shared this social background. A radical elite, however, can not succeed politically without some mass support. The second issue requiring explanation is the relative weakness of caste and class dominance in Bengal. This social–structural condition has enabled the radical elite to extricate a lower caste following. What has finally enabled the radical elite and their followers to displace Congress rule is a well–organized and disciplined political party. How such a party has emerged within West Bengal is thus the third issue area of discussion. I locate the roots of this development in the political traditions of disciplined organizations, especially terrorist organizations, within Bengal. Each of these three issues – the rise of a radical intelligentsia; the weakness of caste and class domination; and disciplined political organizations – are discussed below in a highly condensed form, suitable only for suggesting the flavor and not the details of the argument.[1]

The origins of a radical leadership within Bengal is best understood by focusing both on the culture and the formative historical experiences shared by the regional political elite. Political leadership within Bengal had generally originated from the Bengali *bhadralok* – the high status intelligentsia identifiable as an exclusive grouping by their educational and cultural accomplishments.[2] By the turn of the century the *bhadralok* came to be widely recognized as Bengali community leaders, especially within Hindu Bengal. Products of British education, which was introduced earlier in Bengal than in other parts of India, the *bhadralok* confronted the colonial rulers with demands for political and social reform. The British, in turn, devised various "carrot-and-stick" strategies to cope with increasing vocal political opposition.

What transformed a set of reformist demands into a militant nationalist movement within Bengal was the first attempted partition of Bengal.[3] This partition injured Bengali pride deeply and threatened to severely reduce the scope of *bhadralok* influence. The *bhadralok* reacted with a vengeance; their response was conditioned both by the severity of the threat and the prevailing cultural mood. And the mood was one of romanticization of violence and militancy. Important political and literary leaders such as Bankim Chandra Chatterjee, Aurobindo Ghose and Bipin Chandra Pal successfully interpreted the religious traditions of Kali and Durga as providing a guide to militant action. Violence and militancy came to be regarded as expressions of self-sacrifice for a higher good, and thus as political actions inviting the admiration of Bengali society.[4]

The eventual reunification of Bengal was interpreted by many within Bengal as a victory for militant tactics. As a legacy of the anti-partition movement, sections of Bengali *bhadralok* also came to deeply distrust the British and, related to this, viewed the prospect of participating in British-controlled parliamentary politics with suspicion. Extra-parliamentary militancy thus gained considerable legitimacy as a political strategy within Bengal. The British reacted characteristically to the *bhadralok* militancy, sought to divide-and-rule, and increasingly came to ally with Bengali Muslims. The Muslims, first as part of the Congress, and later as part of Jinnah's Muslim League, thus occupied the political "center" and dominated legislative politics in Bengal during 1920-40. After the creation of Pakistan, however, as the Muslim leadership departed, this pattern of politics created a situation wherein the Congress and a "center-moderate" leadership, capable of forging a consensual alliance, were relatively weak within West Bengal.

Throughout the nationalist phase the Bengali *bhadralok* were, moreover, not as enamored of Gandhi and the Congress as other regional leaders of India. A strong regional identity led Bengali leaders to view Gandhi as primarily representing the Hindi-speaking heartland of India.

Because domination by Hindi-speaking India is a prospect most Bengalis have traditionally sought to avoid, Gandhi's leadership was not easily embraced by the *bhadralok*. Gandhi's penchant for non-violence and reconciliatory attitude towards the Muslims also did not mesh well with important strains within Bengali political culture. As a consequence, not only was Congress a weaker force in Hindu Bengal than in the Hindi-speaking heartland of India, but Bengali "moderates" were also at a distinct disadvantage; legitimacy of their leadership was undermined by its association with the unwelcome leadership of Gandhi and the Indian National Congress.[5]

Regional nationalism and the romanticization of violence were thus two important themes within the Bengali *bhadralok* political culture prior to Independence. Why should these political preferences, however, lead a segment of the *bhadralok* to embrace the left-of-center ideologies of communism and socialism? The link is nebulous and indirect but real; it is best understood by focusing on the fact that attachment to militant Bengali nationalism precluded the acceptance of the "moderate" leadership of Gandhi and the Congress. Having forsaken the political "center," the radical-left and radical-right were the available ideological options. And Bengali leadership was periodically attracted to both. The political careers of M.N. Roy and Subhash Bose thus highlight a more general tendency among the Bengali *bhadralok*, namely, the search of an oppositional elite for radical ideologies.

A number of factors eventually influenced the conversion of Bengali militant nationalists to communism. As most of those who became communist leaders in the 1940s and 1950s were from a "terrorist" (read militant-nationalist) background, interviews with them reveal the factors that led to their breaking away from such terrorist organizations as the Jugantar group and to joining the Communist Party.[6] First, there was general sympathy for the "downtrodden" and the "poor" within Bengali political culture; even the much revered Tagore had socialist sympathies. Second, the Russian revolution had a profound impact on Bengal's militant nationalists. The Bolshevik victory was widely interpreted as a defeat for western imperialism. Sympathy with Bolsheviks and Bolshevik strategy was readily equated with a strategy of militant and heroic nationalistic struggle against British imperialism. Third, there was material help from the new Bolshevik rulers of Russia. And lastly, because a militant strategy distinguished Bengali radicals from the "soft" and "compromising" Congress of Gandhi and because the ideas of communism linked the cause of political heroism to a "higher" good — the creation of a strong and classless society — many former terrorists were slowly but surely attracted to the Communist Party.

If the above discussion gives an inkling of why a significant section of Bengali *bhadralok* were not attracted to Gandhi and the Congress but rather to more militant ideologies, and of why a significant minority among the militant nationalists eventually embraced communism, the next issue is why and how did a radical leadership extricate a sizable lower class following. The question is especially important because radical leaders in other parts of India, save Kerala, have not been very successful in attracting lower class support. The social structural condition best explaining lower class radicalism is the relative weakness of caste and class domination within West Bengal. Since this argument can easily become a tautology, what is meant by "weakness of social domination" requires explication.

The early support of the communists within West Bengal was among the unionized working class. Why should the communists have had greater success in attracting union support within West Bengal than in other parts of India? Numerous factors help explain this outcome. First, there was simply the issue of timing. Industry and a working class emerged earlier in West Bengal than in most parts of India (with the important exception of Bombay and parts of Maharashtra). While Congress leaders were busy organizing against the British, communist leaders, who were in abundance in Bengal in any case, penetrated and gained control over important segments of the trade union movement. Second, the continued weakness of the Congress party within West Bengal made it difficult for non–communist forces to extricate the trade unions from communist control. And third, and most important, there has been the Bengali link between the communist leaders and the working class, pitched against the non–Bengali entrepreneurs within West Bengal — the Marwaris and the Parsis. Because industry and commerce within West Bengal have been controlled by non–Bengali "outsiders," the Marwaris and the Parsis have found it difficult to legitimize their privileged position within the social hierarchy. Bengali leaders and followers have thus organized against non–Bengalis in a struggle which is simultaneously ethnic and class–oriented.[7] Weakness of class domination has, in other words, facilitated lower class radicalism.

The peasantry within West Bengal has also over the years proven to be more susceptible to radicalism and communist appeals than in other parts of India. This is not only manifest in such major peasant struggles as

Tebhaga and Naxalbari, but also in the less dramatic — though more consequential — fact of widespread rural electoral support for the communists.[8] Why should this be so? While this is a complex historical issue, the answer again revolves around the failure of the privileged to legitimize their position and, therefore, their domination over subordinates within the Bengali countryside. This failure is in turn rooted both in the weakness of caste as a mode of social organization within Bengal and in the specific form of absentee landownership that the *zamindari* system came to represent.

Weakness of caste in West Bengal is a well–known fact. This weakness manifests itself sociologically in the relative freedom of social association among Bengalis, and politically, in the fact that no major party within West Bengal utilizes caste appeals for electoral mobilization. This weakness of caste within Bengal is in turn associated with weakness of caste–Hinduism in Bengal, and is rooted deeply in the history of this area. The long historical chain of causation responsible for this significant social outcome can only be hinted at here: Bengal remained outside the zone of Aryan culture from ancient times; egalitarian Buddhism survived much longer in Bengal than in other parts of India; mass lower caste conversions to Islam in the middle ages not only highlighted the weakness of and rebellion against caste domination in the area but also gave rise to numerous Hindu reform movements aimed at softening the repressive elements of caste–Hinduism; and Tantrism, Vaishnavism, Kali and Durga worship, Brahmo–Samaj, and the reformism of Ramakrishna and Vivekananda all represented periodic religious movements against mainstream Hinduism with an anti–caste, egalitarian thrust.[9] While none of this is to suggest that caste–Hinduism does not exist in West Bengal, historical distinctiveness and repeated reform movements have made caste a weaker principle of social organization in Bengal than in other parts of India. The major consequence of this for the argument being developed here is that lower caste positions within a hierarchical structure were not deemed to be very legitimate in this part of India.

Weakness of domination was also reenforced by the *zamindari* system of land tenure introduced by the British. As a result of the *zamindari* system, landowners became far removed from concerns of land; they not only lived away from where their lands were, but they also came to disdain manual and agricultural work. Thus arose within Bengal a class of landowners whose life style was devoted, not to agriculture and production, but to music, poetry, literature, art, philosophical concerns, social criticism and even radical politics. Not being an integral part of the agricultural scene, the owners found it difficult to cover their economic privileges with ideological cloaks. The more radical of the *bhadralok* would later exploit this situation to undermine the economic privileges of their more fortunate brethren, while enhancing their own power position in society.

Both in the cities and in the countryside of Bengal, then, the domination of the privileged over their subordinates was not as consolidated as in many other parts of India. As a consequence, Bengali lower castes and classes provided radicalizable political material. While one should not overestimate lower class radicalism within contemporary West Bengal, the fact is that mere elite radicalism, without peasant and worker support for the Communist Party, could not have led to a democratically elected communist government.

In addition to radical leaders and radicalizable lower social groups, another important factor in the contemporary success of the left within West Bengal has been an effective, centralized political party. What historical factors are responsible for the emergence of such a political force? In a part of the world where personalities, factions, and fragmented parties dominate the political scene, what helps explain the existence of a relatively cohesive political organization? In addition to the obvious role of radical political leaders in organizing democratic–centralist parties, it is also important to take account of the Bengali terrorist past.

By the turn of the century, many of Bengal's militant nationalists, utilizing terrorism as a mode of political activity, organized themselves into highly secretive and disciplined groups. The Anushilan and the Jugantar *samitis* or groups were two of the prominent "underground" organizations.[10] What is interesting about these organizations is the uncanny resemblance they have with the democratic–centralist organization of a communist party. These similarities were clearest in the principles of organizational recruitment, socialization and discipline. To become a full member of the *samitis*, for example, participants had to go through three stages, taking different sets of vows at each stage. Each of these stages involved growing commitment to the organization. The longer the participants remained with the organization, the more they learned to downplay personal interests and familial loyalties on the one hand and to abide by organizational principles on the other. In many instances, *samiti* members committed political murders to punish what was conceived to be a breach of membership principles by newer members. And all this before Lenin's idea of democratic–centralism had reached this part of the world.

Such secretive and disciplined organizations reflected in part the security needs required to carry on terrorist activities against the British, and in part a Bengali tradition of secretive organization of social and religious dissent. Those attracted to terrorism and militancy in Bengal thus acquired an organizational ethos stressing discipline, secretiveness, respect for hierarchy, and self-sacrifice as the political act of highest virtue.

The programs of terrorist organizations in the early part of the century were primarily nationalist with religious and conservative overtones. Slowly, however, many of the terrorists were attracted to left ideologies. The role of Moscow-returned Bengali communists was quite significant in this process. Leaders of terrorist parties were not necessarily attracted to communist ideology. Their interest in the foreign emissaries was primarily the prospect of securing arms and money from the Bolsheviks. These contacts, however, put the returning communists in close touch with intermediate leaders and even the rank and file of the terrorist organizations. Foreign-returned communists had all the necessary ingredients to facilitate ideological conversion: intellectual sophistication; commitment to anti-imperialism; the blessings of the greatest revolutionary leaders, the Bolsheviks; and most of all, readiness to court danger and risk their lives for a higher social good.

Foreign-returned communists, as well as the ideas inspired by the Russian revolution, had the impact of converting many members of the Anushilan and Jugantar Samitis to communism. When jailed in the 1930s, committed communists further converted other jailed terrorists to communism. Such were the beginnings of the original conversions to communism in Bengal. Some of these early converts later became leaders of India's Communist Party. Individuals such as Pramode Das Gupta, Hare Krishna Konar and Binoy Chowdhury are all old terrorist revolutionaries who converted to communism and then devoted their lives to building the communist movement in Bengal.

Thus, a significant minority of Bengali political activists already understood the significance of disciplined organizations when they were introduced to communism. Having embraced the new ideology, the organizational principles of democratic-centralism must have come very easily to this group. Discipline, hierarchy, and party before all else, were values integral to the terrorist political sub-culture. In all probability, these political cultural traditions have facilitated the growth of relatively cohesive parties in contemporary West Bengal. Of course, this is not to ignore the legendary factionalism and sectarianism of the Indian left. Nevertheless, the Communist Party of India(Marxist) (CPM) in West Bengal stands out today as one of the more cohesive political forces in all of India. Long traditions of disciplined organization are, at least in part, responsible for this political characteristic.

By the time of Independence, radical politics had already established strong roots in Bengal. A small but significant number of the political elite had embraced communism, and the lower classes — workers and peasants — had indicated ample susceptibility to radical appeals. The political traditions of the area further enabled the radical elite to organize a small but disciplined party, which would in time grow into the ruling party.

Since Independence the emergence of communists as a ruling force within West Bengal is a function of two related but separate conditions: the weakness of Congress; and the growing electoral popularity of the CPM. Both of these require explanation.

Prior to Independence, Muslims had dominated Bengal's electoral politics. Muslims had also secured the support of the Hindu lower castes and classes by promising them agrarian reforms in the 1930s. As Muslim leaders left for Pakistan, the West Bengal Congress found itself weak, fragmented and with little established grass roots support. Individuals like Atulya Ghosh and B.C. Roy could still muster electoral majorities by their association with Nehru and the Congress, but they had little or no autonomous power base within the state.[11]

Congress general strategy for generating electoral majorities throughout India was to co-opt local influentials — often of higher caste and landed backgrounds — into a large patronage network. The success of this formula rested on the assumption that local influentials could control the electoral behavior of their numerous dependents. This assumption was not as valid in West Bengal as it was in many other parts of India. Caste and class domination had been weaker in West Bengal. Many of the lower classes had already exhibited their political independence in acts varying from strikes and rebellions to bestowing support upon a Muslim government promising agrarian reforms. From the very beginning, therefore, Congress was handicapped in West Bengal.

Furthermore, Congress continued to be thought of as a party of Hindi–speaking India. The partition experience reinforced the belief held already by many in West Bengal that Congress and New Delhi did not have Bengal's interests at heart. Not only was lower class support not universal for Congress, but many of the elites, touched by regional nationalism, held Congress suspect. As the euphoria of national independence fell into the background, issues of regional nationalism resurfaced; they became important electoral issues and further undermined Congress' support.

The Bengali elite and masses alike were thus not incorporated as easily into Congress as in other states of independent India. The very factors which undermined Congress' support, moreover, worked in favor of the communists. Cultural proclivity to radicalism and Bengali nationalism ensured that the new generation of political activists would continue to be attracted, not to Congress, but to left politics. Bengali propertied classes continued to take little interest in production and thus also failed to encourage production–oriented politics. Redistribution and equality, not production and efficiency, became the dominant political themes. Non–Bengali capitalists tended either to withdraw capital or secure central support to ensure their interests. Either of these moves inflamed Bengali passions and created further distrust of capitalism. The lower classes exhibited political independence and quite a few were attracted to left parties. Cumulatively, these trends continued to benefit West Bengal's communists.

With a few minor swings, West Bengal's communists have steadily improved their electoral support. The splits within the communist movement actually worked to the benefit of the long term interests of the CPM. The CPM was on the one hand able to distinguish itself from the CPI, which had over the years been moving closer and closer to the Congress party under Moscow's directions. On the other hand, the CPM also successfully disassociated itself from the more extreme Naxalites. The CPM thus struck a popular image of a party which was both radical and responsible. At the same time, as it did not have the record of collaboration with New Delhi, it could capitalize on regional nationalist themes. Radical, responsible and West Bengal's alternative to Congress: these were the images which eventually enabled the CPM to secure electoral majorities.

It is important to note that the CPM finally swept to power in 1977 only when anti–Indira sentiments were sweeping India as a whole.

The sentiments which worked to Janata's advantage in other parts of India enhanced the CPM's electoral position within West Bengal. This suggests that while the CPM has a strong political base within West Bengal, its dominant position is also a result of electoral caprice. Moreover, the CPM emerged victorious in the first–past–the–post electoral system in which a divided opposition — Congress and Janata - is always punished. The reason the CPM has been able to consolidate its position since 1977, of course, has to do with its effective performance. Nevertheless, electoral caprice and distortions of the electoral system have benefitted the CPM. As the opposition can reunite and electoral popularity can be affected by numerous factors, the CPM may well be voted out of power in the future. Those are the necessary hazards of democratic politics. That outcome, however, would not in any way deny the significant political position which a "radical but responsible," or a reformist–communist party, has come to occupy within West Bengal.

THE CPM REGIME IN WEST BENGAL[12]

The Communist Party of India(Marxist) returned to power in West Bengal in 1977. Unlike the previous United Front ministries, the CPM this time had a clear majority, having won 177 of the 293 assembly seats. With its other partners in the Left Front, the CPM now controlled a solid majority of 230 seats. The 1982 elections were a near repeat performance. These "parliamentary communists" have since sought to use their power to introduce elements of redistribution into the process of development. Central to their political–economic strategy has been a concerted attack on the rural poverty of West Bengal. Restructuring local government, establishing programs for sharecroppers, facilitating credit for small holders and mobilizing the landless for higher wages are all part of the strategy. While many other leaders in India have discussed these redistributive goals, only the CPM has made a systematic and impressive effort to implement them. This reformist thrust reflects the pattern of leadership, ideology, and organization of the CPM regime.

The leadership is neither concentrated in the hands of an individual nor, as might be expected in a communist regime, in the party alone. While the party wields great influence, leadership is shared by the three "wings" of the CPM — the party organization proper, the Kisan Sabha (the peasant wing), and the parliamentary wing. Since the CPM has to compete for votes in an electoral system, the organizational wing of the party cannot simply dictate party policies. The party line has had to take account of both the Kisan Sabha, which provides the crucial link to rural voters, and the parliamentary leaders, who run the government.[13] This sharing of power has not led to the intense conflicts so characteristic of other Indian states. Two important factors have kept such conflict under control. First and foremost has been party discipline. The party is of course organized along democratic-centralist lines. The party position, therefore, once adopted, is binding on all party members. Since members of the government generally belong to the party, party discipline imposes consensus upon the government. In other words, while factionalism exists, and at times threatens the process of government, it has not precluded the pursuit of coherent policy. Second, there is a shared perception of a common enemy: the central government of India in alliance with business interests and the landlords. The process of securing and maintaining power is thus conceived of as an ongoing struggle requiring political unity.[14]

The CPM's ideology over the years has shifted from a revolutionary to a reformist orientation. Instead of emphasizing "class confrontation" as a means of establishing the "dictatorship of the proletariat," the CPM now seeks to preserve democratic institutions while using state power to facilitate "development with redistribution." This "democratic-socialist" tilt is spelled out in the party program, which recommends mobilization of "the broadest possible support" against "authoritarianism," including "elements who do not support the economic program of the party."[15] Moreover, the party's "agrarian program" now seeks the support of "the rich and the poor" peasants; besides the "land question," it addresses the problems of "irrigation, seeds, and fair prices for produce." No longer does the CPM define its friends and enemies strictly by class: even "exploiting" classes are not "enemy" classes as long as they are productive and willing to extend political support.

Underlying this ideological shift are several factors. First, as the CPM has sought electoral success, there has been greater need for broad-based political support. Recognizing that the rich and the middle peasants are not only numerically significant but, if alienated, can mobilize considerable opposition, the CPM has sought to soften its ideological position. Second, the CPM has learned from experience. Having seen earlier United Front ministries in West Bengal and Kerala collapse because of class hostility that the communists unleashed but could not control, and because of pressure by the central government, the CPM has now decided to "go slow," while reassuring the propertied by specifying the limits of the party's "socialist intent." And lastly, there is the problem of economic growth. Regime positions perceived as radical will discourage privately controlled economic activity. But regime legitimacy remains dependent on the demonstrated prudence of the rulers as economic managers. To gain power and to survive within the framework of democratic capitalism, the CPM has learned that it cannot be a revolutionary party.

At the core of the CPM as an organizational force is a tightly knit and relatively small party. Party membership is about 100,000 in a state with a population of 50 million. In the recent past, the bulk of this membership came from urban professional groups. The peasantry was only "discovered" systematically in the late 1960s. With the spread of commerce in the countryside, landlords have further lost their control over the dependent peasantry. This change has been rightly perceived as an opportunity to gain the support of this newly released political resource. Further, the CPM has found itself competing for peasant support with such "Maoist" groups as the Naxalites. As the CPM has made inroads into villages, however, its rural base has continued to develop with the help of groups other than the poorest of the poor. The key linkage groups are students with rural roots who come to the cities for education, get politicized, and go back to rural areas to teach and serve as party organizers and propagandists. As these students often come from middle-income backgrounds, the social base of the CPM in both the city and the countryside rests on the middle stratum.

While the core membership comes from the middle stratum, party support is widespread among lower-income groups. A series of "interest group" organizations are affiliated with, support and are supported by the party. These include the student movement in universities, the teachers' movement in secondary and primary schools, the women's movement, the trade union movement, and the peasant and landless laborers' movements organized under the Kisan Sabha. These organizations provide important links between the party and the society at large. Electoral and other types of political support are mobilized through the various movements, and those representing the movements expect rewards from the party, once it comes to power.

Underlying the CPM's electoral success in 1977 were not only its own deepening political base but the failure of other parties. Once in power, however, the CPM sought to extend and consolidate its base further, especially in the rural areas. To incorporate the lower rural classes more effectively, the CPM restructured local government. The

West Bengal CPM government was the first in India to allow political parties to compete for local government positions. Well aware of its new popularity, the CPM hoped that its own candidates would be successful. The strategy paid off. Eighty-seven percent of the seats at the district level, 74 percent at the block level (the block is an administrative unit between the district and the village), and 67 percent at the village level were captured by those running on the CPM ticket. The results of the 1983 panchayat elections were of a similar order. These "red panchayats" (panchayat being the Indian term for local government) are very important in CPM's overall political and developmental strategy.

While the majority of new office holders are party sympathizers rather than party members, a large majority are small landholders and teachers and therefore from rural lower-middle income groups.[16] This is an extremely significant shift from past patterns. Never have local governments in West Bengal, or, for that matter in much of India, been so free of the domination of landlords and rich peasants. The CPM has done what no other Indian political force has been able to do: throughly penetrate the countryside without depending on large landowners. The CPM regime, along with the newly recreated local governments, thus represents two interlinked patterns of political change: an organizational penetration by the "center" into the "periphery," and a simultaneous shift in the class basis of institutional power.

The CPM has utilized its newly consolidated position to initiate rural reforms. The bulk of the rural poor in West Bengal are sharecroppers and landless laborers. Reform programs have been aimed primarily at these groups, especially the sharecroppers (*bargardars* in Bengali). Tenancy in the past has been based largely on informal arrangements. As a consequence, laws designed to cut back the size of the share of the crop that the sharecropper must hand over to the landowner, and laws to increase the security of tenure, have been ineffective. To alter this situation, the CPM regime has undertaken a concerted effort to legally register the sharecroppers, in the hope that this will improve their incomes and provide them greater security.

One of the early acts of the CPM government was to amend the land reform laws so as to transfer the burden of proof of land-sharing arrangements from the sharecropper to the landowner. With this law on the books, the government undertook a special drive called "operation *barga*" to facilitate rapid registration of the *bargardars*, the sharecroppers. Teams of bureaucrats and/or party members, activists, and Kisan Sabha members were sent out to the countryside to announce the laws and to register the sharecroppers on the spot. The "operation" enjoyed considerable success. Whereas over the previous three decades, fewer than 60,000 sharecroppers were registered in the areas where the CPM is now operating, in its first five years the CPM succeeded in registering over one million.[17] Compared to the past performances of Congress and other regimes in the area, therefore, the CPM's current success has been spectacular. Given the size of the problem — there are nearly 1.5 million families of sharecroppers in West Bengal — more, of course, remains to be done. Nevertheless, the CPM has taken an impressive first step toward improving the living conditions of the sharecropper.

What can explain the CPM's success in registering so large a number of sharecroppers? The mere legalistic act of registration challenges class relations in the countryside. It is aimed at reducing the landowner's control of and income from his property. The act, therefore, is bound to provoke considerable opposition. The sharecroppers are generally afraid to participate in the process without the support of forces outside of the village community. And it is this crucial role of "outside support" that the CPM regime has played. The power of both the party and the government is being utilized to improve the condition of the sharecroppers. The role of the party has been especially significant. "Operation *barga*" has thus had the greatest success in those parts of Bengal where the party is strongest. The crucial variable, very likely, has been party–initiated politicization. As a consequence of sustained party activity, the sharecroppers come to understand the laws, trust the party, and take the final and important step of registration. This act of defiance against the traditional patron perhaps does more to help implement the sharecropping laws than the refinement of the laws themselves.

Modest increases in income and greater security for the sharecroppers have been the short run consequences of registration.[18] The CPM regime has also striven to make it easier for registered sharecroppers to get institutional credit. The government has negotiated with the commercial banks and secured an agreement "in principle" that banks will lend money not only against land but also against a share of the crop. Furthermore, the government has promised to "subsidize" the labor–intensive aspects of the banking costs. The party–controlled local governments will prepare lists of registered sharecroppers and specify their legal share of the crop. This information will be provided to the banks and will save them considerable labor cost. The banks will then offer loans — part in cash and part in vouchers — for agricultural inputs.

The government will also subsidize the interest the sharecropper must pay. The program is a novel one, and it is too early for it to be judged a success or a failure. In 1982 approximately 3,000,000 registered sharecroppers received institutional credit.[19] If the offering of credit can be sustained and expanded, it will demonstrate how a well-organized, left-of-center government can imaginatively and systematically intervene in a private enterprise economy so as to strengthen the position of the lower classes.

In addition to the program for the sharecroppers, the CPM's efforts have been aimed at providing extra employment and better wages for landless agricultural laborers. The Food for Work Program (FWP) — a public works-oriented, employment-generating scheme, in part supported by the wheat/rice grants from the centrally controlled surplus — has been implemented with considerable effectiveness in West Bengal. As a consequence of this, about one month of extra employment for one third of all the landless households has been generated per year. Considering that most of the landless usually get no more than four months of employment per year, this increment is by no means insignificant. The implementation of the program has been facilitated by the party-controlled local governments. Much of the money is channelled through these "red panchayats." In consultation with the local party cadres, the panchayats decide which projects will be undertaken, choose who will be employed, and administer the funds. As the political fortunes of the CPM are closely tied to the success of such distributive schemes, sustained pressure through the party has minimized the commoner problems of corruption and the frittering away of funds in the backyards of local notables.

Party-initiated wage struggles have been the other "non-governmental" mode of increasing the incomes of landless laborers. As a party in power, seeking to maintain broad-based political support, however, the CPM's efforts at organized, union-supported agitation in the countryside have not been very significant. The socio-economic conditions are also hard. With a massive labor supply, only the peak employment season offers the laborers a favorable bargaining position. Nevertheless, in some parts of West Bengal, where party organization is strong, unionization has led to a small rise in wages. My own interviews revealed that wage levels in the unionized blocks tended to be somewhat higher than in the non-unionized ones.

None of the above is meant to imply that rural poverty in West Bengal is on the verge of being eradicated. The problem is massive. The

CPM has only made a small but impressive beginning towards a solution. They have clearly demonstrated a capacity to implement incremental reform policies. The ultimate effects of these policies will take some time to be felt. Within the Indian context, however, where poverty stubbornly persists, any small success at redistribution deserves attention.

The CPM's reform approach has four major characteristics. First, their rule is coherent. The relatively unified leadership has made for clear policy thinking, and for sustained political attention to issues of poverty and development. Second, the ideological goals and the organizational arrangements of the CPM deny the upper classes direct access to the political arena. While the upper classes remain powerful, and significant concessions are made to them, they do not directly control the political process. As a consequence, there is a degree of separation between social and political power. This reduces the possibility that reform programs will be co-opted by the socially powerful. Third, the CPM's organization is both centralized and decentralized. While the decision-making power is concentrated, through newly structured local government local initiative and knowledge can be incorporated within the framework of central directives. And fourth, the CPM's ideology is flexible enough to accommodate the continued dominance of propertied classes in the social and economic sphere. This makes the prospect of reformism tolerable for the upper classes.

Central to an understanding of the CPM's reforms and approach are the characteristics of the CPM as a party. A well-organized, left-of-center party can allow a reformist orientation to be institutionalized within the ruling regime. Political power can thus be used to push through some systematic reforms of the agrarian social order.

RELATIONS WITH NEW DELHI AND FUTURE PROSPECTS

So far I have analyzed the historical origins and the features of the current CPM regime within West Bengal. The subject of this volume suggests that two more issues ought to be discussed: the relations of the CPM regime with the Center; and the future prospects of the CPM within West Bengal. Both of these are discussed below in turn.

The current relationship of West Bengal's communist rulers with Mrs. Gandhi is best described as one of strained coexistence. What factors help explain elements of strain in the relationship, and what constrains both actors into reluctant coexistence? It is important to note right away that the strained relationship of the CPM and Mrs. Gandhi masks what is essentially a struggle over power and influence. The reason to state this seemingly obvious fact is to distinguish what is going on — a naked power struggle — from how it is characterized by the contending actors.

Mrs. Gandhi often labels West Bengal's communists as irresponsible rulers creating problems of law and order. By contrast, the communists characterize their struggle with Mrs. Gandhi either as a struggle against the attempts of the Center to dominate states, or as a struggle against the attempts of reactionary bourgeois–landlord forces to dislodge a set of progressive rulers. While Mrs. Gandhi thus appeals to sentiments favoring effective government, Bengali communists invoke regional nationalism and class hostility. These charges and counter–charges are essentially without substance. If effective government were to be characterized by stability, coherent policies, minimal corruption and orderly elections and assumption of power, then the CPM in West Bengal is probably a more effective government than most state governments in India. So much for Mrs. Gandhi's claims of the CPM as "irresponsible"! Similarly, the CPM is not really a revolutionary force anymore. It can hardly, therefore, blame all its problems away as problems of class hostility represented by the Center.

Why has Mrs. Gandhi been reluctant to repeat the earlier strategy utilized against the "united front" governments within West Bengal, namely, an imposition of President's Rule? While there is nothing to definitely prevent Mrs. Gandhi from undertaking such an action in the future, a number of conditions militate against such a move. First, the CPM offers a much more "responsible" government today than it did in the earlier period. Having forsaken organized "land grabs" and therefore the more destabilizing aspects of "class struggle" in the countryside, as well as having discouraged militant labor activities in Calcutta and elsewhere, the CPM has now become a more acceptable government to the socially powerful than in the earlier years. As a matter of fact, representatives of some of the Chambers of Commerce within West Bengal have requested Mrs. Gandhi to let the CPM rulers continue in power. They have argued that the CPM is likely to initiate greater labor militancy when in opposition than when in power.

Another crucial factor discouraging direct central intervention in West Bengal is probably the widespread state–level popularity enjoyed by the CPM. West Bengal might well prove to be ungovernable if Mrs. Gandhi were to forcibly dislodge the CPM from power. The CPM not only has "hardened" support in the labor unions but increasingly also in the countryside. If forced out of power, the CPM might easily revert back to more revolutionary tactics. At a future date, it is conceivable that Mrs. Gandhi may actually wish this outcome; she would then have a "legitimate" excuse to eliminate a large number of opponents from the political scene. For now, however, she has a number of other regional crises at her hand; she probably has no wish to create another one while Assam is still simmering and a solution to Sikh demands in Punjab is not visible.

For now, therefore, the CPM and Mrs. Gandhi coexist in a strained political relationship. A power struggle continues but manifests itself in less dramatic ways than the imposition of President's Rule. Mrs. Gandhi's strategy seems to be to weaken both the electoral and the coalitional base of the CPM. The periodic termination of central funds for the Food for Work Program — which as a patronage resource brings the CPM considerable popularity in the countryside — highlights Mrs. Gandhi's attempts to do what she can to undermine the CPM's electoral support. Similarly, well-publicized "leaks" about discussions between Congress(I) and minority partners in the CPM-led Left Front government reflect Mrs. Gandhi's continued attempt to split "left unity." These efforts take on considerable meaning for the CPM if one keeps in mind that the Congress(I) in the 1982 elections secured nearly one third of the popular vote.

The CPM's counter-strategy rests mainly on consolidating its electoral base by incorporating the middle and the lower classes. This has been discussed above. Additionally, however, the CPM has gone out of its way to give significant cabinet level appointments to relatively minor partners of the Left Front. This is to guard against any breakup of the Front and prevent any future alliance between minor parties and the Congress(I). The other aspect of the CPM's counter-strategy has been to join forces with non-Congress states to demand basic changes in center-state relationships. All of these demands aim to enhance the scope and control of the state governments vis-a-vis the central government of India.

If strained coexistence best describes West Bengal's relations with Mrs. Gandhi, what speculations can be made about CPM's continued capacity to attract future electoral support within West Bengal? While unforeseen and discrete events always affect electoral behavior, two issues are likely to be of considerable consequence for the CPM's support. First, the CPM continues to face the difficult problem of reconciling the interests of middle and small landholding peasants on the one hand and those of landless laborers on the other hand. Because both of these groups are of considerable numerical significance, the CPM must attract their support simultaneously in order to win clear electoral majorities. This, however, is not easy. The demands of the landholding peasantry are for subsidized inputs and price supports; those of the landless laborers are for higher wages and increased public investments in employ-ment–generating projects. Higher wages are resisted by middle peasants because they often employ wage laborers. Public expenditure to subsidize inputs and provide price–support, by contrast, undermines governmental capacity to fund employment–creating public works projects. The CPM's political skills are thus likely to come under considerable strain as it tries to maintain the social coalition crucial for its power maintenance, namely, a coalition of middle and small landholding peasantry and the landless laborers.

A second problem which the CPM is likely to face in the future is a premature bureaucratization of the party. While the bureaucratization of communist parties in power is a common phenomenon, the CPM's would be "premature" in the sense that it might become bureaucratized without any "revolutionary" accomplishments. A set of relatively privileged party elites, without major accomplishments to legitimize their power positions, might then not only create strains within the party but also become electorally unpopular. Of course, the very knowledge of this potential outcome may militate against the creation of a "new class" within West Bengal. Such foresight, however, even if it existed, may not be a powerful enough deterrent to counter the temptation of consolidating the privileges of power.

CONCLUSION

In the foregoing I have addressed three issues of West Bengal politics: why have radical politics and communism been a significant force in Bengali politics; what are the features of the contemporary CPM regime within West Bengal; and how does one assess the CPM's relations with Mrs. Gandhi and its future prospects within West Bengal. In light of the above discussion I will now conclude by very briefly addressing this symposium's theme of "change and continuity in Indian state politics."

Politics in West Bengal represent both elements of continuity and change over the last several decades. The most salient elements of continuity are the relative weakness of Congress and, by the same token, the relative strength of radical politics. What has changed, however, is more significant: a communist party has consolidated its power position and, in the process, has turned reformist. A permanent and viable alternative to Congress rule has therefore emerged within West Bengal. And as far as politics within West Bengal is concerned, this change is for the better. The so-called communist party is providing a stable and a reformist government, the like of which has certainly never been provided by the Congress in West Bengal, nor maybe in any other Indian state. The present situation may well in the future take a turn for the worse. This outcome may result either due to the CPM's own incompetence and inability to solve crucial problems, or it may be precipitated by central intervention. Whatever the future outcome, the present political situation in West Bengal has moved in a desirable direction when judged by the criteria of relative political stability and relative policy effectiveness in reconciling distributional concerns within the framework of democratic capitalism.

NOTES

1. For the details of the historical argument, see Atul Kohli, "From Elite Radicalism to Democratic Consolidation: The Rise of Reform Communism in West Bengal," paper presented to a conference on "Caste, Class and Dominance in India," Philadelphia, May 3–11, 1984. A considerably revised version of this paper will appear in *Caste, Class and Dominance: Patterns of Political-Economic Change in India*, ed. Francine R. Frankel and M.S.A. Rao (tentative title, forthcoming).

2. See J.H. Broomfield, *Elite Conflict in a Plural Society: Twentieth Century Bengal* (Berkeley: University of California, 1968), esp. pp. 5–6.

3. *Ibid.*, chapters 2–5.

4. See R.C. Majumdar, *History of Modern Bengal, Part Two* (Calcutta: G. Bhardwaj and Co., 1978), chapter. I.

5. For a detailed discussion of the antipathy towards Gandhi and the weakness of the Congress within West Bengal, see Marcus Franda, *Radical Politics in West Bengal* (Cambridge, Mass.: MIT Press, 1972).

6. A number of such useful interviews have been collected at the end of Gautam Chattopadhyay, *Communism and Bengal's Freedom Movement* (New Delhi: People's Publishing House, 1970).

7. This argument has also been made by Marcus Franda, *Radical*

Politics in West Bengal.

8. For a discussion of the Tebhaga movement, see Hamza Alavi, "Peasants and Revolution," *Socialist Register,* (1965); The revolt in the Naxalbari areas has been discussed in Mohan Ram, *Maoism in India* (Delhi: Vikas Publications, 1971), and the electoral support for the communists among Bengali peasantry is documented in Bhabani Scn Gupta, *CPI-M: Promises, Prospects, Problems* (New Delhi: Young Asia Publications, 1979).

9. I have depended heavily for such an interpretation on the four volume history of Bengal by R.C. Majumdar. See his *History of Ancient Bengal* (Calcutta: G. Bhardwaj and Co., 1971); *History of Mediaeval Bengal* (Calcutta: G. Bhardwaj and Co., 1973); *History of Modern Bengal, Part I* (Calcutta: G. Bhardwaj and Co., 1978); and *History of Modern Bengal, Part II* (Calcutta: G. Bhardwaj and Co., 1978).

10. For details of how these organizations functioned, see Majumdar, *History of Modern Bengal, Part II,* chapter. V.

11. For an analysis of politics in West Bengal during the 1950s and the 1960s, see Marcus Franda, "West Bengal," in *State Politics in India,* ed. Myron Weiner (Princeton N.J.: Princeton University Press, 1968); and Nirmal Chaudhry, "West Bengal: Vortex of Ideological Politics," in *State Politics in India,* ed. Iqbal Narain (New Delhi: Meenakihi Prakashan, 1967).

12. This sub-section appeared earlier as part of another article. See Atul Kohli, "Regime Types and Poverty Reform in India," *Pacific Affairs,* 56:4 (Winter 1983–84), pp. 651–658. For a more detailed analysis, see Atul Kohli, "Parliamentary Communism and Agrarian Reform," *Asian Survey* 22:7 (July 1983), pp. 783–809.

13. Interview with Abdullah Rasool, Calcutta, 14 March, 1979.

14. Interview with Ashok Mitra, Calcutta, 16 March, 1979.

15. See Communist Party of India (Marxist), *Political Resolution,* Xth Congress, 2–8 April 1978, (Jullundur City, Punjab), p. 18.

16. See Kohli, "Parliamentary Communism and Agrarian Reform," p. 793.

17. See Government of West Bengal, *Land Reforms in West Bengal: A Statistical Report,* V (Calcutta: Land and Land Revenue Department, 1981).

18. I have documented this conclusion with a survey of 300 households of registered sharecroppers. These results are being published in Atul Kohli, *The State and Poverty: Politics of Social Reform in India* (forthcoming), chapter. III.

19. Government of West Bengal, *Land Reforms in West Bengal.*

5
The Rise and Decline of the Left and Democratic Front in Kerala

Ouseph Varkey

Kerala, situated on the southwest corner of India, is one of the smallest states in India.[1] It has an area of 38,864 square kilometers and a population of 26 million.[2] Christians constitute 21 percent of Kerala's population, compared to the national figure of less than 3 percent. They are educationally and economically more advanced than the Hindus and Muslims in the state. Traditionally, Kerala Christians have overwhelmingly supported the Indian National Congress. Although various splits in the Congress Party have shattered their political cohesion, Christian churches, particularly the Catholic Church, wield considerable influence in Kerala politics.[3] Muslims constitute 20 percent of Kerala's population, compared to the national figure of about 12 percent. They are educationally and economically behind the Christians and high caste Hindus. But numbers, organization and the fact that they are heavily concentrated in some areas make them a major factor in Kerala politics. Two Muslim League parties in Kerala claim to represent the Muslims, and practically all the support for both comes from Muslims.[4] But large numbers of Muslims in Kerala support the two Congress parties and the two communist parties.[5] Hindus, who constitute almost 60 percent of Kerala's population, consist of scores of castes. They may be divided into three broad groups — the high castes (mainly Brahmins and Nairs), middle castes (mostly Ezhavas), and low castes (castes below the Ezhavas). Most high caste Hindus in Kerala have traditionally supported the non–communist parties, though a substantial number of them now do so. Most of the middle and low castes support the communist parties, though large numbers of them support the Congress parties.

Politically, Kerala is not the typical Indian state. Socialists and communists captured governing power in Kerala when an alternative to Congress rule was unthinkable in India.[6] Political participation in Kerala has been consistently the highest in India, and politics is a passion for Keralites. Kerala is also a political paradox in that powerful churches and powerful communist parties coexist.

When the present state of Kerala was formed in 1956, Kerala had a multiple party system. The two largest parties were the Congress and the Communist Party of India. Neither was strong enough to get a majority in the state legislature, and thus, from the beginning, governments in Kerala have had to be coalitions. The making of coalitions was less difficult when the parties were few. But from the mid-1960s, parties multiplied. Ideological, personality, religious and communal differences and the readiness of elites to exploit these differences for political purposes have contributed to the chaotic growth of new parties in Kerala.

Despite the inevitable confusion this muddle of parties will cause to the outsider, to Keralites, their politics has the clarity and convenience of a polarity. That is, for most Keralites, politics in their state is a struggle for power between two distinct forces — the communists and their allies on the one side and the anti-communists led by the Congress Party on the other. Voting in Kerala has seldom been an act of affirmation since voters have usually rejected their previous rulers. Most voters seem to be activated by the negative impulses of either anti-communism or anti-Congressism. The excesses of communist radicalism which explode when the communists are in power produce pervasive anti-communist sentiment in the state; alternatively, the ineptitude of the Congress Party and its factionalist struggles generate widespread anti-Congress feelings. The challenge for party leaders in Kerala is to gauge the strength of these two contradictory impulses of the electorate and to fashion alliances that can fully exploit them. Such alliances have been the key to power in Kerala politics.

In the first election in Kerala, held in 1957, the communists allied themselves with several resourceful independent candidates. Together, they secured a majority in the legislature and formed the government. In 1959, the Congress Party in the state put together a broad anti-communist alliance.[7] Its massive agitation against the communist government led to the latter's dismissal by the central government. In the mid-term election of 1960, the anti-communist alliance decisively defeated the communists and their allies. But the alliance soon disintegrated. The Congress Party continued in power for some time, but, deserted by some of its own supporters in 1964, the government lost its majority in the legislature and resigned.[8] The Kerala Congress Party was born from the desertion. In 1964, the Communist Party of India also suffered a split, resulting in the formation of the Communist Party of India (Marxist) or CPM. The ferocity with which these two new parties attacked their mother-parties and the passions they aroused in the state made the formation of alliances a vain hope in the mid-term election of 1965. Each party contested alone, none got a majority in the state legislature, and the state was placed under President's Rule.

In the general election of 1967, the CPM formed a broad anti-Congress alliance in Kerala and inflicted on the Congress Party the most humiliating defeat in its history.[9] A coalition government led by the CPM came to power, but within two years the anti-Congress alliance crumbled. Some parties in the alliance deserted it and collaborated with the Congress Party to form an anti-Marxist (anti-CPM) alliance.[10] The perennial theme of anti-communism in Kerala politics persisted with a new nuance, namely, anti-Marxism. For the next decade, politics in Kerala became a struggle between an anti-Marxist alliance and the Marxists and their allies.[11] The anti-Marxist alliance began with the advantage of forming a government in November 1969. But dissensions within the alliance led to the resignation of the government in August 1970. In the mid-term election of 1970, the anti-Marxist alliance won a comfortable majority and formed the government. This was the only government in Kerala which completed a full term of five years. The declaration of Emergency in India in 1975 extended the life of this government. In the general election of 1977, the anti-Marxist alliance was broadened and it won an impressive victory over the CPM and its allies.[12] But the victory soon proved to be a barren one. Between 1977 and 1979, Kerala had four governments headed by four different political parties.[13] In the 1970s, several parties in Kerala suffered splits and many new parties were formed.[14] By the end of the 1970s, anti-Congressism had become widespread in Kerala.[15] The CPM seized the opportunity and formed a broad anti-Congress alliance.

THE FORMATION OF THE LDF

The formation of the "Left and Democratic Front" (LDF) in Kerala in late 1979 represented a significant political breakthrough. The

Front brought together the Communist Party of India (Marxist) (CPM), the Congress(S), the Communist Party of India (CPI), the Revolutionary Socialist Party (RSP), the Kerala Congress (Mani Group) (KCM), the Kerala Congress (Pillai Group) (KCP) and the All India Muslim League (AIML).[16] Together, these seven parties constituted a formidable political force in Kerala in 1979.

The CPM, the CPI, and the Congress(S) — the three major parties in the Front — had been advocates of the unity of the left and democratic forces in the country since 1978,[17] but they differed on how to achieve it. The CPI and the Congress(S) had argued that the LDF could be formed in Kerala by including the CPM in the ruling front,[18] but the CPM insisted on starting with a "clean slate."[19] The inclusion of the CPM would strengthen the Front, already weakened by the split in the Congress Party.[20] But the CPM would be in third position, below the CPI and the Congress(S), in the broadened front. The CPM did not want to play second fiddle to any party in the state. The "clean slate" argument revealed its motive: to establish its preeminent position in any front it would join in Kerala.

Since the CPM was in the opposition, it had nothing to lose, and much to gain, by starting with a "clean slate." It was not so in the case of the CPI and the Congress(S). They already had power, and would lose it with the resignation of the government. Yet, that was the precondition set by the CPM for the formation of the LDF. The CPI and the Congress(S) knew that the formation of the Front with the CPM would make the CPM the most powerful force in the Front. They wanted to minimize the gains of the CPM as such gains would be at their expense. They thought they could do that by negotiating with the CPM from their position of strength.

Several political developments in the state in 1979 compelled the parties in the ruling front to change their tactics. Four by-elections to the state legislature were held in May, and the opposition front led by the CPM won all four.[21] In September, elections to the panchayats and municipalities were held. The results confirmed the growing popularity of the CPM and the declining popularity of the ruling front.[22] These election results compelled the CPI and the RSP to accept the "clean slate" demand of the CPM. The ruling front government headed by CPI leader P.K. Vasudevan Nair resigned in early October. The Congress(S) and the KCM then decided to support a minority government headed by C.H. Muhamed Koya of the Indian Union Muslim League.[23] The purpose of the KCM was to pass the land gift bill, which it soon accomplished.[24]

Then the KCM withdrew its support for the Koya government and joined the negotiations for the formation of the LDF. The Congress(S), faced with the practical necessity of allying with its archenemy, the Congress(I), also later withdrew its support for the Koya government in order to join the LDF. The Koya government resigned and the Governor dissolved the state assembly. A mid-term election thus became certain, and that accelerated the formation of the LDF.

The Common Program which the LDF adopted reflected the diverse interests of the seven parties in the Front and the efforts of the leaders to offer something to all important segments of the Kerala population. The parliamentary election held in early January 1980 tested the strength of the two fronts – the LDF, and the United Democratic Front (UDF) led by the Congress(I).[25] Of the 20 seats from Kerala, the LDF won 12 and the UDF 8.[26] Coming on the heels of Indira Gandhi's astounding victory in the national election, the subsequent state assembly election acquired extraordinary significance. Since she had become the Prime Minister, many wondered whether she would be able to win Kerala for her party. She had campaigned in Kerala in late December for the parliamentary candidates of the UDF, but she chose to go to Kerala again to campaign for UDF assembly candidates. Three days after her swearing in as India's Prime Minister, she rushed to Kerala. Fortified with the power and prestige of the office of the Prime Minister of the country, she visited dozens of constituencies and addressed about twenty-five public meetings. She warned the audience that the communists would foment trouble, and advised them to elect a government that would cooperate with the central government – that is, a government of the UDF. The leaders of the UDF echoed her words. The leaders of the LDF replied that the UDF was a hodgepodge and would soon crumble because of its irreconcilable internal contradictions. They said that what Kerala needed was a government that would bargain from a position of strength with New Delhi, and claimed that only the LDF could form such a government.

There were 602 candidates, most of them inconsequential independents, for the 140 seats. The real fight in all the constituencies was between the candidates of the two fronts. Out of 13.2 million eligible voters, 75 percent voted.[27] The result of the election (see Table 5:1) was a signal victory for the LDF, especially in the context of Indira Gandhi's redoubled efforts to defeat it.

Table 5:1

Kerala State Assembly Election Results, 1980

Party	Seats contested	Seats won	Percentage of votes
LDF (Left and Democratic Front):			
Communist Party of India (Marxist)	50	35	19.33
Congress(S)	30	21	10.94
Communist Party of India	22	17	7.79
Kerala Congress (Mani Group)	17	8	5.24
Revolutionary Socialist Party	8	6	3.02
All India Muslim League	11	5	3.50
Kerala Congress (Pillai Group)	2	1	0.80
	140	93	50.62
UDF (United Democratic Front):			
Congress(I)	54	17	17.34
Indian Union Muslim League	21	14	7.10
Kerala Congress (Joseph Group)	19	6	4.94
National Democratic Party	11	3	3.66
Praja Socialist Party	6	1	1.29
Socialist Republican Party	7	0	2.00
Janata − UDF ally	29	5	7.62
	147	46	43.95
Others − mostly Independents −	315	1	5.43

Source: *Manorama Election Guide, 1982,* and *Kerala Kaumudi*

Notes: (1) The Janata Party was not formally in the UDF, but it was in electoral alliance with the UDF. In seven seats there was contest between the Janata and the UDF.

(2) The Governor nominates one member to the assembly to give representation to the Anglo-Indian community. The Congress(S) got this seat.

THE LDF IN POWER

On 24 January 1980, an LDF ministry headed by E.K. Nayanar (CPM) assumed power in Kerala. In a broadcast to the state, Nayanar admitted that the popular majority of the LDF was extremely thin – 50.62 percent – and that many Keralites had no faith in communism. He appealed to them to cooperate with the elected government to solve the problems of the state. The major purpose of his speech was to relieve the widespread fear, fanned by UDF propaganda, that the LDF government would create confrontations with the central government, that it would ride roughshod over the rights of religious minorities, and that its policies would lead to lawlessness in the state.

A by-election in May was the first test of the popularity of the government. Opposition leaders campaigned against the LDF by arguing that law and order in Kerala had broken down and that the interests of the religious minorities were unsafe. But the LDF candidate won the election with a majority of 17,841 votes.[28] In September, elections were held in six municipalities and fifty panchayats. Of the 625 seats involved, the LDF won 308 and the UDF 105. The LDF also won control of all the municipalities and most of the panchayats.

During the first year, the Nayanar government took many steps to give relief to the poor and middle classes. Opposition leaders charged that some of the measures were demagogic and showed the fiscal irresponsibility of the government, while others were administered for the benefit of the supporters of the CPM. Reviewing the record of his government at the end of its first year, Nayanar wrote that it was working as an effective team and that he was satisfied with its progress.[29]

In an editorial on the first year of the Nayanar government, the *Kerala Kaumudi* wrote that the government had nothing to be apologetic about. "On the contrary, it has plenty to be proud of."[30] A critic of the government admitted that it had implemented some social welfare measures, but he argued that the government was weak and compromising, that it had no control over the administrative machinery, and that its members lacked mutual trust. He credited Nayanar with averting "explosions" in the LDF.[31] But the tact and skill of Nayanar were not sufficient to sustain the team spirit of the LDF for long. In November 1980, an attack on the Congress(S) office by the members of the CITU – a labor union connected with the CPM – pushed the LDF to the precipice.[32] The following January, a scandal in which a CPM minister was allegedly involved caused a major crisis in the LDF government.[33] In the following months, an increase in violent clashes in the state, particularly between followers of the CPM and the Rashtriya Swayamsevak Sangh (RSS), severely strained the relations between the CPM and the other parties. The opposition under K. Karunakaran, leader of the Congress(I), meanwhile, was determined to oust the government by any possible means. In the first session of the legislature, the Chief Minister complained that the Congress(I) was seeking central intervention in the state. One month later, the Congress(I) decided to agitate against the "wrong policies" of the government and Karunakaran said that it was the beginning of a massive popular movement to liberate Kerala from "Marxist misrule." Thereafter, agitation against the government became the preoccupation of the opposition.

Opposition leaders used a variety of arguments to whip up public sentiment against the government. They tirelessly argued that law and order had broken down in the state and accused the government of dividing the citizens into two classes, of ignoring the interests of religious minorities, and of misusing the administrative machinery, particularly the police, for the benefit of the CPM. During their visits to Kerala, some central ministers also openly criticized the LDF government on these grounds. The Congress(I) leaders also brandished the threat of central intervention resulting in the dismissal of the state government. The purpose of such threats was not so much to intimidate the LDF government (whose leaders often scoffed at them) as to boost the morale of the opposition which was headlong in the struggle against the government.

Opposition leaders later realized that the central government would not intervene unless there was a collapse of law and order in the state. So in September 1981, they started a new propaganda offensive against the LDF government charging that it had led Kerala to the brink of civil strife and that the CPM, after neutralizing the police, had let loose violence throughout the state with the result that in the agrarian and industrial sectors an explosive situation existed. As a remedy, they planned a "save Kerala" campaign which was to culminate in demonstrations before police stations in the state on September 28.

The LDF was thrown into crisis when on September 16, A.K. Antony, leader of the Congress(S), issued a statement sharply criticizing the police policy of the LDF government. The Home Minister replied that Antony's criticisms were baseless. But Antony repeated his charges and accused the CPM of fomenting class struggle in the rural areas. Other Congress(S) leaders also openly criticized the CPM. The widening rift between the Congress(S) and the CPM threatened the survival of the LDF. Alarmed, the Coordination Committee — the policy–making body of the LDF — asked the government to take effective measures to ensure peace and order in the state. The police acted swiftly and captured a variety of weapons from unauthorized persons. But Antony called the police action a "farce" and added charges against the Home Minister and the CPM. The strain in the LDF had begun to weaken the will of the government. "There is government," the *Kerala Kaumudi* caustically commented, "but no administration."[34]

THE FALL OF THE LDF GOVERNMENT

As charges and countercharges, accusations and refutations by the Congress(S) and the CPM continued, rumor spread in the state that the Congress(S) might leave the LDF after its meeting on October 14. The meeting was a gathering of the Congress(S) elite in Kerala. They came feeling deeply injured and insulted by an article in a CPM weekly ridiculing and attacking the Congress(S) and Antony personally.[35] The vast majority of them argued at the meeting that it was suicidal for the party to continue in the LDF.

On October 16, Antony announced his party's decision to leave the LDF. Reacting to the decision, Nayanar said that the LDF still had a legislative majority. But the exit of the Congress(S) from the LDF had reduced the LDF's strength from 93 to 71 in an assembly of with 141 members, including the speaker. That pushed Kerala politics into a "cliffhanger" phase, and all eyes turned to the KCM. The decision of the KCM to leave the LDF would deprive the Front of its majority (of one) in the legislature and would precipitate the fall of the government. That possibility brought enormous pressure on the KCM and after five days of deliberations, the KCM decided to quit the LDF. Explaining the decision, George J. Mathew, chairman of the party, said that the KCM was compelled to leave the Front because the party realized that its continuation in the Front would not be beneficial to its supporters or to the state. The Nayanar government resigned that evening. The Chief Minister had not expected the adverse decision of the KCM. He was so confident of the continued support of the KCM that, while the party was deliberating, he informed the Governor that the cabinet would meet the next day and fix the date for the next session of the legislature.

The KCM leaders had been strong supporters of the LDF in the beginning, but as law and order in the state deteriorated, the party reminded the government of its responsibility to make the police vigilant against the danger. Thereafter, KCM leaders continued to prod the government to act more vigorously to maintain law and order, while at the same time accusing the Congress(I) leaders of exacerbating conditions by their public statements and by trying to exploit the issue for political purposes. Mani even said that the greatest enemy of the Indian people was the Congress(I). In early October 1981, the KCM thoroughly evaluated the performance of the LDF. In a public meeting that followed, Mani claimed many achievements for the Front, but said that there might be deficiencies in the Front which should be corrected. He added that the KCM would stand firm in the Front, correct the deficiencies, and make the functioning of the Front smooth. On November 10, Mani secretly met Nayanar and discussed his party's prescription for the ills of the LDF. Its essence was that the CPM should give up the Home portfolio. The CPM rejected it. According to Mani, if the CPM had accepted it, the government could have been saved and the LDF strengthened.[36]

THE CONGRESS(S) AND THE FALL OF THE LDF GOVERNMENT

What proved fatal to the LDF was the decision of the Congress(S) to quit the LDF. Would the transfer of the Home portfolio from the CPM have averted that decision? Perhaps. That would have saved the face of the Congress(S), possibly giving it a temporary sense of triumph in its duel with the CPM. Without such a tangible victory, Congress(S) leaders could not have appeased the rank and file in their party who had turned against the CPM by October 1981.

In a joint statement, leaders of the CPM, CPI, RSP, and AIML alleged that the breakup of the LDF was the result of a conspiracy of the central government, and that both the Congress(S) and the KCM had become tools in the hands of the enemies of the LDF. E.M.S. Namboodiripad, General Secretary of the all-India CPM and a native of Kerala, alleged that the Congress(S) left the LDF because it could not get the police to serve the interests of the capitalists and the landlords and to suppress the mass struggles.

The Congress(S) is not a Marxist party. Its intellectual heritage is Nehruism. In domestic politics this means belief in parliamentary democracy, democratic socialism, and secularism. It stands for substantial changes in Indian society brought about by peaceful means. In Kerala, the Congress(S) gets much of its support from the poor, lower middle, and middle classes. The leadership of the party in Kerala is young and is adept in the use of radical leftist rhetoric for political purposes. A.K. Antony is a past master in this game. He was able to create a new image for the party, making it appear as a party of dynamism and radicalism. C.M. Stephen, a Union minister and a native of Kerala, once described the Congress(S) in Kerala as the "Communist Party of Antony."

But distrust of the communists was always in the hearts of most Congress(S) leaders in Kerala. Most of them had developed their political ambitions and skills as active participants in the struggle against the first communist government in Kerala in the late 1950s.[37] Since the formation of the CPM in late 1964, they had seen the CPM as their chief rival in the state. That perception continued to shape their political outlook till the end of the 1970s when the Congress Party split. Then the leaders of the Congress(S) in Kerala saw the rival Congress(I) as their chief enemy. This led to a search for new allies, which resulted in the Congress(S) Party's decision to join the LDF. It was political pragmatism, not political conviction, that led the Congress(S) to the LDF. The Congress(S) was the last party to join the LDF, and it joined only at the eleventh hour. Its entry into the LDF was preceded by weeks of exchanges of bitter words with the CPM.[38] It joined the LDF in awkward circumstances and against the will of some of its most prominent leaders.[39] It was the desire to win the 1980 election that pressed the Congress(S) and the CPM into a team. A common program helped to camouflage their differences. The chant against Indira Gandhi's authoritarianism induced in them an illusory sense of harmony. The LDF was thus able to erect a facade of unity. The flush of victory in the election, the flexibility of the CPM in dividing the spoils, and some common grievances against the central government helped to maintain that facade almost intact for a few months.

But several developments had begun to change the conditions that had prompted the Congress(S) to join the LDF. First, there was the triumphant return of Indira Gandhi to power in January 1980, followed in May by the sweeping victory of her party in mid-term elections in nine states. These victories of Indira Gandhi shook the Congress(S)' faith in the LDF as a viable alternative to her party in Kerala. Second, the death of Sanjay Gandhi in June 1980 eliminated a phenomenon in the Congress(I) which the Congress(S) leaders in Kerala had hated and feared. Third, the return of some Congress(S) leaders like Y.B. Chavan to the Congress(I) made many in the Congress(S) nostalgic for the days when the Congress Party was united and they had the protection and patronage of Indira Gandhi, who had again become the "Empress of India."

These developments strengthened the anti–LDF clique in the Congress(S) in Kerala led by Vayalar Revi. Revi had been unhappy with the party's decision to join the LDF. He had said that the LDF could be formed in Kerala only over his dead body.[40] He also had a personal grudge against the leftist parties in the LDF because his defeat in the parliamentary election was attributed to the lack of whole–hearted support from them. Ambitious, Revi was determined to destroy the LDF, whose structure had no niche for him. Some Machiavellian moves by the Congress(I) leaders facilitated Revi's machinations against the LDF. C.M. Stephen said that the Congress(I) was ready to make any compromise to form an anti–communist alliance in Kerala. He then publicly invited all in the Congress(S) "to return to the family," and promised that they would be received with a "red carpet." Karunakaran later confirmed Stephen's invitation. Stephen's "red carpet" temptation emboldened the enemies of the LDF in the Congress(S), swayed to their side the unsure, and caused doubts and confusion in those who remained faithful to the LDF. These developments strengthened the Revi clique.

But it was the aftermath of the police policy of the LDF government that ensured Revi's victory in sabotaging the LDF. The Common Program of the LDF had said that the police would not interfere in the "agitations and struggles of the people for the needs of their livelihood," and that the police would be given "the freedom of organization."[41] The way the CPM Home Minister applied this policy caused widespread criticism. In a bizarre episode, the police held a demonstration shouting, along with other slogans, "Inquilab Zindabad" ("Hail Revolution," the one sure slogan in all Indian communist demonstrations). Opposition leaders argued that the new police policy would destroy discipline in the police. Ironically, Antony was one of the first who had so argued. But criticism had no effect on the Home Minister, who was only implementing his party's well–known police policy. The result was that the police in Kerala ceased to be a "preventive force." The escalating violence in Kerala prompted the *Malayala Manorama* to write an editorial entitled, "Atmosphere of Terror."[42] The *Kerala Kaumudi* bluntly reminded the government that it had the responsibility to ensure a peaceful life to the people.[43] The police policy and the Home Minister's statement that the police would not intervene in labor disputes emboldened many workers in the rural areas to take the law into their own hands. In many places the headload (porter) and agricultural workers, mostly members of the CITU, demanded exorbitant wages and used extortionary tactics. That made normal life impossible for merchants,shopkeepers, farmers, and others in the middle levels of society. They were the mainstay of the Congress(S) in Kerala. Revi articulated with eloquence the frustrations and fury of these people. Their growing alienation from the LDF corroded the Congress(S) Party's faith in the LDF. As these groups became hostile to the CPM, the Congress(S) leaders found it imperative to leave the LDF.

THE KCM AND THE FALL OF THE LDF GOVERNMENT

The KCM is a regional party in Kerala. It gets much of its support from lower, middle and upper class Christians, particularly the Catholics, in the rural area. Its aim is to keep the status quo in its essentials, and it advocates and accepts reforms for that purpose. It is widely believed in Kerala that the party is patronized by Christian planters and Catholic bishops, to whom Marxism is anathema and the CPM a dreadful force in Kerala. The KCM believes that the central government in India is too strong and the state governments too weak. It would like to correct the imbalance. Its main complaint against the central government is that it ignores the interests of Kerala, particularly of its cash crop farmers. The CPM holds similar views. But it was the desire for power on the part of the KCM leaders that brought the party into the LDF. The KCM's alliance with CPM was a perfect case of politics making strange bedfellows. The police policy of the LDF and the militancy of the CITU turned most supporters of the KCM against the CPM. Meanwhile, the Catholic Church leaders kept up their pressure on the KCM to leave the LDF.[44] When the Congress(S) left the LDF, the future of the Nayanar government became uncertain, and the political intrigues of the Congress(I) suggested possibilities for a non-communist alternative government. That brought more pressure on the KCM both from inside and outside.[45] The chance to enter the alternative government was a temptation hard to resist for the KCM leaders. They finally succumbed to it and left the LDF.

THE CPM AND THE FALL OF THE LDF GOVERNMENT

Antony alleged that the full responsibility for wrecking the LDF rested with the CPM. But the CPM wanted to maintain the LDF and was eager to expand it by including the Janata Party and the other Muslim

League. It appeased the Congress(S) and the KCM by conceding their demands or yielding to their pressures. Remembering the unhappy and untimely end of the left united front in 1969, the CPM was also careful to avoid the image of "big brother." On the whole, the CPM's behavior in the LDF was marked by compromise and conciliation. But the CPM was steadfast and uncompromising in its police policy and that caused irreparable damage to the LDF. There is something special about the police policy of the CPM. On all three occasions that the CPM was in power in Kerala, its police policy became highly controversial and it was a major factor in the fall of the three governments.[46] It is superficial to argue that the CPM in Kerala has not learned from its experiences. The CPM's police policy is a well thought-out one, and it is a cornerstone of its LDF program.

There was a fundamental difference between the CPM's views on the LDF and those of the Congress(S) and the KCM. As B.T. Ranadive, a CPM theoretician and Politburo member, has written, for the CPM, united fronts and coalition governments are "an instrument of changing the balance of class forces impelling the mass movement forward."[47] For the Congress(S) and the KCM the LDF was primarily a means for electoral gains and participation in the government in Kerala. For the CPM, with its grand vision for all of India, the LDF was only an important step in its long march to power. For it, the LDF was just the beginning of the People's Democratic Front which would usher in the People's Democratic Revolution, which in turn would be a prelude to the establishment of communism in India.[48] The CPM is not convinced that its ultimate goal, making India communist, can be achieved by parliamentary means alone. So its commitment to parliamentarism is qualified and conditional. The LDF is an instrument to further its goals of polarizing society into its supporters and irreconcilable class enemies. As a CPM document bluntly put it, united front governments are "instruments of struggle" in the hands of the people, and the CPM's participation in such governments is a "specific form of struggle" to win more support for the proletariat and its allies in the struggle for a "people's democracy" and later for socialism.[49] It is this perspective of the CPM that led the party to the controversial policy of "administration and agitation together" and resulted in the breakup of the left united front government in Kerala in 1969. In 1980 also this perspective continued to guide the CPM. The result was the party's police policy, which was objectionable to both the Congress(S) and the KCM from the beginning and which finally became intolerable to them.

The CPM's police policy had two aspects. First, the CPM believes in the orthodox Marxist view that the police in a capitalist society are an instrument of oppression in the hands of a dominant class. So it is ideologically opposed to an active police that would prevent social conflicts or intervene in them. At the practical level, CPM followers expected the LDF government to use the police to further the interests of the communists. The result was that the CPM was unwilling to allow the police to play its traditional role in law enforcement. If it had done otherwise, the CPM would have alienated many of its own supporters and made the party more vulnerable to the attacks of the ultra-left.

The CPM strategy was to build a firm alliance of workers and peasants and to win over to its side all except the small upper class and the handful of the super rich. But its efforts to mobilize the rural poor in Kerala threatened the lower and middle classes.[50] The politicized poor ignored traditional social relations which included deferential treatment of the propertied classes and aspects of patron-client behavior. The politicized workers in the rural areas demanded from their employers unrealistically high wages and benefits. Most of these employers were small farmers with only a few acres of land. They resisted the new demands of their workers as the demands were economically ruinous to them. The CPM tried to channel the frustrations of these farmers against the central government by arguing that New Delhi's policies favoring big industrialists were the root cause of agrarian problems. But its success was limited and momentary. The central government was a remote entity to farmers in Kerala. The relevance of central nation-wide policies to their economic plight was not self-evident to them; it needed explanation. But such political education of the farmers did not take place in sufficient degree. There were not many economic issues on which the farmers and their workers closed ranks and fought together against the central policies. Instead, acute conflicts developed between them. The farmers faced their workers almost daily. They saw the new militancy of their workers as an immediate menace. Their old recourse in such circumstances was to the police. Feeling helpless, the farmers blamed the CPM for their woes — for organizing their workers and infecting them with the idea of class struggle and for depriving farmers of the help of the police in protecting their vital interests. These farmers had never trusted the CPM, but they had acquiesced in the decision of the Congress(S) and the KCM, parties which most of them supported, to join the LDF. That acquiescence was essential for the survival of the LDF. But the CPM's police policy and the militancy of some of its trade unions turned this silent majority in the Congress(S) and the KCM into implacable enemies of the CPM and thus of the LDF. This development was the most decisive factor in the decision of both parties to quit the LDF.

The LDF strategy was profitable for the CPM. It helped the party to escape from the political wilderness and reach the paradise of power. The party's strength in the legislature rose from 19 to 35 and party membership in the state from 67,000 (1978) to 104,000 (1981).[51] The LDF helped the CPM to solidify the leftist forces in Kerala and to split the Congress(S) and thus weaken a major non-communist force in the state.[52] The breakup of the LDF was a great disappointment for the CPM, but that did not lessen the party's faith in that model. A resolution the CPM passed after the fall of the LDF government in Kerala reaffirmed the party's commitment to the LDF. In fact the mid-term election in Kerala in 1982 showed that the CPM was eager to expand the LDF.

THE 1982 MID-TERM ELECTION: PREPARATIONS

After the fall of the LDF government, the Congress(S), the KCM, and a faction of the Janata Party decided to join the UDF to form a government. The UDF claimed the support of 71 members and formed a government with K. Karunakaran as the Chief Minister in December 1981. In March 1982, a member of the KCM withdrew his support for the government. The government thus lost its majority of one in the legislature and resigned. This led to the mid-term election of May 1982.

Anticipating an election in May, the two fronts had already begun their preparations. Both tried to wean away parties from the rival front and to coax into their front those parties that were not aligned with either front. The most difficult problem the two fronts faced was how to divide limited seats among partners without causing too much dissatisfaction to anyone.

When the UDF was formed to fight the election in 1980, it consisted of five parties.[53] Two years later, when it formed the government, the number of parties increased to nine.[54] By March 1982, the number of parties in the UDF had grown to a dozen.[55] This influx of parties made the division of seats very difficult for the UDF. The newcomers could be given seats only at the expense of old members. This led to intense competition between the newcomers who aggressively tried to maximize their gains and the old-timers who doggedly fought to keep what they had. Most parties in the UDF advanced unrealistically high claims for seats and few were willing to compromise. There arose other complications as the various parties scrambled for the maximum number of safe seats. Some old members of the UDF grumbled that the Congress(I), the leading party in the UDF, was too solicitous to powerful newcomers to the UDF like the KCM and the Congress(A), and was more ready to placate them than to protect the legitimate interests of old loyalists. Meanwhile, the small parties in the UDF felt ignored amidst the wheeling and dealing of the big parties whose politics had pushed them to the fringe of the UDF and reduced them to being spectators.

The UDF first decided to give each party those seats it had won in the previous election. That settled the problem for half of the total of 140 seats. It faced almost insurmountable difficulties in the division of the other seats, however. Only the claims of the Indian Union Muslim League (IUML) sounded reasonable, as they were based on the indisputable superiority the League had in some constituencies. The Congress(A) insisted on an equal number of seats with the Congress(I). Since it was widely rumored that the merger of these two parties was only a matter of time, other parties in the UDF suspected that the Congress(A) and the Congress(I) were acting in collusion to maximize their seat allocation at the expense of others.[56] The Congress(A) also wanted to maximize its seat allocation as more seats would enhance its bargaining power with the Congress(I) when negotiations for the merger would begin.

During the intrigues that had led to the withdrawal of the KCM from the LDF and its subsequent joining of the UDF, a deal had been struck between G.K. Moopanar, General Secretary of the Congress(I), and K.M. Mani, Chairman of the KCM. In the deal, Moopanar had promised the KCM twenty–two seats in the coming election. Mani now demanded his pound of flesh. P.J. Joseph, Chairman of the Kerala Congress (Joseph Group) or KCJ, and the arch political rival of Mani, demanded that his party should get one seat more than Mani's party. Joseph argued that his party had stood with the UDF through thick and thin, whereas Mani's party only joined the UDF very late and for opportunistic reasons. The adamant attitude of Joseph on this issue made any progress in the negotiations impossible. Under intense pressure from the UDF leaders, Mani agreed to settle for eighteen seats. The UDF decided to give twenty–seven seats to the two Kerala Congress parties — sixteen to the KCM and eleven to the KCJ. But Joseph insisted on parity with the KCM and he demanded some specific seats. That was unacceptable to the UDF. The negotiations thus reached a deadlock.

The wide rift between Joseph and the UDF was clear at the press conference which the UDF convened on April 15 to release its election manifesto. The absence of Joseph on the occasion was conspicuous. The next day Joseph publicly threatened that his party would leave the UDF unless it was given an "honorable share" of the seats. By this he meant fourteen seats. A feeling of betrayal at the hands of the UDF leaders, particularly of the Congress(I), was fast spreading in the rank and file of the KCJ. Some party units expressed their resentment by passing resolutions urging the leadership to quit the front if the party did not get its due share of seats. At a press conference on April 20, Joseph detailed his party's bitter experiences with the UDF during the course of the negotiations for the division of seats. He alleged that Karunakaran was inconsistent in his words and that in some of the constituencies which the UDF had offered his party, the party had no organization or followers. That meant, in effect, the UDF had offered his party only ten seats. On the same day, the *Kerala Kaumudi* reported that the KCJ was ready to leave the UDF.[57]

As Karunakaran appeared to be at his wit's end and the UDF faced its gravest crisis, Indira Gandhi intervened.[58] The result was dramatic and almost miraculous. The next day, Joseph hurriedly convened a press conference and announced that his party would never leave the UDF for whatever reason. The threat of the disruption of the UDF thus vanished. By the end of April, 1982, the UDF completed the allocation of seats.

The LDF, meanwhile, completed the allocation of seats more easily than did the UDF. When the LDF was formed in late 1979, it consisted of seven parties. In late 1981, the Congress(S) and the KCM left the LDF and joined the UDF. The departure of these two parties from the LDF left enough space to comfortably accommodate the smaller parties that joined the LDF in 1982. The LDF started negotiations for the allocation of seats in late March. First it decided to give each party the seats it had won in the previous election. That accounted for half of the total of 140 seats. It divided the rest of the seats on the basis of which party had the best chance for victory in each constituency. The LDF also decided to support nine independent candidates. On April 18, the LDF sources claimed that they had finalized "everything," but postponed the publication of the list of seats for each party for "strategic" reasons.[59]

On April 12, the LDF released its election manifesto. The manifesto blamed the Congress(I) and the central government for most of the political and economic problems of Kerala, and accused them of destroying the federal character of the country and the democratic rights of the people. It promised that the LDF government would promote the industrialization of Kerala, introduce many welfare measures to help the workers and the poor, give special attention to the problems of women, protect the rights of religious and linguistic minorities, decentralize administration and effectively attack corruption. The UDF released its manifesto on April 15. It accused the CPM of fanning class conflict, subverting the rule of law and misusing power. It promised a variety of measures to help farmers, workers, fishermen, and the unemployed poor. There was no significant difference between the economic programs of the two fronts. However, they differed on center–state relations and on priorities. The LDF manifesto accused the central government of a policy of omission and commission against Kerala and pledged that the LDF would organize and lead the struggle against New Delhi. The UDF stood for "friendly relations" with the Union government. The UDF manifesto gave the highest priority to the maintenance of law and order and the protection of the lives and property of citizens. The LDF manifesto emphasized welfare measures and trade union rights.

THE 1982 MID–TERM ELECTION: THE CAMPAIGN

Two statements issued on the eve of the election, one by A.K. Antony, leader of the Congress(A), and the other by K. Karunakaran, leader of the Congress(I), succinctly announced the general position of the UDF. Antony's statement said that the main issue in the election was the future of Kerala and the Keralites. All those who desired peace should vote for a UDF government. Three times in Kerala's history – in 1957, 1967 and 1980 – Keralites voted for governments in which communists had the upper hand. It was under these governments that Kerala experienced the highest number of violent conflicts and murders. The LDF was, in effect, a communist front. Its victory would mean the rule of the CPM. Kerala would then return to the plight of 1957 when violence was endemic in the state. Karunakaran's statement, meanwhile, argued that the mid–term election became necessary because the LDF, which had won the 1980 election, deteriorated into a Marxist dictatorship. Kerala had similar experiences in 1957 and 1967 when the communists controlled the government. The UDF promised a government that would be stable, incorruptible, and progressive. It would ensure justice for all. If peace and harmony were to prevail in Kerala, if the state were to develop economically, if the people were to attend to their business and live in dignity, the UDF must win.

The election caused an influx of political leaders from other parts of the country into Kerala for campaigning. Prime Minister Indira Gandhi came to Kerala twice. In four days of hectic campaigning she traveled through most of the state's twelve districts and addressed more than fifty public meetings. She also found time for prayer at the famous Guruvayur Hindu Temple and for lunch with a bishop. In her speeches, Indira Gandhi severely criticized the previous LDF government. She alleged that during its twenty-one months' rule in Kerala, "chaos, anarchy and lawlessness" were the order of the day and that its misrule was the cause for the growth of rightist forces in the state. She singled out the CPM for her harshest rebukes. According to her, the CPM never believed in democracy, its creed was to crush "all opposition by any means," it did not know how to rule according to the Constitution, it knew only how to rule for its cadres, and it was following the politics of violence. She reminded her audience of the country's progress, tried to explain away its difficulties, disclaimed any desire to establish a one party political system, and vowed that her government would work for the poor, the downtrodden, the minorities and the backward classes.

Central ministers used a variety of tactics, from alluring promises to outright threats, to influence the voters in favor of the UDF. The Deputy Minister for Railways announced in late April that an existing railway line in the state would be extended to a town located in a constituency from which a UDF leader was contesting. The Minister of Civil Aviation announced the construction of a new airport in Kerala. Opponents of the LDF pointed out that such announcements were "naked and deliberate" violations of the Election Commission's code of conduct which prohibited government personnel from making any new promise to the voters after the election date was announced. But such complaints had no effect on central ministers. Just four days before the election, the central Minister for Petroleum and Chemicals announced the government's decision to start a couple of new industries in Kerala.

Prime Minister Gandhi harped on the theme of possible center-state conflicts in the event of an LDF government in Kerala. Union Communications Minister Stephen, a native of Kerala, told an election rally that the election results would decide whether Kerala would get more industries from the central government. The implication was that an LDF victory would imperil Kerala's chances of getting them. Union Deputy Law Minister Rehim, another native of Kerala, warned at an election meeting that the CPM and other leftist parties should remember very well that it was Indira Gandhi who was in power at the central level.[60]

The UDF leaders claimed that their front represented all the democratic forces in the state. They depicted the LDF as an alliance dominated by the communists and the election as a struggle between democracy and communism. Their chief target of attack was the CPM. One UDF leader argued that the CPM would not adopt progressive policies that were beneficial to the people and that the party did not know how to govern. Another argued that the CPM was the chief enemy of those who believed in democracy and desired peace. A third warned that if the CPM came to power after the election, even the fetuses would not forgive the voters. A fourth argued that the CPM had no faith in democracy but was resorting to the ballot box because it had no alternative. A fifth accused the CPM of practicing the politics of murder.

The three major themes in the UDF campaign speeches and propaganda were the issues of law and order, center–state relations and the communist profession of democracy. The UDF leaders argued that law and order in Kerala would collapse if the LDF came to power, and they frequently referred to the days of the previous LDF government in support of this argument. Secondly, they argued that a LDF government would follow a policy of confrontation with New Delhi and that would be detrimental to the interests of Kerala. Thirdly, they argued that the communists did not really believe in democracy and they would undermine democratic institutions and practices if they came to power.

There was nothing new in these arguments. The argument that law and order would break down if the communists came to power has been made in Kerala politics since the days of the first communist–led government in the state in 1957. That a communist–dominated government would follow policies that would entail conflicts with the New Delhi has been a major allegation made against the communist governments since the days of the second communist–led government in 1967. Anti–communists in Kerala have questioned the sincerity of the communist profession of democracy since the Communist Party entered electoral politics in the early 1950s.

The communists largely ignored the first and third arguments; however the second provoked a sharp response from them. E.K. Nayanar, who had headed the LDF government, said that the warning of the Prime

Minister and others regarding conflicts between the center and the states was only a cheap threat. C. Achutha Menon, a prominent communist and former Chief Minister of Kerala, argued that it was when the central government denied the legitimate demands of the states that conflicts developed, and that as long as the Congress(I) was in power at the central level such conflicts would continue. The LDF leaders argued that what Kerala needed was a government that would be vigilant about the needs and rights of the state and would boldly bargain with the central government. They claimed that only an LDF government would do that.

The leaders of the LDF characterized the UDF as a federation of vested interests and caste and communal forces. They derided it as a camp of defectors. They argued that there was neither unity nor democracy in the UDF, that its member parties had conflicting views and goals, that its leaders would not work together, and that it was an obstacle in the path of socialism and the unity of the working class. They praised the record of the LDF government, asked the voters to compare it with the record of the UDF government, and claimed that only the LDF could give Kerala a government that would protect the interests of minorities, farmers, workers and the poor. Some leaders of the LDF, especially the communists, expressed doubt whether the election would be conducted fairly. N.E. Balaram, Secretary of the state unit of the CPI, warned that the Congress(I) might resort to violence, intimidation and fraud. E.M.S. Namboodiripad, General Secretary of the CPM, expressed the fear that under the incumbent Governor the election might not be free and fair.

The UDF had to face the election with some disadvantages. First, the political intrigues that paved the way for the formation of the UDF government under Karunakaran in 1981 and the political maneuverings by which it struggled to survive had caused widespread revulsion in the state, particularly against the Congress(I). It was during the days of this government that political propriety reached its nadir in Kerala.[61] The Congress(I) had had to stoop to much political horse-trading to keep a bare majority in the State Assembly. Some of the actions of the Governor became highly controversial. The opposition charged the Governor, who was supposed to be above politics, with acts of blatant partisanship. The Speaker of the Assembly, who was also supposed to be non-partisan, had had to save the government with his casting vote seven times in a single day. All these moves had not ensured the survival of the UDF government for long. After eighty days of precarious and paralytic existence it had fallen when one member of the UDF returned to the LDF. The fall of the government led to the imposition of President's

Rule, which is very unpopular in the state. Many Keralites blamed the UDF for this detested outcome. Second, the UDF was an ideological hodgepodge. It consisted of reactionary, conservative *and* reform–minded parties. There were irreconcilable conflicts of interest between some of them. Some parties in the UDF professed socialism, others were averse or hostile to it; some claimed to be secular, others were based on religion; yet others, by their own admission, were formed to protect and promote the interests of particular castes.[62] The UDF thus created the impression that it was a creature of political opportunism. Third, the hard bargaining during the allocation of seats, the open squabbles among some of the parties, and the feelings of betrayal expressed by some strained the unity of the UDF and tarnished its image. Fourth, the division of seats and the selection of candidates caused widespread dissatisfaction in some parties. The district committee of the KCM in Alleppey rebelled against the decision of the central leadership of the party. Many discontented party leaders filed nominations in defiance of the official candidates and there were resignations from some parties in the UDF. Though the central leadership of the concerned parties was able to solve most of these problems by persuasion, pressure, promises and threats, some rebel candidates remained in the field and the morale of the UDF generally suffered. Finally, the bold decision of the Bharatiya Janata Party (BJP) to contest in scores of constituencies threatened the prospects of many UDF candidates.

The BJP's attempt to carve out a distinct place for itself in the state political system was one of the most noteworthy developments of the 1982 election in Kerala. In earlier elections, the Jana Sangh, predecessor of the BJP, used to put up a few candidates to make its presence in the state known. But the BJP's aspirations had grown much bolder by 1982, mainly because of the widespread popular disillusionment with the performance of the front governments led by the CPM or Congress(I). The BJP might have also felt encouraged by the spectacular rise in the militancy of the RSS and its new popularity in the state.[63] The BJP's goal in Kerala was to become the nucleus of a third force that could "combat the corruption and decadence of the Congress(I) on the one hand and fight the Marxist violence and regimentation on the other."[64] Its efforts to create such a third force by bringing together all the parties in Kerala except the Congress(I) and the communist parties failed because no party of any significance in Kerala politics was interested in a third force. All of them wanted to join either the Congress(I)–led front or the CPM–led front. Openly scorned by the leaders of both the Congress(I) and the CPM, the BJP ended up with two allies, the Janadhipatya Socialist Party and the National Democratic Socialist Party, two paper parties in Kerala.

More than one hundred persons filed nominations as BJP candidates, but the party finally decided to contest in only sixty–eight constituencies. The BJP election manifesto promised the voters a clean, efficient and upright administration, and spelled out the specific measures it would take if it came to power. They were designed to attract voters of all religions, castes and classes. All the important national leaders of the party, all of them north Indians, came to Kerala for campaigning. In their speeches they severely criticized both fronts, particularly their leading parties, the Congress(I) and the CPM. On the whole, the north Indian leaders of the BJP were more critical of the Congress(I) than of the CPM. Ram Jethmalani, Vice President of the party, even said that the LDF was the lesser evil and that the BJP would support it to form a government if neither front secured a majority.[65] The BJP leaders claimed that the election result would upset many calculations and expressed confidence that this time the voice of their party would be heard in the Kerala legislature.

THE 1982 MID–TERM ELECTION: THE OUTCOME

Political alignments in Kerala had changed significantly since the previous election when the LDF won a decisive victory over the UDF. On the whole, the changes were favorable to the UDF mainly because of the defection of the Congress(A) and the KCM from the LDF to the UDF. But the large number of BJP candidates was a new factor in Kerala politics. Since the BJP was likely to draw more voters from the UDF than from the LDF, confident prediction of the 1982 election result became difficult. Yet, leaders of both fronts publicly expressed full confidence in the victory of their fronts. P.V. Kunhikannan, Coordinator of the LDF, claimed in late March that the LDF would win by a landslide. E.M.S. Namboodiripad in early May, and the CPM Kerala State Secretariat a few days before the election, made similar claims. The UDF leaders were more specific, though a bit boastful, in their claims. In late April, Karunakaran said that the UDF would win 110 seats out of the total of 140. Kidangur Gopalakrishna Pillai, leader of the NDP, repeated Karunakaran's claim. Later, M. Neelakantan Nair, Coordinator of the UDF, predicted that the UDF would get no less than 95 seats, and the LDF from 35 to 40 seats.

Table 5:2
Kerala State Assembly Election Results, 1982

Party	Seats held	Seats contested	Seats won	Percentage of votes
LDF(Left and Democratic Front):				
Communist Party of India (Marxist)	35	51	26	18.9
Communist Party of India	17	26	13	8.8
Congress(S)	6	18	7	5.7
All India Muslim League	5	12	4	3.1
Revolutionary Socialist Party	4	8 .	4	2.8
Democratic Socialist Party	1	1	1	0.4
Kerala Congress-Socialist	1	1	1	0.4
Lok Dal	0	1	0	0.2
LDF Independents	3	9	3	2.7
Janata (Arangil Group)	2	13	4	4.3
	71	140	63	47.3
UDF (United Democratic Front):				
Congress(I)	17	35	20	11.9
Congress(A)	16*	28	15	9.6
Indian Union Muslim League	14	18	14	6.2
Kerala Congress (Joseph Group)	6	12	8	4.5
Kerala Congress (Mani Group)	8	17	6	5.8
National Democratic Party	3	8	4	2.7
Janata (Gopalan Group)	3	8	4	2.8
Socialist Republican Party	0	6	2	2.1
Revolutionary Socialist Party (Srekantan Group)	1	4	1	1.2
Praja Socialist Party	1	1	1	0.3
National Revolutionary Socialists	0	1	0	0.4
UDF — supported Independents	1	2	2	0.8
	70	140	77	48.3
Bharatiya Janata Party	0	70	0	2.8
Independents	1	349	0	1.6

*Including one nominated member

Source: *People's Democracy*, 30 May 1982, and newspapers.

There were 699 candidates for the 140 seats. About half of them represented two dozen political parties. The rest were independents, most with no hope of winning. Of the 13 million voters, 70 percent voted. The overall result was no surprise. The victory of the UDF was foreseeable as the result of the defection of the Congress(A) and the KCM from the LDF and the broadening of the UDF. The UDF was a combination of important political parties and important communal and religious forces in Kerala. It was the small size of the UDF victory that surprised many. The UDF got 77 seats and 4.6 million votes; the LDF got 63 seats and 4.5 million votes (see Table 5:2). The actual difference between the two fronts was 95,227 votes, which was less than one percent of the total valid votes polled.[66]

The prestige of the LDF, particularly of the two communist parties, suffered severely because of the defeat of many leaders. The defeat of T.K. Ramakrishnan, a former Home Minister, and of K. Anirudhan and M.K. Kannan, both prominent trade unionists, reflected popular dissatisfaction with the police policy of the previous LDF government and disgust with the militancy of some CPM–controlled labor unions. The defeat of communist candidates in Alleppey and Shertallay and in the industrial heartland of Kerala stretching from Ankamali to Ernakulam was a crushing blow to the parties of the proletariat. The UDF also lost a few prestigious battles. But the fact that the UDF won a majority of the seats and that Karunakaran won in both the constituencies he contested overshadowed the defeats.

Of the fourteen reserved seats the CPM won five and the CPI three (see Table 5:3). That confirmed the popularity of the communists among the most underprivileged castes in Kerala society. In the Malabar area, traditionally the communist stronghold in the state, the communists retained the seats they had won in 1980 and captured four more in 1982. Here the alliance with the Congress(S), the Janata(A) and the All India Muslim League benefited the communists. It was in the Travancore–Cochin area, particularly in the districts of Ernakulam, Alleppey, and Quilon, that the communist losses were severe. Whereas the communists had secured twenty seats from these three districts in 1980, they could get only eight seats in 1982 (see Table 5:4). The defection of the Congress(A) and the KCM and the alliance the UDF had made with communal parties like the National Democratic Party and the Socialist Republican Party proved fatal to the communists in this area. In terms of seats, which are what ultimately count in the game of parliamentary politics, the greatest loser was the CPM. The CPM's seats

Table 5:3

Reserved Seats Won by the Various Parties in the 1982 election

Constituency	CPM	CPI	Congress(A)	Congress(I)	Janata(G)	AIML
Chelakkara	X					
Devikulam	X					
Hosdurg		X				
Kilimanur		X				
Kunnamangalam						X
Kunnathur					X	
Kuzhalmannam	X					
Narakal			X			
Neduvathur	X					
North Vayanad				X		
Pandalam	X					
Thrithala				X		
Vaikom		X				
Vandur				X		
Total	5	3	1	3	1	1

Source: Compiled from *Manorama Election Guide 1982*, and newspapers.

Table 5:4

Seats Won by the Two Communist Parties in the Various
Districts of Kerala in the 1982 Election

District	Total Seats	Seats secured by the LDF	Seats secured by the CPM	Seats secured by the CPI
Aleppy	14	4	3	0
Calicut	12	9	3	1
Cannanore	15	11	6	2
Ernakulam	14	3	1	1
Idukki	5	2	2	0
Kottayam	10	3	0	2
Malapuram	12	1	0	0
Palaghat	11	9	5	2
Quilon	16	6	2	1
Trichur	14	7	2	2
Trivandrum	14	8	2	2
Vayanad	3	0	0	0
Total	140	63	26	13

Source: Compiled from the *Manorama Election Guide 1982*, and newspapers.

in the legislature fell from 35 (1980) to 26 (1982). But the CPM retained its position as the number one party in the state both in terms of seats and votes. Despite the significant drop in its seats, there was no decline in its votes.[67] Both the Congress(S) and the Janata(A) increased their seats as a result of the alliance with the communists.

Politically, the greatest winner was the Congress(I). Its seats rose only slightly, from 17 (1980) to 20 (1982). Its vote fell from 17 percent (1980) to 12 percent (1982), but it was able to transform itself from an opposition party to the backbone of the government.[68] The instrument with which it achieved this feat was the expanded UDF. Whereas the UDF in 1980 consisted of only five parties, in 1982 its membership had grown into a dozen parties. Many of the new members were just splinter groups, but their help was invaluable in snatching victory from the LDF in several constituencies. With the sole exception of the KCM, every party in the UDF was able either to maintain the strength it had in the previous legislature or to improve it slightly (see Table 5:2). The KCM's seats fell from eight (1980) to six (1982), though its votes remained virtually unchanged. Thus the KCM hardly gained anything tangible by deserting the LDF. It now suffered psychologically as it fell behind its chief rival, the KCJ, which increased its seats from six (1980) to eight (1982).

The BJP, which entered the electoral fray with a bang, had to leave it with a whimper. It could not win a single seat. All but two of its candidates, including the President of the state party, forfeited their deposits. It did relatively better in the Malabar area, from where more than half of its candidates contested, though Malabar accounted for only 38 percent of the total seats in Kerala. In twenty constituencies the BJP votes exceeded the difference between the votes of the LDF and UDF. The UDF won eleven of these twenty seats. In most of the other nine constituencies, the BJP was the major factor in the defeat of the UDF candidates.

Supporters of the UDF interpreted its success as the victory of the common people who loved democracy and wanted a government that would protect their lives, property and dignity. Antony claimed that the election result was the clear verdict of the people against the Nayanar government. Supporters of the LDF argued that the UDF was able to get a small majority by patching together an alliance of religious and communal forces in the state, through the intervention of church authorities, and through the misuse of governmental machinery. They also argued that, in the end, the BJP supported the UDF candidates in many constituencies.

The victory of the UDF was a severe setback for the CPM. One of its chief goals in forging the LDF was to isolate the Congress(I) and to confine it to the opposition. But the Congress(I) outwitted the CPM; it became the kingpin of a broad anti-communist alliance and recaptured power in Kerala. On 24 May 1982, a UDF ministry with Karunakaran as Chief Minister came to power. It was the thirteenth ministry in Kerala's history of 26 years and the third one Karunakaran had headed in six years. Karunakaran's position in his party was now secure; he controlled the Congress(I) in Kerala. But the coalition he led contained parties with conflicting programs and leaders with vaulting ambitions.[69] Some of his cabinet colleagues were old foes who were in no mood to forgive and with no wish to forget.[70] These were potentially fatal weaknesses.[71]

An experienced political leader of Kerala recently told me that 95 percent of Keralites will be contented if the government maintains law and order and ensures an adequate supply of rice at a subsidized price.[72] I think his remark is essentially correct. No government in Kerala has been able to provide enough rice at a price affordable to the poor. Hence the unpopularity of all governments in Kerala. But beyond that, few governments in Kerala were such intolerable failures in the maintenance of law and order as was the LDF government. Hence its fall and defeat in the election that followed.

Nonetheless, the LDF is still a formidable political force and the CPM is the best organized party in Kerala.[73] The LDF can regain power by broadening itself, which is possible only by enticing some of the parties from the ruling front. The past suggests that the CPM may eventually succeed in doing so. But the greater challenge the CPM will face is how to maintain unity when the LDF is in power. The CPM will have to undergo a metamorphosis to do that. It must accept the inevitability of gradualness inherent in Kerala's political culture and inescapable in democracy. That will be very difficult for a party which believes that it was born out of revolt against revisionism in the Communist Party of India.

NOTES
    1. I am thankful to Ronald J. Herring, James Manor, and Koshy Chacko for their comments on the earlier version of this paper.
    2. *The Manarama Yearbook, 1982* (Kottayam (Kerala): The

Malayala Manorama Company, 1982) is the best source of general information on Kerala; but it is in Malayalam, the language of Kerala. For a general introduction to Kerala in English, see George Woodcock, *Kerala* (London: Faber and Faber, 1967). For Kerala politics, see P.M. Mammen, *Communalism vs. Communism in Kerala, 1892-1970* (Calcutta: Minerva Associates, 1981), Victor M. Fic, *Kerala, the Yenan of India* (Bombay: Nachiketa Publications, 1970), and T.J. Nossiter, *Communism in Kerala* (Delhi: Oxford University Press, 1982).

3. The splits resulted in the creation of the Kerala Congress (1964), Congress(O) (1969), Congress(I) (1978) and Congress(S) (1978). The Congress(O) eventually disintegrated as its supporters joined other parties. The Kerala Congress, Congress(I), and Congress(S) all suffered splits later.

4. A split in the Muslim League in 1975 produced the All India Muslim League and Indian Union Muslim League.

5. A split in the Communist Party of India 1964 produced the Communist Party of India (CPI) and the Communist Party of India(Marxist) or CPM. Both the CPI and CPM suffered splits resulting in many communist splinter groups. · Only the CPI and CPM are electorally significant in Kerala.

6. In 1954, the Praja Socialist Party (PSP) formed a minority government in the former Travancore-Cochin state, most of which became part of Kerala in 1956. The PSP government existed because the Congress Party supported it, and fell within a year when the Congress withdrew its support. In 1957, the Communist Party, with the support of five Independents, formed the government.

7. The alliance consisted of Congress, PSP, and the Muslim League and it had the support of the high caste Nairs and the Christian communities.

8. Within two years, first the League and then the alliance; but Congress had a legislative majority and continued in office.

9. Congress got only 9 seats out of 133, though it got 34 percent of the votes.

10. These included the League, the Socialists, and the CPI.

11. There were three fronts in 1970, but the real fight was between the CPM-led front and the Congress-led front. In Kerala, "Marxists" have become synonymous with the CPM.

12. The anti-Marxist alliance won 111 seats and the Marxist alliance 29.

13. These included the Karunakaran government, March-April 1977 (Congress); the Antony government, April-October 1978 (Congress-S); the Vasudevan Nair government, October 1978-October

1979 (CPI); and the Muhamed Koya government, October–November 1979 (Muslim League).

14. Splits occurred in the Kerala Congress and the Muslim League. The National Democratic Party (NDP) and the Socialist Republican Party (SRP) were the two important new parties that were formed.

15. See pp. 124–25.

16. The KCP merged with the KCM in November 1980. The CPM, the CPI, and the RSP are considered leftist parties; the Congress(S) as centrist; and the KCM and the AIML as right of center.

17. See *Political Resolution: Adopted by the Tenth Congress of the Communist Party of India (Marxist)* (Calcutta: CPI(M) Publication, 1978), p. 37; *Political Resolution: Adopted by the Eleventh Congress of the Communist Party of India* (New Delhi: Communist Party Publication, 1978), p. 18; and the *Kerala Kaumudi* (hereafter, *Kaumudi*) 12 October and 19 November, 1978.

18. The ruling front in 1979 consisted of the Congress(S), the CPI, the RSP, the Indian Union Muslim League, the KCM, and the Praja Socialist Party.

19. A "clean slate" meant that the ruling front must resign and dissolve the legislature for a new election before negotiations to form the LDF could start.

20. Following the split in the Congress Party in January 1978, the followers of Indira Gandhi in Kerala chose K. Karunakaran as their leader and left the ruling front.

21. The four seats were, Tellichery, Parasala, Thiruvalla, and Kasarkode.

22. Of the total of 3,911 seats the CPM won 2,961. See *Kaumudi*, 24 September 1979.

23. The Congress(I), the party that accepted Indira Gandhi as the leader, also supported the Koya government. Koya's party, the Indian Union Muslim League, had 12 members in the state legislature of 141 members, including the speaker.

24. This bill, which would have helped some land owners, was opposed by the CPM.

25. The UDF consisted of the Congress(I), the Indian Union Muslim League (IUML), the Kerala Congress–Joseph Group (KCJ), the National Democratic Party (NDP), and the Praja Socialist Party (PSP).

26. The LDF got 51.2 percent of the votes; the UDF, 46.4 percent. *Kaumudi*, 9, January 1980.

27. *The Times of India,* 22 January 1980.

28. *Kaumudi*, 1 June 1980.

29. *Deshabhimani,* Feature, 25 January 1981.

30. *Kaumudi,* 25 January 1981.

31. R. Chummar in *Malayala Manorama* (hereafter, Manorama), 24 January 1981.

32. Following a clash in Trivandrum between the student organizations of the Congress(S) and the CPM, the CITU members chased the Congress(S) supporters into the Congress district committee office and caused considerable damage. See *Kaumudi,* 21–24 November 1980.

33. The scandal arose from the illicit import of rectified spirit to Kerala from Tamil Nadu. The Opposition alleged that M.K. Krishnan (CPM), the LDF excise minister, was involved and demanded his resignation. The CPM felt annoyed when the youth wing of the Congress(S) demanded a judicial enquiry into the matter. See *Kaumudi,* 21 January 1981.

34. *Kaumudi,* 29 September, 1981.

35. *Deshabhimani Weekly,* 11 October 1981.

36. *Kaumudi,* 17 October 1981.

37. Government policies during 1957–1959 provoked opposition from the churches, the Nair Service Society and the middle and upper classes. Most leaders of the Congress(S) were then students. They actively participated in the popular struggle against the government.

38. The Congress(S) leaders charged that the CPM was trying to split their party and slander them. For Antony's remarks, see *Kaumudi,* 15 October 1979. For Namboodiripad's, see *Ibid.,* 8 November 1979.

39. The circumstances were awkward because first the Congress(S) supported the minority government of Koya, then within two months, it withdrew the support in a hurry. Among the Congress(S) leaders who opposed joining the LDF was Vayalar Revi.

40. See Namboodiripad's speech reported in *Kaumudi,* 3 December 1981.

41. *People's Democracy,* 20 January 1980.

42. *Manorama,* 3 April 1981.

43. *Kaumudi,* 22 May 1981.

44. Catholic Bishop Sebastian Mankuzhikary confessed: "We had put pressure on K.M. Mani to pull out. We do not want any alliance with atheists and anti-social elements. We are happy that the Ministry had fallen by God's Grace." See *India Today,* 15 November 1981, p. 59.

45. According to one rumor, two legislators of KCM threatened to defect to the opposition; this would have deprived the LDF of its majority in the legislature. According to another rumor, Mani used the critical position of his party to bargain hard with the Congress(I) and he got a written assurance that his party would be given 22 seats in the next

election. See *Kaumudi*, 18 October 1981.

46. The three governments were: the first Namboodiripad government, 1957–1959, the second Namboodiripad government, 1967–1969, and the Nayanar government, 1980–1981. Actually, there was no CPM until the CPI suffered the split in 1964.

47. *Right Communist Betrayal of Kerala U.F. and Government: A Collection of Documents* (Calcutta: CPI(M) Publications, 1969), p. 101.

48. *Programme of the Communist Party of India (Marxist)* (Calcutta: CPI(M) Publications, 1964), p. 101.

49. *New Situation and the Party's Tasks* (Calcutta: CPI(M) Publication, 1967), p. 70.

50. These classes in rural Kerala have some land which they cultivate, either with hired labor or with the help of hired laborers. For an explanation of the predicament of the CPM in this respect, see Ronald J. Herring, *Land to the Tiller* (New Haven: Yale University Press, 1983) pp. 210–16.

51. A.S. Abraham, "Comrades All At Vijayawada," *The Times of India*, 5 February 1982.

52. The decision to join the UDF split the Congress(S) into two – Congress(A) and Congress(S). Congress(A) joined the UDF, and Congress(S), the LDF.

53. Congress(I), IUML, KCJ, PSP, and NDP.

54. In addition to the five, the UDF now included Janata (Gopalan Group), or Janata(G), KCM, Congress(A), and RSP (Sreekantan Group) or RSPS. The last resulted from a split in RSP in 1981.

55. The three new ones were the Socialist Republican Party (SRP), the National Revolutionary Socialist Party, which was born out of a split in RSPS, and the Democratic Labor Party. The last was not formally in the UDF, but was an ally. The UDF also had the support of the All India Communist Party, which had no candidate of its own.

56. The two finally merged in December 1982.

57. *Kaumudi*, 21 April 1982.

58. According to one report, Indira Gandhi expressed concern at the deadlock of the UDF. Her private secretary, Dr. P.C. Alexander, a native of Kerala, telephoned Joseph and invited him to Delhi for a meeting with Indira Gandhi. New Delhi also contacted Karunakaran and put pressure on him to accommodate the demands of the KCJ. Meanwhile, Chevalier Kannamthanam, a prominent lay Catholic leader and a confidant of Archbishop Gregorios of Trivandrum, presumably acting for the Catholic hierarchy, met both Joseph and Karunakaran and tried to patch up their differences. The crisis ended in an anti-climax when the KCJ gave back to the Congress(I) two of its fourteen seats and

decided to contest twelve seats only. See *Kaumudi*, 22 and 28 April 1982.

59. *The Times of India*, 19 April 1982. The main reason appeared to be the hope of the LDF that the KCJ might seek the help of the LDF. See *Kaumudi*, 22 April 1982.

60. *Ibid.*, 9 May 1982.

61. Karunakaran was able to form a UDF government because of the defection of the Congress(S) and the KCM from the LDF, and their decision to join the UDF. The Congress(I) played a key role in engineering the defection. The decision of the Congress(S) to join the UDF split that party — those who joined the UDF came to be known as Congress (Antony Group) or Congress(A); others continued as Congress(S). The decision of the Janata Party to join the UDF split that party also. Those who joined the UDF came to known as Janata (Gopalan Group) or Janata(G), others as Janata (Arangil Group) or Janata(A). Even with the support of these parties, it was not clear whether Karunakaran had a legislative majority. Opponents of the UDF severely criticized the governor for allowing Karunakaran to form a government under these circumstances.

62. For example, the SRP is for the present system of reservation, while the NDP is against it. Both Congress parties in the UDF profess socialism, others, except perhaps the SRP, are either averse or hostile to socialism. The Muslim League parties are based on the Islamic religion, the NDP on the Nair caste, and the SRP on the Ezhava caste. The two Kerala Congress parties get much of their support from Christians, particularly from Catholics.

63. Many Keralites who opposed the goals of the RSS wondered whether it was not the effective answer to the tactics of intimidation and violence which CPM supporters often used. The BJP has close links with the RSS.

64. *The Times of India*, 9 May 1982.

65. *Manorama*, 16 May 1982. Raman Pillai, Secretary of the state unit of the BJP, dissented and said it was just Jethmalani's opinion and not the BJP's. See *Kaumudi*, 17 May 1982. For the Kerala BJP leaders the CPM is their chief enemy as the CPM is very powerful in their state; for the north Indian BJP leaders the Congress(I) is their chief enemy as Congress(I) is powerful in north India and the CPM a negligible force there.

66. For election coverage and results, see *Kaumudi*, 28 March–23 May, 1982.

67. In 1980, the CPM got 19.33 percent of the votes; in 1982, it got 17.78 percent. But in 1982, the various LDF independent candidates together got about 4 percent of the votes, a large part of which was for the

CPM. *Kaumudi,* 23 May 1982.

68. In 1980, the Congress(I) contested from 50 constituencies; in 1982, it contested from only 35 constituencies. The decline in its votes should be seen in light of this fact.

69. The SRP and the NDP are examples the first; Vayalar Revi and K.M. Mani are examples the second.

70. K.M. Mani and P.J. Joseph are examples of this.

71. Splits in three member parties (the Congress(I), Janata(G), and SRP), the death of two UDF legislators, a defeat in one by-election, charges of corruption and the relentless pressure tactics of some UDF parties and Karunakaran's desperate attempts to appease them, have subsequently weakened the UDF and tarnished its image. On a couple of occasions, the government reached the brink of collapse as the KCJ prepared itself to withdraw from the UDF. But Karunakaran has shown an extraordinary political will to survive. In December 1983, the legislature rejected an opposition no-confidence motion by 72 to 63 votes. When the latest session of the legislature ended in March 1984, the government had the support of 72 members and the opposition of 65. By-elections are due in three constituencies, two of them caused by the death of UDF members and one by the invalidation of an LDF member's election.

72. Interview with Ommen Chandy, August 1983. Chandy is the deputy leader of the Congress(I) Party in the Kerala legislature.

73. Congress(A) merged with Congress(I) in late 1982. Thus Congress(I) replaced CPM as the largest party in the legislature.

6
Blurring the Lines Between Parties and Social Bases: Gundu Rao and the Emergence of a Janata Government in Karnataka

James Manor

It may be helpful, before turning to a discussion of events in Karnataka; to outline what I see as the framework within which recent changes in this and almost all other Indian states have occurred. It is well known that India is a nation of immense variety. It is marked by huge differences among (and within) its many regions — differences in language, ecology, religious and cultural traditions, the very composition of society, agrarian relations, literacy, political identity and a host of other things. Given these daunting complexities, each region or state in India has had its own distinctive political logic, its own very particular language or culture of politics. In the absence of an organizational instrument capable of rigorous, relatively centralized control of the regions (of the kind which the Chinese Communist Party has at times possessed but which has never been developed in India), leaders at the national level have been able to make their influence penetrate down to the regional level and below most effectively by means of *compromise* and *bargaining* with powerful groups in regional and sub–regional arenas, rather than by means of *diktat.*

Since 1970 or so, Mrs. Indira Gandhi has tended to depart from this method of dealing with the states. She has attempted, by and large, to abandon the old system of compromise with powerful groups at the regional level and has attempted to operate by *diktat* on the erroneous assumption that this will enable her first to make her influence penetrate more effectively to regional and sub–regional levels and second to homogenize the politics of these varied regions. In reality, as I have argued elsewhere,[1] her efforts have tended to produce the opposite results to those that were intended. There appear to be a small number of exceptions to this generalization. In a few parts of Hindi-speaking India — notably in Uttar Pradesh, as Paul Brass has shown[2] — where her own direct involvement in regional and sub-regional arenas equipped her to understand the particular political logic, her influence did penetrate effectively. But in the vast majority of regions, including several Hindi states, her attempts at centralization have eroded the corporate substance of her party and have cut her off from those regional arenas, so that her influence over them has declined. In the absence of the restraints which the old system of compromises had imposed upon the various regions or states, the natural heterogeneity of the states has asserted itself. States have tended to diverge from one another. The emergence of regional parties in some states is one sign of this, but so is the radical divergence among states supposedly run in a consistent manner by Mrs. Gandhi's own Congress Party. The so-called state units of the Congress have themselves operated like regional parties, often without Mrs. Gandhi's knowledge.[3] It is in this context that the events in Karnataka and other states discussed in this book must be viewed.

This chapter should be seen as an initial report on the internal political developments in the south Indian state of Karnataka between the first week of 1980 and early 1984. It is impossible in the space available to deal exhaustively with the numerous issues and events that arise, so the chapter should be regarded as an invitation to others to pursue things more fully.

One purpose of this book is to discuss whether events in our various states lead us to believe that state politics in India are "in crisis." If we are discussing center-state relations in India's federal system or India's national party system, then from where I sit, something approaching a crisis appears to exist. But politics *within* Karnataka are not now in crisis. They are in great *confusion* which may eventually lead to a crisis. And they were brought very near to crisis by an exceedingly unintelligent and destructive Chief Minister, R. Gundu Rao, whom Mrs. Gandhi visited upon the state between 1980 and 1983. But that crisis was averted by the voters of Karnataka in January 1983 when they turned Gundu Rao and the Congress(I) out of office in a state assembly election.

Another purpose is to consider whether the general election of 1980 or events since then have constituted a return to "normality" in the politics of our various states. In the case of Karnataka, the short inadequate answer is "no," but a more satisfactory reply is best left until after we have reviewed the very considerable changes that have occurred in the state since January 1980. It is worth noting here, however, that an important preoccupation of this paper is with the connections between Karnataka's political parties and their socio-economic bases. On that front, "normality" has certainly *not* returned to the state's politics — indeed, in some important ways the opposite has occurred.

THE DEMISE OF GUNDU RAO'S CONGRESS GOVERNMENT

Until the fall of Devaraj Urs in January 1980, the ruling party in Karnataka had always had — more or less — a clearly identifiable constituency or socio-economic base. Until 1972 this consisted mainly of the two locally-dominant landed *jati*-clusters, the Vokkaligas and the Lingayats.[4] In that period, the regional Congress Party's political machine saw to it that other groups in the state received modest portions of political patronage which was the life's blood of the machine. But the Lingayats and Vokkaligas got the lion's share because they had considerable numerical strength (comprising roughly 32 per cent of the population), because they were better organized and educated than most groups, and especially because they owned a great deal of land and could therefore influence the votes of their poorer neighbors in the villages. This changed in and after 1972. In that year, Devaraj Urs led the Congress(R) to victory, partly because he was the representative of Mrs. Gandhi who was then riding high after her 1971 national election victory and the Bangladesh war. But he also managed to attract the votes of a great many disadvantaged voters by promising them reform and a more substantial share of the spoils.

Between 1972 and 1980, he offered these groups a number of programs which were intended to fulfill, to varying degrees, these promises. He also kept some patronage flowing to elements of the old dominant landed groups — particularly to Vokkaligas and to Lingayat cultivating groups in northern districts — in order to minimize the backlash from those quarters. But it was the disadvantaged majority of voters that he sought out as his main socio-economic base and, by the mid-1970s, many such people had developed enough political sophistication to disregard the advice of locally dominant land-owning groups and vote for Urs.[5] This was demonstrated at the state assembly election of 1978 which the Congress won, despite the strong national swing in 1977-78 in favor of Janata. Until late 1979 the links between socio-economic groups and the major parties were reasonably clear. Lingayats and (to a lesser degree) Vokkaligas tended to back Janata or other opposition parties, while Congress drew most of its support from among the less prosperous groups.

In June of 1979, the alliance between Devaraj Urs and Indira Gandhi broke down. For some months, Urs had faced mounting interference and insults from Sanjay Gandhi and Sanjay's allies in Karnataka. These included increasing demands for massive payments to the national leadership — despite the fact that Urs had outdone every Congress Chief Minister at "fund-raising" since 1972. Still more frustrating were the demands that he allow young men in the Congress — some of whom he had brought into the party, but who were now developing into a force beyond his control under his Transport Minister, R. Gundu Rao — to engage in violent and illegal protests in support of Mrs. Gandhi in the streets of Bangalore.[6] These things and his own ambitions to be a force in national politics persuaded Urs to break with Mrs. Gandhi. Had he known that only a few weeks later at the national level Janata would collapse and a general election would be called, his decision would have been different. But it was impossible to foresee those things in June.

When he split with Mrs. Gandhi, Urs managed to retain the support of most Congress legislators so that he did not lose his majority in the State Assembly. But Gundu Rao immediately set up a rival Congress Party in the Assembly which was loyal to Mrs. Gandhi and he took 42 legislators (MLAs) with him. Despite various comings and goings during late 1979, this situation persisted until the general election results became known on 6 January 1980. Urs knew that Mrs. Gandhi's victory would mean a new wave of defections to Gundu Rao which would give the latter a majority, so within hours he resigned as Chief Minister. The defections of another 146 MLAs followed soon after and Gundu Rao became Chief Minister — a post which he was to hold for three years until the defeat of his Congress(I) Party in the State Assembly election of January 1983.

It was in January 1980, when this spate of defections carried Gundu Rao to power, that the clear links which had alway existed in Karnataka between major parties and distinct socio-economic bases were thrown into confusion. This occurred in a rather complicated fashion. First of all, the legislators who now provided Gundu Rao with his majority in the State Assembly were a rather variegated group. Most of them were ex-Urs supporters who had been elected on and were therefore enthusiastic about the reformist programs to assist less prosperous social groups. But during his campaign to attract enough defectors to assemble a majority between June 1979 and January 1980, Gundu Rao had also welcomed into the Congress(I) a number of defectors from non–Congress parties or from the ranks of the independents. And, during those few days of opportunism and fluidity in January, after the general election result became known, he allowed a number of other MLAs from outside the old Urs group to join him. This left him with a very motley legislative delegation. And once Gundu Rao had become Chief Minister, Urs naturally sought to make common cause with other elements of the opposition. That brought him and the legislators who remained loyal to him — mainly people who were from or who favored aid to disadvantaged groups — into a loose alliance with the Janata Party which had heavy Lingayat support. And then to complicate matters further, Gundu Rao began cultivating the Lingayats, with mixed results.

This rather confused situation existed throughout Gundu Rao's three years as Chief Minister. It was compounded after Devaraj Urs' death in mid–1982. While he lived, he had stood in many people's eyes as a symbol of a regime that had sought to extend at least some aid to the disadvantaged — a role which Gundu Rao's blundering, unresponsive and at times brutish government (of which we shall say more in a moment) could not fulfill. Once Urs had died, he became the object of tearful praise from all sides, so that both the Gundu Rao government and various opposition groups posed as his political heirs.

To understand how, once the lines between parties and social bases had been blurred, Gundu Rao came to lose the state election of 1983, we must examine his performance in office. The fundamental problem of this government was an extreme overcentralization of power in the hands of a Chief Minister who was breathtakingly incapable of the most elementary tasks.[7] Gundu Rao's colleagues were astonished to learn, for example, that despite many years as a minister under Urs, he found it enormously difficult to draft basic discursive statements. And yet he insisted on keeping for himself an unprecedented number of major ministerial portfolios — indeed he held every important spending portfolio except education. This meant, of course, that he was faced with a monstrous work load which would have severely taxed even the most brilliant and industrious of ministers — and Gundu Rao was neither of these things. This meant, according to one high authoritative source, that roughly two hundred official files crossed his desk every day. And yet, given his limitations, he was seldom able to comprehend the issues that they raised. The result was either very random and often bizarre decisions or — increasingly as time wore on — no decision at all, so that things were left in the hands of civil servants. They in their turn soon came to recognize the Chief Minister's disabilities and his disinclination to look too closely into the workings of the state machinery. They therefore set about taking effective control of vast areas of government which had been the preserve of elected politicians since 1947.[8] It was in this way that civil servant raj of a kind unknown in Karnataka since British and princely times began to take hold. As we shall see presently, that process was completed not by the Chief Minister's *in*action, but by his conscious choice.

Gundu Rao's possession ("control" would obviously be too strong a word) of so many government departments prevented the development of the sort of minimal solidarity within his party and cabinet that would have served the interests of everyone concerned. It also made it impossible for the Chief Minister to gain the backing of several important social groups to whom various ministers had connections. Given that Gundu Rao was a Brahmin from that remote and most idiosyncratic part of the state, Coorg, he badly needed to cultivate such intermediaries as allies. But he appears to have lacked the imagination to see even this, and the temperamental inclination to engage in that kind of political bargaining. Gundu Rao's tendency to take impulsive decisions without consulting fellow ministers — as when he promised the Farmers' Lobby 850 million rupees in special concessions without a word to his Revenue Minister who was theoretically responsible — caused profound alienation among his colleagues. (That promise, like many others,[9] went wholly unfulfilled and did Congress immense damage among cultivators at the 1983 state election.)

Gundu Rao's distrust of and disregard for fellow ministers was matched by similar feelings for Congress legislators. This might seem rather surprising since in theory he was dependent upon them for his majority in the State Assembly, but in practice he was not and did not feel dependent upon them at all. He had been chosen not by the legislators but by Mrs. Gandhi and Sanjay — indeed, he knew that most legislators and most Congress Party workers would have preferred other men, who had done the hard spade work of party organization, to lead them. He believed — correctly, given the extreme (and ultimately self-defeating) overcentralization within the all-India Congress(I) — that he was secure at least until the next state election if he kept Mrs. Gandhi happy. He knew that the way to achieve that was to offer her slavish loyalty and frequent massive tributary contributions to the apex of the system.

Gundu Rao surpassed all rivals in abject protestations of loyalty to his chief. Indeed it was for these, for the observation that he was merely a humble player in Indira Gandhi's drama troupe and the like, that he first became famous or notorious. The need to raise funds for his masters impelled him to throw his own weight behind the move towards civil servant raj which began as a result of his inaction and incapacities as Chief Minister. By giving bureaucrats near–total immunity to pressure from his legislators, and by cutting legislators off from access to political spoils and private profiteering, Gundu Rao could centralize and personalize control over "fund–raising" to an unprecedented degree. Civil servant raj brought no diminution of corruption in Karnataka politics. On the contrary, new devices were developed which required the participation of civil servants. For example, minimum wage laws were manipulated by having official inspectors extract from firms substantial contributions to "fund–raising" campaigns in order to prevent punitive action by government. Opposition critics and even Congressmen complained that such contributions were passed up to the apex of the state's political system (and thence on to New Delhi) instead of being dissipated among Congressmen in the legislature. The need for massive fund–raising intensified after the death of Sanjay Gandhi, Gundu Rao's great patron, in June 1980. Others at the national level – especially Rajiv Gandhi after his emergence – were less tolerant of the Chief Minister's penchant for maladroit public statements and for actions such as the siege of the *Deccan Herald* newspaper office by Congress(I) toughs which achieved little except grotesque publicity.

Not surprisingly, Gundu Rao's reliance upon civil servants caused deep frustration among legislators and other Congressmen. They found themselves with little or no influence over bureaucrats whom they had controlled for decades. The old gambit of threatening an official with a transfer was rendered impossible by the Chief Minister's announcement that he would prevent such things – and this was one promise that he *did* keep. Since there was a radical decline in the amount of political spoils passing through legislators' hands and a radical curtailment of opportunities for them to make profits by peddling influence or by skimming off a percentage of spoils for themselves, legislators now began to squeeze what spoils did come their way far more ruthlessly than before. This meant that smaller proportions of funds for development or welfare projects actually reached the people for whom they were intended. And – to look at the legitimate side of things – legislators had so little influence over bureaucrats, they were unable to get constituents' needs attended to according to democratic convention. Indeed, they often found it impossible even to get appointments with relatively minor civil servants. This eventually convinced many citizens that the government was hopelessly unresponsive, and stored up major trouble for Gundu Rao's Congress(I) at the 1983 state election.

Gundu Rao's wrongheaded notions of the proper role of a Chief Minister and of ways to win public support also contributed to popular resentment against his government. He was much given to theatrical pronouncements and initiatives of a symbolic nature which cast him in the role of a decisive, forceful leader in the "action"-oriented, Sanjay Gandhi mold. Many of these actions were, somewhat paradoxically, intended to bring the Chief Minister closer to the people and at the same time to inspire awe by depicting him as a man who lived at a level far beyond the aspirations of ordinary folk. For example, he regarded his decision to hold meetings of the state cabinet in various district headquarters towns as one of his greatest achievements, and he took a great deal of trouble, particularly as the 1983 election neared, to show himself to people in a great many localities. But the fact that he would arrive at most of these occasions by helicopter — a mode of transport that was little used (indeed, it was scorned as needlessly and obviously self-indulgent) by his predecessors and his successor — rather spoiled the image of accessibility.[10]

This impression of Gundu Rao's lavish life-style was reinforced by a widespread awareness that he had built himself at great expense a plush retreat in Bangalore where he would repair for lively parties and, as eminent journalists and Congress leaders have attested to this writer, that he insisted upon drinking champagne every day that he was Chief Minister. This popular impression fitted logically alongside the air of scandal that surrounded his government. As one observer put it, under Devaraj Urs there were two or three ministers who became involved in scandals, while under Gundu Rao there were only two or three who did not. Nor were his ministers very adept at dealing with allegations of misconduct. One who was accused of illegally collecting four lakhs of rupees publicly took issue with the amount but not with the crime itself. And the evidence of corruption in the allocation of cement was so ill-concealed that even the Congress(I) majority on the State Assembly's Public Accounts Committee felt compelled to sign the report indicting the Chief Minister.

His exercises in decisiveness often yielded negative results. His famous decision to seal off the Vidhana Souda, the legislative and administrative headquarters, until the entire backlog of government files was dealt with, predictably led to a great many hasty, arbitrary and irrational decisions on matters that often affected people's lives very deeply. His insistence that land reform tribunals vastly accelerate their decision–making also led to rulings being made at an insane pace with no hope of proper enquiries into evidence or inspections of sites, so that a great many injustices were done.[11]

The callous ineptitude of the Gundu Rao government is perhaps best exemplified by its bungling and monumental insensitivity in dealing with farmers. Many examples of this could be offered, but two will suffice to illustrate the point. The first is Gundu Rao's typically rash, unconsidered promise of a revision of procurement policy on paddy which led paddy growers to expect a major change for the better whereby they would get something close to the market price for their grain instead of a lower rate fixed by government. Their euphoria soon gave way to exasperation when the government announced that 50 per cent of the grain grown must be sold at their lower fixed price. *Then* it announced that the 50 per cent was not just of *marketable* paddy as in the past, but of *all* paddy including that which the farmer kept for his own consumption. This left growers no better and in many cases decidedly worse off than before. It hit small and marginal paddy farmers especially hard and since they outnumber rich farmers, it caused widespread resentment against the government.

The second example is more startling. Gundu Rao did not understand how previous governments had dealt with cultivators. When he saw that many farmers were late in repaying loans from the state, he did not realise that every government since Independence had written off such arrears in order to subsidize agriculture and win the support of rural voters. To Gundu Rao, this seemed an example of administrative slackness which should be sorted out with a dose of the decisive action in which he took such great delight. Therefore in 1981, he abruptly instructed the bureaucracy to be very strict in insisting upon the recovery of loans.[12] When farmers did not respond promptly, prosecutions were instituted. Then, in an action which even the princely autocracy of old Mysore would have regarded as political lunacy, Gundu Rao sent revenue officials accompanied by armed detachments of police into rural areas to seize moveable property of defaulters. When the High Court ruled that such actions went beyond existing laws, the government took no notice and continued the seizures. The results were often "heartrending," as one hardened journalist put it, with small farmers having their few animals and tools carried off. Not surprisingly, this sudden and wholly unexpected rupture of the understanding, which had existed between cultivators and the government since the late 1940s (and, in spirit though not specifically in terms of loan arrears, since 1831), produced violence. It also led cultivators to express their much–intensified suspicion of the state by concealing a great deal of their produce, so that in one of the Gundu Rao years, the government managed to collect only 20 per cent of their target figure in essential food grains.[13] Several cultivators' protests were met with draconian police action. This was the main source of more than 80 police firings in which over 120 people were killed. Both of these statistics were so high as to be scarcely credible in a state which had seen little strident conflict since independence, and they generated widespread anger against the government.

It is worth noting at this point that Gundu Rao conforms to one of several divergent types of chief minister which have emerged under Indira Gandhi since 1972. The emphasis here should fall upon the word "divergent" since Mrs. Gandhi's overcentralization of power within the Congress had tended to cut her off from state–level units of the party and has caused understanding of and influence over those units to diminish. With the decline of the center's influence, the natural heterogeneity of the regions has, as we have noted, asserted itself and regions have therefore diverged from one another.[14] (Hence the very different stories that the contributors to this book have to tell.) One symptom of that divergence is the emergence of regional parties, but another is the increasingly varied nature of the state units and the chief ministers in Mrs. Gandhi's own party. Gundu Rao's centralization of power and his adoption of civil servant raj at the expense of the Congress organization is similar to the trend in Maharashtra under S.B. Chavan in the mid–1970s[15] and to the Congress(I) government in Punjab in the early 1980s before the imposition of President's Rule. But it should be stressed that Congress governments in other states were operating in *radically* different ways, and that Mrs. Gandhi was far less aware of these variations than she should have been.[16] Thus when Myron Weiner writes:

> India has many different party systems, reflecting the
> varied social cleavages, class structures, and historical
> circumstances of each of the states. All they share is a
> national Congress party. . . . [17]

we should remember that the way in which that national party has been run since 1971 has contributed to the diversity among various state–level systems.

The blurring of the lines between parties and social bases in Karnataka which resulted from the defections to the Congress(I) in 1980 might have served as an opportunity for the Gundu Rao government to cultivate support from a very broad range of interests. It would not have been easy to succeed at such a strategy since the political appetites and the level of awareness of such groups greatly exceed those of a few years ago, but it might have been possible to construct a workable electoral coalition in that way if political patronage had been carefully distributed. Nothing of the sort happened, however. Instead, by mishandling things, the government alienated a remarkably broad array of groups. Civil servants, freed of pressure from politicians to deliver goods and services to constituents, dragged their feet on a great many programs. Poorer people (and their more prosperous patrons who had often supervised the allocation of goods to them) became frustrated when the Janata housing scheme to provide houses to deprived families "stopped dead," in the words of one observer, as a result of bureaucratic inaction and when similar welfarist initiatives dried up. At the same time, developmental programs which mainly benefited more prosperous groups also wound down as numerous government departments significantly underspent their budgetary allotments. Public gestures by the Chief Minister also provoked anger from diverse groups. Perhaps the most important example was his signal to Lingayats that he intended to give their appeals for patronage much greater consideration than had Devaraj Urs. The signal itself alienated non–Lingayats and the Chief Minister's subsequent failure to deliver adequately on this promise alienated many Lingayats.

The Gundu Rao government's problems did not end there. The Karnataka Congress(I) was weakened by factional divisions,[18] and at times these led to intra–party violence or threats of violence.[19] The party also acquired a reputation, even among Congressmen, for thuggery and criminality. Thus when over 300 people died in Bangalore and Mysore after drinking adulterated liquor in 1981, seven Congress(I) MLAs asked Mrs. Gandhi to initiate a police investigation because they feared that the judicial enquiry set up by their own government would be a whitewash. (For their pains, they were disciplined by the party.) Senior Congress legislators complained when the government quashed a police investigation into allegations of abducting and molesting a young woman against Minister C.M. Ibrahim, whose continued presence in the state cabinet was highly embarrassing, and when no action was taken against Gundu Rao's confidant F.M. Khan after he assaulted a high police official in front of witnesses.[20] This sort of thing led former Congress Chief Minister Kadial Manjappa — a man of unblemished reputation whom many regard as the conscience of Karnataka politics — to send appeals to Mrs. Gandhi to clean out the "gangsters and corrupt adventurers," the "hooligans" and "politics of plunder" in the state.[21]

A great many other examples of the Gundu Rao government's mismanagement could be presented and many of those which have already been offered could be further elaborated and quantified. But by now it should be apparent that there were ample reasons for the people of Karnataka to reject this government at the State Assembly election in January 1983. That, essentially, is the explanation for the election results. It was far more a case of Congress(I) losing than of Janata winning. Indeed given greater space, I would argue (and have begun to do so elsewhere[22]) that this has become a common feature, something like the norm, in national and state elections since 1971 — the tendency for voters to reject poor or ineffective incumbent governments. Re-election has become increasingly difficult to win given the two main themes in India's recent political history: the *decay* of most parties' organizations and the *awakening* of the electorate to greater awareness.[23] But that is a discussion for another day. It is necessary now to turn to the other side of our story, the Janata government of Ramakrishna Hegde which swept to power in January 1983.

THE EMERGENCE OF A JANATA GOVERNMENT

It is important, first of all, to explain very briefly that the absence of Devaraj Urs from the political scene at the 1983 state assembly election greatly facilitated the emergence of the two internally heterogeneous electoral blocs — Congress(I) and the Janata-Kranti Ranga alliance — which confronted one another. This was true in two ways. First, many prominent figures in the Janata Party before the formation of the alliance with the Kranti Ranga felt considerable animosity towards Urs for his actions and some of his successes as Chief Minister. Urs had founded the Kranti Ranga as a regional party consisting mainly (though not entirely) of minority and backward class politicians who shared his reformist views. Had he lived, he would have remained its leader and this would have made an electoral alliance between the Kranti Ranga and Urs' foes in Janata — many of whom were dominant caste politicians from the old Congress(O) — virtually impossible. Second, after Urs' death, the coalition of disadvantaged groups that he had assembled could not find a leader capable of replacing him. None of the Muslim, Scheduled Caste or Brahmin politicians who were in the Urs camp could have replaced him because people from those communities would not have been acceptable to the coalition as a whole. Urs' own daughter, Mrs. Chandraprabha Urs, was too much of a newcomer and lacked her father's political weight.

Two other potential successors – S. Bangarappa and Veerappa Moily – were each disqualified on other grounds. Bangarappa had something of the personal drive and vision that was needed. But unlike Urs (who came from such a tiny *jati* that he could not be accused of diverting a major share of state resources to his fellow–castemen) he came from a sufficiently large and politically ambitious *jati*–cluster that many within the old Urs coalition regarded him as a prisoner of his community. And some of Bangarappa's actions in the run–up to the 1983 election – particularly his preference for candidates from his community – reinforced this distrust. Veerappa Moily on the other hand, came from a *jati* which was similar, at least in terms of its size, to that of Urs. But he appeared to many people to lack the vision and immense self–confidence which had enabled Urs to maintain the precarious balance of forces within his coalition, so that he was also unacceptable. It was therefore almost inevitable that the old coalition of disadvantaged groups would break up – indeed Urs himself would have been *very* hard–pressed to keep it together had he lived. All of this demonstrates how extremely difficult it is, at this point in the social and political evolution of Karnataka and India, to sustain the sort of alliance which Urs hammered together for a time during the 1970s.

The Congress(I) went into the 1983 state assembly election holding 184 seats against Janata's 12, the Kranti Ranga's 9 and the Bharatiya Janata Party's 4. The two Communist parties had an electoral understanding with the Janata–Kranti Ranga alliance. The B.J.P. did not have an electoral understanding with other parties but they indicated that they intended to support Janata–Kranti Ranga if the latter won the election.

The results of the election, which deserve further study, can be seen in Table 6:1.[24] They represent a serious defeat for the Congress(I), the first time that a Congress government had lost in Karnataka. Gundu Rao and several of his ministerial colleagues lost their seats, and Congress candidates were beaten in almost every constituency which had been visited during the election campaign by Mrs. Gandhi and her son Rajiv.

Table 6:1

Karnataka State Assembly Election Results, 1983

Party	Seats	% of Seats	Votes	% of Votes
Janata(KR)	94	42.0	4,292,469	33.22
Congress(I)	81	36.2	5,164,395	39.97
BJP	18	8.0	1,026,178	7.94
CPI	3	1.3	161,006	1.25
CPI(M)	3	1.3	115,320	0.89
MES	5	2.2	189,947	1.47
Independents and others	19	8.5	1,890,246	14.63
	223	99.5	12,919,561	99.37

Notes: Bharatiya Janata Party, CPI(M)=Communist Party of India(Marxist),
      CPI=Communist Party of India, MES=Maharashtra Ekikaran Samithi
Source: See note 24.

Soon after the result became known, the Bharatiya Janata Party and the Communists reiterated that they would support the Janata–Kranti Ranga alliance in the Assembly. This ensured that the alliance would be able to form a government. But amid their jubilation Janata–Kranti Ranga leaders found themselves off balance, since they had not expected to win the election and they were less than fully prepared to govern. The two most palpable indications of this were the state of their election manifesto, which offered voters an impossibly ambitious set of proposals which had been drawn up on the assumption that they had little hope of victory, and — most tellingly — the fact that they had no leader. The manifesto could wait, but a leader had to be found quickly so that the Governor would know whom to summon to form a government. At first glance, there were three main candidates for the post: H.D. Deve Gowda, a formidable and experienced Vokkaliga in the Janata group; S.R. Bommai, a former Leader of the Opposition and the most prominent Lingayat, also from Janata; and S. Bangarappa, the Kranti Ranga leader and a former lieutenant of Urs from the Idiga (or Bilava) community, a backward group akin to Kerala's Ezhavas containing a number of members who have gained great wealth in the liquor trade.

The Janata Party in New Delhi sent Biju Patnaik, former Chief Minister of Orissa, to Bangalore on 8 January with instructions to guide the new legislators quickly to a consensus. It was to be an exceedingly hectic day. Patnaik promptly arranged a formal merger of the Janata and Kranti Ranga to ensure that they would be perceived by the Governor as a single bloc and not as two smaller parties, but it was immediately obvious that none of the three contenders for the leadership enjoyed the support of the fifty or so MLAs needed to carry the day. A small deputation of Bangarappa's supporters called on Patnaik to argue that since their man had attracted backward class votes to the alliance, he should become the Chief Minister. These claims were far from convincing, however. Bangarappa *had* campaigned far more widely beyond his constituency than any other backward class leader, but his headstrong ways and his preference in candidate selection for dubious members of his own caste had alienated other backward class groups and led to several needless defeats for the alliance, even in areas of great Idiga strength. It also quickly became clear that only 10 of the 30 Kranti Ranga MLAs supported Bangarappa, since most of the others soon spoke of proposing the Urs-oriented Muslim, Abdul Nazir Sab, as a candidate.

Deve Gowda, the Vokkaliga, claimed to have 40 supporters — probably a slight overestimate. Bommai, with former Chief Minister S. Nijalingappa rallying Lingayat MLAs behind him, appeared to have a slightly smaller number since Vokkaligas outnumbered Lingayats in the newly-merged Janata legislators' group. Deve Gowda sought talks with Bangarappa to secure a deal that would put him over the top, but Bangarappa — recklessly overplaying his hand, as he did throughout this period — brusquely refused to negotiate. The 20 or so anti-Bangarappa MLAs from the Kranti Ranga made it plain that they wanted neither Deve Gowda nor Bommai, and the first priority of each of the latter two camps was to prevent the other from succeeding. The day ended in complete deadlock.

On the morning of 9 January, the Janata legislators were to hold their first full conference. Just before the meeting, Deve Gowda announced his support for Ramakrishna Hegde as Chief Minister. It rapidly became clear that Hegde was an acceptable second choice in the eyes of most legislators and at the meeting, Bommai formally proposed his name, to wide agreement. The following day Governor Govind Narain — after very scrupulously fulfilling his constitutional duties, a refreshing change after the chicanery in Haryana the previous year — called Hegde to form a government which had assurances of support, and hence a .

legislative majority.

Ramakrishna Hegde had not expected to be chosen to lead the new government; indeed, he had not even been a candidate at the assembly election. He had spent the last few years as a General Secretary of the Janata Party in New Delhi, and he intended to stand from a Karnataka constituency for the Lok Sabha at the next general election. He was 55 years old and had served with distinction as the state's Information Minister and Finance Minister between 1962 and 1972. But his long absence from Karnataka and the fact that he was from the tiny Haviya Brahmin *jati* from the marginal and somewhat eccentric coastal district of Uttara Kannada (North Kanara) made him at first glance an unlikely choice. On the credit side, he had earned a reputation during his years as a minister as an exceedingly adroit political manager – an image which gained credence from his thorough and intelligent planning of Janata's campaign in Karnataka before the 1983 election. It was anticipated that, as a Brahmin, he would have no natural independent social base and would therefore need to be a balancer of interests. This expectation was reinforced by his exceedingly cosmopolitan background. He came from a staunchly nationalist family, having been jailed twice in his student days during the struggle for Independence, and having spent time studying law at Banaras Hindu University and Lucknow University where he learned Hindi.[25] His first two children had married outside their caste – one to a Sindhi and the other to a Marwari – and the third was planning to do likewise, to an Iyer Brahmin. His interest in work in New Delhi notwithstanding, he was prepared to serve if summoned and he promptly set about constructing a government capable of surviving, despite its precarious majority and the Janata Party's very heterogeneous composition and socio-economic base.

Hegde was concerned about a possible attempt by Lingayats and Vokkaligas both to dominate his cabinet and to channel the lion's share of resources to their fellow castemen at the grass roots. Rivalry between Lingayats and Vokkaligas may have prevented agreement on a candidate for Chief Minister, but they had a common interest in both of these other matters. Despite his concern, however, Hegde had no option but to include Deve Gowda and Bommai in his cabinet and to give them very prominent posts. Deve Gowda requested and got Public Works, a portfolio with major patronage powers in both urban and rural areas, including major outlays in road–building and irrigation. Bommai received the Ministery of Commerce and Industries which gives him control over huge resources, although few that can be deployed among mainly rural

Lingayats. (Bommai comes from the powerful, cultivating Sadar Lingayat sub-group of northern Karnataka.) Having made sizeable concessions to them on these fronts, Hegde chose to assert himself in response to their appeals for numerous ministerial posts for Vokkaligas and Lingayats. He argued for the need to give the Kranti Ranga (which had numerous Lingayat and Vokkaliga legislators, but not in prominent roles) substantial representation in the cabinet as a means of minimizing the number of portfolios which went to those two communities. (As a result, the Kranti Ranga is somewhat overrepresented.) He had only limited room in which to maneuver in assigning portfolios to other Vokkaligas. But one who received a prized position, Agriculture Minister B.L. Gowda, is generally regarded as less than effective, which may explain the appointment. Hegde also managed to find two non-chauvinistic Lingayats for prominent ministries, so that Bommai could not develop a Lingayat bloc in cabinet. The first of these was M.P. Prakash, Minister of Transport, who comes from the priestly and heavily urbanized Jangama Lingayat *jati* which does not share all of the concerns of the three large cultivating sub-divisions.[26] The second and more important was Minister of Power and Excise J.H. Patil, an exceedingly urbane and secularized man with a reputation for integrity who comes out of the Lohia-ite socialist tradition and who does not relish being described as a Lingayat. He operates as an impediment to efforts to restore dominant caste preeminence in state-level politics.

Hegde then saw to it that a number of Urs-ite or Lohia-ite or minority or backward class ministers (these categories overlap quite considerably) were chosen to act as counterweights to the Vokkaligas and Lingayats. Prominent among these are Abdul Nazir Sab, a genuinely reformist Muslim at Rural Development and Panchayati Raj; Mrs. Chandraprabha Urs (daughter of Devaraj Urs) at Social Welfare and Sericulture; B. Rachiah, the experienced Scheduled Caste Education Minister; another Muslim, Azeez Sait, at Labour and Wakfs; and the articulate Kumbara A. Lakshmisagar, at Law, Parliamentary Affairs, Housing and Public Grievances. The Chief Minister was assisted in gaining the backing of backward class and Urs-ite legislators by the refusal of S. Bangarappa — a potential rival for their loyalties — to enter the cabinet until it was far too late, so that he was left out and became politically isolated. Hegde's initial team of 24 ministers consisted of one Brahmin (the Chief Minister himself), five Lingayats, four Vokkaligas, four members of the Scheduled Castes, two Muslims and one of each of the following groups (most of which are included among the "backward classes"): Arasu, Kumbara, Naidu, Jain and Maratha.[27] Of the 16 ministers holding cabinet rank, 8 were from the old Kranti Ranga. Of the full list of 24, 10 had been Kranti Ranga members.[28] This overrepresentation was, we have noted, the result of Hegde's efforts first to retain support of old Kranti Ranga members despite the continuing (and self-destructive) refusal of their former leader Bangarappa to enter the government, and second to enlist backward class leaders from the Kranti Ranga into the cabinet as a counterweight to Lingayat and Vokkaliga ministers.

To that latter end, Hegde also undertook two initiatives which surprised and annoyed some of his more secularized, cosmopolitan friends and associates. First, he sought to develop a close relationship with H.D. Deve Gowda, the leading Vokkaliga in the cabinet and the most forceful and effective leader among the two traditionally dominant groups. His purpose in doing so was in part to show a little more sympathy to Vokkaligas than to Lingayats, to prevent the two groups from making common cause out of shared exasperation. This was a tactic which Devaraj Urs had used to good effect by, for example, classifying Vokkaligas but not Lingayats among the "backward classes," which made them eligible for concessions from the government. Indeed, Hegde's very first public statement after being selected as Chief Minister stressed that preferment for backward groups was to be sustained, along the lines established by Devaraj Urs. This made sense for Hegde in several ways. Vokkaligas are in reality less advanced than Lingayats, although they are far better off than most other groups in Karnataka. Hegde also recognized that Janata had done perceptibly better in Vokkaliga areas than in Lingayat country. This needs to be discussed in much greater detail than is possible here, but one very crude illustration of it is the fact that Janata won 71 of its 94 seats in 1983 in the districts of former princely Mysore (roughly the southern half of Karnataka) where nearly all Vokkaligas reside and where Lingayats take second place to Vokkaligas in supra-local politics. Hegde also knew that Lingayats — a sect that rejects the sacral authority of Brahmins and has its own priests or *swamijis* — tend to be more anti-Brahmin (and therefore, possibly, more anti-Hegde) than Vokkaligas who accept the ritual position of Brahmins. Finally and probably more importantly, Hegde found Deve Gowda amenable to a close relationship — which, for the Chief Minister, was more a means of containing Vokkaliga power than of enhancing it. Deve Gowda played a very prominent role in organizing the March 1983 by-election in the Vokkaliga heartland which provided Hegde with his seat in the State Assembly.

Hegde's second initiative was to seek issues which he could make his own in order both to acquire a modest independent power base and to contain other potentially threatening political forces. The most important of these was his advocacy of "Karnataka for the Kannadigas."[29] This certainly raised eyebrows among Hegde's friends and even, it is said, his family — coming as it did from south India's first Hindi-speaking Chief Minister. But it made good sense in several ways. It enabled Hegde to gather to himself some of the pro-Kannada excitement which had lately been mounting in the state. Through most of the post-Independence period, Karnataka had been remarkably free of controversy over language issues,[30] but one of Gundu Rao's more stupendous blunders — his maladroit response to the Gokak Report which need not have stirred the passions of Urdu and Kannada speakers — had sparked a modest agitation for greater concessions to the language of the majority and to those who spoke it. By taking it up, Hegde sought to prevent it both from being taken to extremes and from falling into the hands of the opposition. He also sought to reassure a Kannada film idol, Rajkumar, who felt strongly on the issue and who was considering (somewhat diffidently) the possibility of entering politics, that the government would act constructively on this matter. This has so far kept Rajkumar from generating a political movement that first might destabilize the entire party system before Janata had a chance to consolidate its position with important interest groups, and second — since Rajkumar is from the same caste as Bangarappa — might needlessly revive the fortunes of that self-destructively maladroit operator who at this writing has been rendered relatively harmless. Finally, by adopting the cause of Kannada, Hegde has strengthened his image as a regional leader when he joins with other non-Congress Chief Ministers in their effort to develop an opposition front. And by stepping into that latter role, he gains further strength by appearing as the state's main link-man with the wider political world and as a champion of Karnataka's interests.

Since taking office, Hegde has faced attempts by Vokkaligas and Lingayats to regain much of the power which they enjoyed in Karnataka politics before 1972. Some of these have originated within his cabinet, but the main thrust has consisted of attempts behind the scenes by Vokkaliga and Lingayat legislators to get officials from these two groups inserted into numerous administrative posts in their constituencies, at the taluk and development block level. Sources very close to the Chief Minister indicated that requests or, more often, demands from Lingayat and Vokkaliga MLAs for such transfers of officials had become quite commonplace as early as April 1983. And, given the precarious margin by which Janata controls the assembly, the Chief Minister and his colleagues have been compelled to acquiesce in a large number of such cases, despite public assurances to the contrary. This has caused considerable distress among some of Hegde's close associates who see these incidents as affronts to his dignity and as threats to their hope for a government that is free of dominant caste control.

There are, however, at least three reasons for thinking that the result of all of this will not be a return to Lingayat/Vokkaliga dominance over the machinery of state. First, there are simply not enough Vokkaliga and Lingayat officials available at the appropriate levels of the Karnataka Administrative Service (which is the cadre from which such people would, in the main, need to come) to achieve a systematic blanketing of taluk-level posts, even if this were the aim of the Chief Minister, which it is not. Second, Hegde and his allies have been able, in the light of this manpower shortage, to placate Vokkaliga and Lingayat MLAs by offering to appoint their clients to posts in the vast array of government boards and committees which were created for patronage purposes during the Devaraj Urs years. These positions soothe the egos of appointees and often prove profitable, but they carry very little real power.

Finally, even if there were enough officials from the traditionally dominant groups on hand, and even if every Lingayat and Vokkaliga MLA in the Janata Party succeeded in packing posts in his constituency with them, a third factor would prevent this from leading to a reassertion of Lingayat/Vokkaliga control. This is because Janata holds only a minority of seats in the assembly and nearly half of its MLAs are not members of the traditionally dominant groups. Hence, the Lingayat and Vokkaliga legislators in the Janata delegation represent less than one-quarter of the constituencies in the state (and a significant minority of them are not seeking appointments for fellow castemen in their taluks). It is of course true that in previous assemblies during the Lingayat/Vokkaliga heyday, the arithmetic was not always vastly different from that of today. But the key differences in those days were that the leadership of the ruling party was keen to see bureaucrats from the dominant groups present in strength at the taluk level, and — in the time before Urs' recruitment of backward class personnel into the administration — there was no shortage of Vokkaligas and Lingayats to fill those positions. Neither of these things is true today.

Nor are we likely to see a return to a semblance of the old situation, even if one of the leading Vokkaligas or Lingayats in the present

Karnataka cabinet — Deve Gowda is seen as the most formidable — should take over from Hegde. Two rather unlikely things would need to happen before a restoration of the old order could occur. First, the rules governing recruitment to the state public service would need to be revised, to reverse the changes which Urs made. That would cause an almighty controversy which most politicians — even Lingayat and Vokkaliga chauvinists — believe would alienate voters from the backward classes, minorities and Scheduled Castes. Political scientists may disagree about whether voters from such groups are sufficiently aware and independent of dominant caste control to reject a party which proposes to undo those Urs reforms (although this writer believes that an imperfect but quite substantial awakening *has* occurred among them). But what is clear is that most Karnataka politicians *believe* that a major change in the recruitment rules would incur a serious backlash from non–Lingayat/Vokkaliga voters who constitute nearly 70 percent of the population. These politicians are unlikely to take this risk. And even if it were taken, several years would need to pass before enough new recruits had passed into the administration to permit a reassertion of Lingayat/Vokkaliga control.

The other impediment to such a rules change is the widespread belief among politicians from the traditionally dominant groups that if they wish to get to the top in Karnataka politics, they now need to build up networks of supporters, in the Assembly and in the state at large, from all or most important social groups. A Lingayat or Vokkaliga leader without numerous Kuruba, Muslim, Scheduled Caste, etc., MLAs standing at his shoulder seems a highly implausible candidate for ministerial rank. With this in mind, Vokkaliga and Lingayat politicians are unlikely to press too forcefully for a major overhaul of the rules.

Let us now (all too briefly) examine the Hegde government's policies and initiatives in its early months in power, in order both to illustrate some of the implications of the very heterogeneous composition of the ruling party and to bring the discusssion round to the question of whether there has been a return to "normality" in the state's politics. We have already seen that the cabinet contains powerful figures from the locally–dominant landed groups and several ministers who wish to aid less prosperous people, either because they come from less prosperous groups or because they are philosophically inclined that way.

Government policies have been similarly mixed. In its first six months in power, it allocated Rs. 360 million to programs for farmers, most of which aided landowning interests. These include concessions exempting cultivators from payment of new taxes on newly irrigated land for five years, and subsidies on pesticides, rodent and weed control, insecticides and certain seeds. Other government funds will cover the delivery of chemical fertilizers to cultivators and will assist in the development of agro–based industries. Purchase taxes on sugarcane were waived for several months of 1983 and the government agreed to make advance payments for cane.[31] Most of these initiatives were intended in part to defuse the farmers' agitation which arose during the Gundu Rao years. In this they have partially failed, as the conflicts of February 1984 indicate.[32] But it should be emphasised that the farmers' "movement" in Karnataka is a very complex, internally heterogeneous thing which will need to be more fully discussed on a separate occasion. And there are indications that the government's measures outlined above have taken several groups who were once active in the protests out of the campaign. The government also spent Rs. 510 million in its first six months on drought relief, some of which aided landowners, and it has reverted to the lenient policy on recovering loans to agriculture which Gundu Rao so unwisely abandoned.[33] The efforts of ministers like H.D. Deve Gowda to channel resources to landed groups have also yielded clear gains.

Nonetheless, other ministers have sought to aid less prosperous groups. Hegde's pledge, in his first comment upon assuming office, to assist "the oppressed classes"[34] has been backed up with action on many of the reformist initiatives that have come down from the Urs years, and new schemes have been undertaken. A program to aid thirty thousand Scheduled Caste families per year has been introduced, as have others to provide grants to Scheduled Caste students, to aid educated unemployed from the Scheduled Castes and to expedite entry of bright Scheduled Caste students into government service. A major commitment has been made to an *Antyodaya* program to assist the five poorest families in every village. Hegde's government is also accelerating schemes to assist minorities, to build houses for the poor and to sink bore wells in villages that are short of water, with priority to Scheduled Caste colonies. These and several other efforts are reinforced by sympathetic ministers who direct patronage and resources to poorer people, and the presence in the bureaucracy of large numbers of officials from deprived backgrounds — mainly recruited since 1972 — facilitates this to at least a modest extent. It is of course true that the impediments to aiding the poor are still quite substantial, but these initiatives are by no means wholly nullified by resistance from prosperous interests. It should therefore be clear that the Hegde regime is seeking to provide resources to nearly all major interest groups in the state, as we would expect given the social composition of the government.

Finally, to turn for a moment to an issue that is only loosely connected to the problem of the government's socio-economic base, efforts have been made to clean up both the image and the operations of the regime after more than a decade in which corruption grew enormously under Devaraj Urs and, especially, Gundu Rao. The Hegde government certainly contains some ministers who are busy enriching themselves and their clients. But men such as the Chief Minister, the Rural Development Minister Abdul Nazir Sab and J.H. Patil (who, significantly, holds the Excise portfolio which has immense potential for profiteering) — to name only three — are rightly regarded as figures of probity. The government has also created a *Lok Ayukta* (ombudsman) and, for the first time in an Indian state, a separate bureaucratic structure to enquire into public grievances. These initiatives have been matched by attempts to make government seem more democratic. Municipal and corporation elections were held for the first time in over a decade, and the Minister of Rural Development presented a scheme for the creation of new elected bodies close to the local level which are to have substantial resources.[35]

The new situation in Karnataka, in which neither the pre-1972 links between the ruling party and the dominant landed groups nor the links of the Urs years between the ruling party and less prosperous groups are predominant, may be a recipe for political instability.[36] No matter which party holds power, governments that seek to please almost every important interest group are almost certain to spread their resources too thinly. Their policies are likely to seem inconsistent, as indeed they will be. Their priorities will seem muddled. Some might argue that this represents a return to the type of politics practised by Congress in the early years after Independence — but they would be overlooking a fundamental change since the 1950s. In those days, the votes of substantial numbers of disadvantaged villagers could be obtained by winning the support of dominant landed elements who were able to instruct or influence the voting behavior of their poorer neighbors. They are no longer able to do this. Most poorer people now decide for themselves how to vote and they increasingly demand concrete assistance rather than empty rhetoric. So governments that seek votes from all sections of society must commit tangible resources to all sections – hence the danger of spreading resources too thinly.

This is likely to generate political instability because today's maturing electorate is far more inclined to lose patience with governments.

It may therefore become very difficult to win re–election. The increased awareness, appetites and assertiveness of all sections of the electorate make it virtually impossible to keep every important social group happy.[37] Governments which hope to get re–elected must pare down their socio–economic bases to a realistic size, but the present motley composition of both major parties in Karnataka makes it very difficult to do this. Gundu Rao had a large enough majority in the Assembly to attempt it. He could have survived a sizeable defection by legislators who felt that their constituents were being squeezed out, but he lacked the political imagination to understand the implications of the new situation. Hegde certainly understands it, but his precarious majority which Congress(I) has repeatedly sought (largely unsuccessfully) to erode through rather ham–fisted bribery[38] prevents him from taking the risks which a paring down would entail. Given the political awakening that has occurred in India in recent years, it would probably be impossible to maintain public favor with a policy of patronage for all, even if Karnataka's Janata or Congress(I) had efficient organizations for spoils distribution of the kind which existed under the Congress led by Nijalingappa and company in the state before 1972. But neither major party today has anything like that sort of organization.

It is worth noting, although it is probably obvious to most readers already, that the blurring of the lines between parties and support bases was mainly the result of political and not socio–economic changes. So in this case, politics — which I take to be a sphere enjoying a degree of autonomy from socio–economic forces — enjoyed primacy as an agent for change. The political change which caused the lines to be blurred did not occur solely *within* Karnataka but in the interplay of state and national politics. The most important element in this interplay was the attempt by Mrs. Gandhi (and in early 1980, Sanjay Gandhi) to impose personal dominance both upon center–state relations and upon the politics of Karnataka. Throughout India's history, the logic of politics and the needs of politicians at the national level were almost always quite different from the same things at the regional level. But until Mrs. Gandhi arrived at the apex of the national political system, leaders at that level (including most British rulers) understood that an over–energetic imposition of national needs upon regional arenas would prove destructive to the regions and, ultimately, to the strength of national leaders as well. They therefore sought to arrange bargains and accommodations with regional leaders and with conditions in the regions. Mrs. Gandhi and Sanjay abandoned this approach and, in Karnataka, imposed a Chief Minister who was both intellectually unequal and temperamentally unsuited to his task. He was also unwelcome in the eyes even of the Congress(I) rank and file. The remarkable and quite avoidable defeat of Congress at the 1983 state election was the logical result.

CONCLUSION

Let us now look more closely at the question of whether the general election of 1980 or events since then constituted a return to "normality" in the politics of Karnataka. There is no simple answer to this. We need first to determine what "normality" is in the state's politics and that is far from clear. If "normality" means that a party calling itself the Congress and owing allegiance to a member of the Nehru family is in power, then the general election of 1980 triggered a return to "normality." But that is a very superficial notion of "normality" and in any case, Gundu Rao's gross mismanagement led to a revival of "abnormality" when he and Congress(I) were defeated at the state election of 1983. If "normality" means that the landed groups (Lingayats and Vokkaligas) who dominate village life also dominate state politics, then the departure from "normality" occurred in and after 1972 under Devaraj Urs. But again this notion of "normality" is unsatisfactory because in my view (and it is a view shared by almost all of Karnataka's political leaders including those who come from locally dominant groups), Devaraj Urs helped disadvantaged groups to achieve sufficient self-awareness and political experience to remain major, though not necessarily dominant, forces in state politics. He made it exceedingly difficult and probably impossible to restore Lingayat-Vokkaliga political dominance at the state level. In other words, he altered the nature of political "normality."

"Normality" might also imply the existence of a large network of solid, reliable links between political parties — particularly the ruling party — and various social groups. This is a somewhat separate issue from that identified in the title of this paper. Even if a party lacks a limited, logically-composed, manageable socio-economic base — even if it seeks, rather confusedly, to do something for virtually every important social group (as is the case with both the ruling party and the opposition today) — it is still possible that such a party will have good connections with the various sections of society. If we take "normality" to mean this — and until 1980, the ruling Congress in Karnataka always had such links — then the election of Mrs. Gandhi at the national level triggered a marked departure from "normality" in the state. Gundu Rao's government between 1980 and 1983 proved so unresponsive to social groups and indulged in so many wanton and very public acts of normlessness, that leaders of social groups in Karnataka began to turn away from politics. Politicians no longer seemed able or willing to deliver assistance and this inspired public cynicism about politics. Some Congress politicians behaved so outrageously, without being reprimanded, that they seemed unclean even to leaders of social groups whose experience of horse-trading over the years had made them anything but squeamish. Social groups therefore tended to give up hope of any rational, rewarding or even decent relationships with politicians. In other words, Gundu Rao's government — like Congress(I) governments in several other states — caused an erosion of the integration between society and politics, a *divergence* of society and politics.[39] The Hegde government has worked hard, with some success, to reverse this process, but great damage has been done.

Gundu Rao's accession to the Chief Ministership in 1980 brought a departure from "normality" in the way in which bureaucrats and legislators interact. Civil servant raj is hardly normal. But he went to such ill-considered extremes that he ensured his government's defeat and a return to "normality" in bureaucratic-legislator relations in 1983.

Mrs. Gandhi's victory in the Indian general election of 1980 led in another sense to a break with "normality" in that it sparked mass defections that blurred the lines between parties and their social bases. It thereby rendered state politics more irrational and created difficulties for virtually all major parties, in and out of power. A return to "normality" and greater rationality on that front, which requires a realignment of forces, may prove very difficult to achieve.

Finally, it is appropriate to register a word of scepticism (as far as south India is concerned) about one further version of "normality" to which Myron Weiner alluded in his article on the 1980 election. Among the similarities which he sees between the Congress victories of 1971 and 1980 is the following:

> In both instances the electoral coalition was similar. Congress won the support of the very rich and the very poor, from Brahmins to ex-untouchables, from well-to-do businessmen and government bureaucrats to tribal agricultural laborers and Muslim weavers.[40]

The blurring of the connections between parties and social bases in

Karnataka after the first week of 1980 obviously renders this sort of "normality" impossible to achieve in the short term — for example at the State Assembly election of 1983 — but that is not the point that needs emphasis here. What should be stressed is my suspicion that Weiner's generalization is less accurate for south India than for other parts of the country. There is no doubting its explanatory power in Uttar Pradesh, as Paul Brass has ably demonstrated[41](although its relevance to neighboring Rajasthan, where the Janata Party government under Shekhawat which sought to aid disadvantaged groups and which may have altered the pattern somewhat, needs careful investigation). But is it accurate for Kerala where both Congress and the CPI(M) have been unable to break down the strength of communal and caste parties, and where the votes of many disadvantaged people go to the CPI(M) rather than to Congress?

It is also difficult elsewhere in the south to find many areas where a tripartite struggle of the kind described by Brass could develop. He sees Congress drawing support from the "former landlords and rich peasants, on the one hand, and the rural poor, on the other," with opposition parties basing their strength on "the middle · peasantry" in between. These divisions tend to be reinforced by caste factors, since Congress' two strata consist on the one hand mainly of twice-born groups — Brahmins, Rajputs and Bhumihars — and on the other of the Scheduled Castes and very depressed caste Hindus. The opposition meanwhile draws support mainly from Sudra groups.[42] Such conflict tends not to develop in most parts of Andhra Pradesh, Tamil Nadu and Karnataka, partly because large estates and the large blocs of rich peasants (or once-rich peasants) were and are far less common than in U.P., and partly because of the very different composition of society. Brahmins form only a tiny proportion of the population, there are no indigenous Kshatriyas and Vaisyas, and Sudras form a solid majority of the population. These different conditions produce in the south a different political logic (or logics) and a socio-political "normality" that is also distinctive. It should be stressed that to say that Brass' model for U.P. is inappropriate for the south does not wholly invalidate Weiner's thesis in the southern states. He is speaking in more general terms than is Brass (and Brass makes no comment on the south). But it raises very real problems for the Weiner argument.

NOTES

1. James Manor, "Where Congress Survived: Five States in the Indian General Election of 1977," *Asian Survey* (August 1978); and "Party

Decay and Political Crisis in India," *The Washington Quarterly* (Summer 1981).

2. Paul R. Brass, "Division in the Congress and the Rise of Agrarian Interests and Issues in Uttar Pradesh Politics 1952 to 1977," chapter 2 of this volume; and his "Congress, the Lok Dal and the Middle–Peasant Castes," *Pacific Affairs* (Spring 1981).

3. Manor, "Where the Gandhi Writ Doesn't Run," *The Economist* (15 May, 1982), and "Where Congress Survived."

4. Manor, *Political Change in an Indian State: Mysore, 1917–1955* (Columbia: South Asian Books, 1977), chapter 2.

5. Manor, "Structural Changes in Karnataka Politics," *Economic and Political Weekly* (29 October, 1977), pp. 1865–68, and Manor, "Pragmatic Progressives in Regional Politics: The Case of Devaraj Urs," *Economic and Political Weekly* (Annual number, 1980), pp. 201–13.

6. Interviews with Devaraj Urs and others, January 1980.

7. Interviews with a member of Rao's cabinet and journalists in Bangalore, March 1983.

8. These comments, like many more throughout this paper, are based on a large number of interviews with politicians, civil servants, journalists, academics, voluntary association leaders and others on three visits to Karnataka in January 1980, March and April 1982 and August 1983.

9. See the discussion later in this essay of the muddle on procurement prices for paddy.

10. See for example, *Indian Express* (Bangalore), 20 September, 1981 and *The Hindu* (Madras), 21 October, 1981. Each cabinet visit to a district headquarters cost Rs. 200,000, which the Chief Minister thought well worthwhile. *The Hindu* (Madras), 26 September, 1981.

11. These comments are based on interviews with land tribunal members, civil servants and legislators in Karnataka in March–April 1982 and August 1983, and upon statistics provided by officials from the Revenue Department who dealt with land reform.

12. I am grateful to E. Raghavan for alerting me to these two examples.

13. This discussion is based on conversations with bureaucrats, journalists and farmers' and cooperatives' leaders in Karnataka, March–April 1982 and August 1983.

14. Manor, "Party Decay and Political Crisis in India."

15. Manor, "Where Congress Survived."

16. Manor, "Where the Gandhi Writ Doesn't Run" and "Where Congress Survived."

17. Myron Weiner, "Congress Restored: Continuities and

Discontinuities in Indian Politics," *Asian Survey* (April 1982), p. 347.

18. See for example, *Indian Express* (Bangalore), 12 July, 1981 and *The Hindu* (Madras), 12 October, 1981.

19. See for example, *Indian Express* 19 June, 1981, 2 August, 1982, and 29 September, 1982.

20. *Indian Express*, 11, 19, 22, and 23 July, 1981.

21. See for example, *Indian Express* 24 and 28 September, 1982.

22. Manor, "The Electoral Process amid Awakening and Decay: Reflections on the Indian General Election of 1980," in *Transfer and Transformation: Political Institutions in the New Commonweath*, eds., P. Lyon and J. Manor (Leicester: Leicester University Press, 1983).

23. *Ibid.*, and Manor, "Party Decay and Political Crisis in India."

24. The numbers and percentages of votes given in Table 6:1 are open to minor disputes and must be treated as provisional until the Election Commission Report on the election is issued. The turnout was 64.28 percent. This compares with turnouts of 71.96 percent at the 1978 State Assembly election and 57.85 percent at the 1980 parliamentary election. The State Assembly has 224 seats, but in one constituency, polling was countermanded. It should be stressed that Congress(I) received a larger share of the vote than Janata–Kranti Ranga because it contested 222 seats while the latter contested only 191. I am grateful to E. Raghavan and his colleagues at the Bangalore office of the *Indian Express* for these and other statistics, and to K.H. Cheluva Raju and the members of his election analysis team at Bangalore University. See also, K.H. Cheluva Raju et. al., *Karnataka Assembly Elections, January 1983*, Bangalore University, 1983; Karnataka State, *Election Statistics of General Elections to Legislative Assembly, 1978* (Bangalore, n.d.), p. 1; and G.G. Mirchandani, *The People's Verdict* (New Delhi, 1980), appendix xviii.

25. *Indian Express*, 11 January, 1983.

26. The Lingayats and Vokkaligas are disaggregated in James Manor, *Political Change in an Indian State*, chapter 2.

27. *Indian Express*, 17 February,1983 and conversations with political observers in Karnataka, August 1983.

28. Conversations with E. Raghavan and K. Satyanarayana, Bangalore, 24 August,1983.

29. This involved support for the teaching of Kannada in schools, preferment for Kannada speakers in public employment, an extension of the use of Kannada (as opposed to English) in administration, and symbolic actions such as Hegde's decision to head a commission to restore the ancient ruins at Hampi, one of the glories of ancient Karnataka. *Indian Express*, 17 April, 1983.

30. Manor, "Language, Religion and Political Identity in Karnataka," in *Political Identity in South Asia*, eds., D.D. Taylor and M.E. Yapp (London: Curzon Press, 1977).

31. These comments are based on discussions with several government ministers, bureaucrats and political commentators, Bangalore, August 1983. See also Karnataka Information Department, *The Six Significant Months* (Bangalore, 1983), pp. 23–25.

32. For example, *India Today*, 29 February, 1984, pp. 28–9.

33. *The Six Significant Months*, pp. 25–7.

34. *Indian Express*, 11 January 1983.

35. Interview with the Minister, Abdul Nazir Sab, Bangalore, 9 August, 1983.

36. This is certainly the view of Congress(I) leader K.H. Srinivas; interview, Mysore, 14 August, 1983.

37. Manor, "Party Decay and Political Crisis in India."

38. See for example, *Indian Express*, 11 December, 1983 and 1 January, 1984; and *India Today*, 15 December, 1983.

39. For a fuller treatment of this see my essay in *New Society* (12 August, 1982), which draws heavily upon evidence from Karnataka.

40. Weiner, "Congress Restored," p. 340.

41. Brass, "Division in the Congress," and "Congress, the Lok Dal and the Middle–Peasant Castes."

42. Brass, "Division in the Congress," p. 40.

7
One-Party Dominance in Maharashtra: Resilience and Change

Jayant Lele

In 1980, Mrs. Gandhi's Congress(I) came back to power at the Center.[1] In the legislative elections which followed it also won a large majority in Maharashtra. However, between January 1980, and the present, the state has had four Chief Ministers. The first one, Sharad Pawar, left when the legislature was dissolved. The other two, A.R. Antulay and Babasaheb Bhosle, were dismissed by Mrs. Gandhi under a barrage of publicity. Rumors float almost everyday that the departure of the fourth one, Vasant Dada Patil, is imminent. He himself has publicly threatened to resign at least twice.[2] Does this mean that the era of stable Congress governments under seemingly strong Chief Ministers is over? Has the Congress party lost its status of one–party dominance? In this paper I propose to examine the changes in party politics in Maharashtra in terms of the following questions:

1. What are some of the significant trends in the political economy of the 1980s,
2. What is the direction of the development of the party system and of other relevant political structures,
3. What major shifts have occurred in the electoral process as compared to the patterns that had existed before 1970, and
4. In what way are the relations between the state and the Center changing.

My intention is first to review the major developments that have occurred in the last few years and then to examine their long term implications for Maharashtra's polity. Since this is being written during the early part of

169

the decade a certain amount of reasoned speculation seems inevitable.

THE POLITICAL ECONOMY

In terms of many of the standard, aggregate economic indicators Maharashtra is a relatively more developed state than most. Its per capita income is substantially higher than the national average (40 percent over that of India in 1976–77). Its contribution to the national income is also considerably higher than its proportion of the population. It is more urbanized than the rest of the country and it has established a secular trend for increases in per capita income over the last two decades. Much of the rapid growth is to be attributed to the industrial sector, manufacturing in particular, in which substantial diversification has gone hand in hand with increasing volume and rising productivity of investment. A great deal of manufacturing is occurring in enterprises using modern technology and involving complex collaborative arrangments with foreign transnational corporations. This type of growth has left most of the older industrial sector, consisting primarily of textiles, in a state of obsolescence and stagnation. The modern, large scale manufacturing sectoi is complemented by a growing small industries sector which produces a wide variety of ancillaries in small units. It is often able to bypass much of the labor legislation applicable to larger units and thrives by exploiting unorganized and low paid semi–skilled labor.

This picture, as a description of a progressive state, is highly deceptive. Much of the development has occurred in the city of Bombay and in the so–called "Poona–Bombay corridor" involving the districts of Thane and Pune. In spite of the claims and desires expressed in favor of wide regional dispersion of industrial growth and the creation of many fully serviced industrial estates in and around district towns, industrial dispersion has been abysmally slow. Bombay remains the most attractive center for industrial investment in all of India and continues to grow despite severe limits of space and massive pressure on its meager services. It now houses more than twelve percent of the state's population. It also continues to attract large numbers of impoverished rural landless workers who come in the hope of finding some form of employment in the "prosperous" megalopolis. A recent estimate puts the number of incoming people at 650 per day.[3] In 1983, Bombay had 4.7 million unauthorized squatters, a quarter million of whom were regular pavement dwellers.[4] According to the city's municipal corporation, even their minimal demands on the declining services constitute a potential disaster for the health and safety of all citizens. In 1981, people in the working class area of central Bombay protested following a three day failure of water supply. One person was killed in the police firing.[5]

As long as Bombay continues to remain the center of industrial growth it will have to contend with the problem of growing congestion that has defied all proposed solutions. Attempts to provide services and protection to slum dwellers, to evict pavement dwellers, to control rents and prices, to help renovate dilapidated tenements and to create new and inexpensive housing have all been haphazard. Referring only to the problem of slum landlords, a political worker said that it had "become as complex as the agrarian question with a many–tiered structure comprising the landlord, main lessor, sub–lessor, end–lessors and finally the structure owner and then the tenant."[6] The problem of pressures from conflicting interests for favorable state policy is by no means restricted to the slums. The only policy option over which there seems to be a consensus among all interested parties is the continued expansion of the city's economic base. Successive governments have therefore favored proposals for enlarging the size of the city by aquiring large tracts of agricultural land. While the issue of adequate compensation for acquired lands was recently exploited by the various political parties none of them along with the ruling party has been willing to confront the basic question of the long term disastrous consequences for the state of the continued anarchic growth of Bombay's industrialization. Slum dwellers are the prime source of cheap labor for the growing industrial and service sectors of the economy. Organized slum dwellers may also constitute ready vote banks for the various political parties. They as well as the more privileged and better established white collar workers have continued to be the objects of courtship by politicians. Internal divisions among the working classes (for example, slum dwellers on private lands vs. pavement dwellers and squatters, organized industrial workers vs. workers in the informal sector), give political parties an opportunity to divide them on issues and thus nullify their potential impact on state policy.

All of Bombay's problems are, therefore, addressed politically in factional and sectoral terms in response to pressures from the various elements in the competitive arena of democratic politics. Piecemeal solutions, based on reactive strategies, are being found to specific problems as they are brought in focus. Wherever it is convenient, basic issues are deflected and interpreted in ethnic terms. In extreme situations, when popular anger erupts spontaneously, the state has been unleashing its coercive power rather effectively when it is used against the indigent population. In sum, in spite of apparent crises, Bombay is unlikely to produce a serious challenge to the direction set for Maharashtra's political economy by those in control of politics.

The attraction of Bombay, symbolizing the rapid and "successful" urbanization of the state, makes even greater sense in the light of the continuing stagnation of the agricultural sector. Whereas the gross cropped area of Maharashtra under food grains is about 11 percent of the national total its production is only about 7 percent. The major handicap, of course, is the lack of assured water supply. Only about 10 percent of the net sown area in the state had irrigation in 1978-79. With a primarily rain-fed agriculture the vagaries of the monsoon produce not infrequent mass migrations of the most indigent rural landless classes to urban centers such as Bombay and Poona. Since 1973, Maharashtra's agriculture has shown an improving trend in terms of area and productivity, almost entirely as a result of good monsoons. In 1982, however, a severe drought hit the state again, the worst since 1971. At the same time for those with assured irrigation, opportunities for making a fortune in cash crops emerged. They have been very diligently exploited, thus creating a false picture of general agricultural prosperity. In fact, the rest of the state has experienced steady stagnation and decline in productivity since the early sixties, except when favorable monsoons have provided some respite. The sense of euphoria which was experienced by the rural elite during the Nehru era was based on false expectations. Under the ideology of Community Development and Extension, the Congress government created several structures for making generous public resources available to farmers in the form of credit, subsidized inputs and technical advice. In the absence of technological breakthroughs which would improve dry farming, these structures soon became clogged up. Since 1970 they have become unattractive, both economically and politically, to the rural rich. Although they are still controlled and occupied by the same elites, the earlier scramble and competition has disappeared. For the rural poor without work and the rural rich, rising productivity and expansion of industrialization and urbanization have become important avenues for sustenance and for the advancement of careers among the younger generation. At the same time agriculture continues to be the way of life for most. The basic structures of the rural political economy, dominated by the relatively better off rural elites as controllers of *zilla parishads*, cooperative societies, educational institutions and party organization, will continue to dominate Maharashtra's polity for a long time to come.

The exception to the general state of agricultural stagnation is sugarcane and perhaps, on a smaller scale, a few other cash crops such as onions and maybe cotton. Both in terms of area and output sugarcane production doubled between 1960–61 and 1976–77. Its productivity is also substantially higher than the national average. Good soil, plenty of assured water and liberal use of fertilizers and new technology are the reasons. The rapid growth of state–subsidized cooperative sugar mills has provided a guaranteed and lucrative market for cane. The mills have thrived as a result of state–controlled, favorable prices for sugar. Highly favorable treatment by the state in extending credit and favorable terms for imports have also helped. Recognizing the limits on long term profitability of sugar production (the proliferation of cooperative sugar mills across the state, initiated by political elites in control of the ruling party has raised serious concerns about productivity and marketing) several mills have diversified production into industrial alcohol, liquor, potash and cattlefeed. Since they are supposed to distribute their profits among the members as a "final price" for the sugarcane, they pay no taxes, even on the profits from the ancillary industries. And since such favorable terms have not been available to growers of other cash crops (for example, onions, bananas, tobacco and cotton) the latter have been agitating, on behalf of all producers of marketable agricultural surplus for higher prices under the banner of Shetkari Sanghatana (Farmers Organization). There have been many attempts to organize poor peasants and agricultural workers for higher wages or better inputs. So far they have produced few state–wide pressures on the government. Attempts to organize factory workers in rural industries have also been rather unsuccessful. The benefits of state–subsidized inputs, controlled prices and favorable credit facilities have gone to the privileged middle and rich peasants with bigger and better holdings. By and large they have belonged to the hegemonic lineages of the dominant Maratha caste.

The political economy of Maharashtra, as it advances into the 1980s, is characterized by truncated growth trends in industry and agriculture. The problem of regional disparities is routinely raised by the elites from various political parties. The government has routinely responded to their demands by creating review committees and Development Boards. Bombay keeps on producing its own problems of growth and shortages. The attendant opportunities for extension of discretionary patronage are routinely exploited by those controlling the state. Relatively minor industrial growth also continues to occur in and around district towns. The favorable conditions of infrastructural and tax incentives provided by the state are routinely exploited by educated sections of the Maratha and other upper caste clusters. There is sufficient room for the expansion of ancillary small scale industries in small towns, given the availability of cheap labor and a relatively protected market. These developments will continue to follow the pattern set under the Congress system whereby competing elites will gain favorable access to state resources for their constituencies. They will thus maintain their structures of political support. Shifts in the relative fortunes of their alliances will depend on which state–level alliance has the dominant share in political power. There seem to be no compelling reasons to suggest that the current state of peaceful coexistence between urban capital (industrial and commercial), rural privilege (landlords and rich peasants) and those in the service sector (technocrats, bureaucrats and white collar workers) will be disturbed during the 1980s. No major shift in the current pattern of skewed development seems likely, even though agitations for balanced regional development will continue to be mounted as they have been in the last decade. Structures of pluralist competition established in the early 1960s have delivered favorable results to Maratha elites across regions. Regional disparities in agricultural and industrial development are the byproducts of competitive pluralism. The fact that actual irrigated area in 1981–82 was less than 10 percent of the total whereas the expert estimate of the total potential area is about 25 percent may have a lot to do with the nature of democratic polity. Any policies that can effectively end disparities may also call for an end to pluralism and thus threaten privilege.

During the Nehru era, while the new arenas of political competition were being introduced into the rural areas, a number of young elite Marathas who had gone to the cities for education and employment returned to their villages to take charge of the new "opportunity structures." Rosenthal described this phenomenon as "deurbanization."[7] With the clogging up of many of these avenues a reversal of that trend may have emerged. The object of new urban aspirations is not professions or traditional civil service employment any more. Young rural elites now want privileged access to the growing advanced technology sector. That opportunity has remained largely restricted to the upper castes. Consequently, despite the growth of the industrial and service sectors, the student intake of technical institutions in the state has stagnated for over fifteen years while the number of admission seekers has doubled. One of the responses to this dilemma has taken the form of an attack on the long–established policies of protective discrimination for the scheduled castes and tribes. The state has responded only recently with a plan for sanctioning rapid expansion of technical institutions. These are to be run by voluntary organizations, most of them dominated by the competing elites within the Congress system. Although the state government has declared that it has no intention of subsidising these institutions, it is already beginning to relent under pressure. At the same time, the introduction of "capitation fees" has also become a lucrative source of patronage.[8]

In sum, while the political economy of Maharashtra may be headed towards some inevitable long–term objective crisis due to resource scarcity and rising disparities, it will probably not have an impact on political structures, at least during the 1980s. Short run manifestations of that crisis will take the form of demands and pressures from specific, vocal and resourceful interests. The state will be able to provide temporary amelioration through the usual strategies of reactive policy formation. Meaningful change in the direction of the established pattern of rural and urban growth calls for basic structural changes in the political economy. Since such structural changes are detrimental to the interests of those who are currently in charge of the state, both locally and centrally, political parties will not "articulate" or "aggregate" such demands. The major thrust for structural changes will have to come from the urban and rural classes that remain unorganized. Currently, many of their members are deprived of even the basic necessities of life.

Even the nascent challenges to such injustices are effectively vitiated by turning them into issues of ethnic or caste loyalty. The rise and decline in the support for Shiv Sena in Bombay in the 1960s and the 1970s and its recent resurgence, attacks on the lives and homes of defenceless groups, and demands for protective discrimination for the "other backward castes" are some of the indications of how basic structural problems can be transformed into "manageable" political demands. In May, 1984, for example, Shiv Sena was able to instigate major riots in the Bombay region in which, by official estimates, more than 230 people died. It not only exploited the widespread anti–Muslim prejudice of the Hindus but, in particular, mobilized large segments of unemployed youth and elements of Bombay's multi–layered underworld that has grown around activities such as construction, smuggling and bootlegging. While Shiv Sena first gained support in the 1960s by splitting the left–oriented labor movement through a sons–of–the–soil appeal, it lost much of its strength due to its anti–labor stance during the textile and public sector employee strikes in the 1970s. Its recent attempts to regain support across ethnic and linguistic divisions by its anti–Muslim appeal seem to have succeeded. As the recent riots indicate, many Hindus see it as a necessary vigilante organization for protecting their lives and property against the "growing Muslim menace." Its major function thus continues to be the same: to turn basic issues of poverty, unemployment and hunger into temporary emotional appeals against minorities. The state seems both unwilling and unable to confront or curb such organizations because it has no solutions to offer to the real problems. The current political uncertainty in the Congress party often forces some of its leaders to depend on the support of Shiv Sena.[9] The continuing viability of traditional symbols of identity and their availability for elite manipulation are also demonstrated by these events. The new amalgam of rulership strategies of pluralism, populism and centralism established by Mrs. Gandhi after 1971 arose as a response to such structural challenges, but is now serving the purpose of maintaining a viable state apparatus in order to allow the enhancement of privilege through structures of moderated competition. As to which of these three strategies is likely to dominate Maharashtra politics in the 1980s depends to a considerable extent on the various shifts that are currently occurring in the party system and in other relevant political structures.

THE PARTY SYSTEM

I have argued elsewhere that the political process in India resembles, in its essentials, the elite pluralism of Western democracies.[10] Other models, especially the most popular one of one-party dominance seem to make an implicit teleological assumption about the desirability, if not the inevitability, of a two or multi-party political system consisting of "a stable democratic regime with adequate but not excessive participation, adequate but not excessive awareness of issues and adequate but not excessive interest in politics" by the citizens.[11] Where the Indian polity does not resemble this ideal, on either side of the golden mean, the preferred explanatory variable is political underdevelopment (not of the Western democracies, but of India). My evidence from the state of Maharashtra suggests that all the essentials of elite pluralism that can be found in American democracy are present, albeit within different cultural garbs, in Maharashtra. They include, above everything else, the presence of a highly dispersed ruling class — dispersed both spatially and in terms of subdivisions or strata. Because of such dispersion it can be identified only by reference to the extremes of deprivation and privilege. In reality the dispersed ruling class is politically, economically and culturally integrated, as Sweezy has shown in the case of the USA and as I have tried to demonstrate with respect to the hegemony of elite Marathas.[12]

The impact of the dispersed and relatively invisible elite is not to be judged strictly by what they have but by how and how effectively they restrict participation by the larger segments of population in the distribution of a society's resources. Not only the initial advantage but also the strategies of exclusion are characteristic of pluralist democracies. This exclusion results not only because of overt elite control of resources that are necessary for effective participation (as many since Bentley have pointed out with respect to Western democracies) but also due to cultural hegemony, a consensus on values, presumably shared by the non-participants. The predominance of the goals of civic privatism (with career, consumption and leisure as prime goals) among the privileged and a sense of fatalism among the poor have been well demonstrated for the West. The behavioral theory of democracy kept pace with these developments by becoming a scientific justification of apathy and fatalism demonstrated by the "spectator-sports" orientation to political events by "modern" citizens. For India, the theory of "one-party dominance" has served a similar purpose in explaining the behavior of its "traditional" citizens.

In Maharashtra competitive democratic pluralism was synonymous with Congress Party politics up until 1971. The Congress Party was responsible for monitoring the competition for access to public resources. The major competitors were the established elites of the dominant Maratha caste. The Maratha caste has been, historically, a relatively homogeneous unit of social identity which effectively conceals substantial economic and cultural disparities. Potential conflict zones are systematically dissolved by conscious application of the communal ideology. Out of this hegemony Y.B. Chavan had fashioned and managed democratic politics in Maharashtra through a hierarchy of formal structures. These arenas of participation, including local governments, cooperative societies, educational institutions and party organization, have been in existence since the early sixties. In order to ensure their smooth functioning in a manner conducive to hegemonic interests, a hierarchy of informal structures of influence also came into existence. Public resources, to which there is universal access in theory, are transformed into discretionary allocations, based on the relative political power of various interests, by a mechanism that is usually described as patronage. The hierarchy of formal and informal structures ensures a graduated distribution of resources.

Such a system requires an arbitrator. Since resources are scarce and stakes are high, competition has a tendency to go beyond self-imposed limits. Instead of leaving the outcomes entirely to the electoral process (as is the case in Western democracies) the Congress system seeks to first work out compromises within its own boundaries. This is true of competition within and between states. In spite of appearances to the contrary, the arbitrators who arise at the apex, in states and at the Center, can never really be the "bosses." They must lead where their followers choose to go. They must lead by their skills of persuasion. They must also display an acute sense for the strength of various political forces and to pick and support the winners while, at the same time, ensuring that contending competitors, the losers, are also assured of a place and a share.

Chavan's success in establishing this system in Maharashtra brought him to the central cabinet during the Nehru era. In 1966, he was one of the several state leaders (the Syndicate) who settled on Indira Gandhi as the successor to Shastri. As someone without a base in state politics they expected her to be a weak arbitrator, in fact a mere implementor of compromises, to be worked out by them in the traditional Congress style. Mrs. Gandhi, who had been close to Nehru and had seen his management of politics, had other intentions. While he had also followed the Congress pattern, Nehru was, in addition, blessed with the admiration and affection of the masses. The latter gave him a cutting edge in making difficult decisions that at times displeased many of the state level leaders. It seems Mrs. Gandhi wanted to be able to emulate her father in this respect.

The period beginning with the mid-1960s presented to her both a challenge and an opportunity. Despite the difficulties of the early post-Independence period, the Nehru era was a period of rapid and steady economic growth. The Center had played a key role in the creation of the industrial and agricultural infrastructure. The viability of competitive pluralism was predicated on the availability of resources to feed the demands of the expanding, politically conscious middle classes which included not only the rapidly expanding urban intelligentsia but also, and more importantly, the elites of the dominant castes in rural areas. The latter had, since the mid-1930s, flocked to the Congress fold and started to take over its grass roots organization. Pluralist competition ensured a steady distribution of the rewards of growth to the upper and middle classes in rural and urban areas. In turn that success ensured that the recipients developed a vested interest in its stability and continuation. Nehru's role as the supreme arbitrator of pluralist politics was made easy by this objective situation of economic expansion.

By 1966 the disastrous side effects of the previous policies were already being felt. Rising disparities regions and classes in the industrial sector, stagnation for want of structural changes in agriculture and rising and visible economic disparities in urban and rural India were beginning to show the limits of planned growth. At the same time competition for access was growing far more rapidly than the rate at which the resources were likely to grow. The famine–like conditions that prevailed for two successive years in 1965–67 brought these limits to growth into a sharp focus. It became obvious to many that pluralist politics had served the interests of the rich peasantry from the dominant castes in the rural areas and of those who were already well equipped to exploit new opportunities in the urban sector. It had been mostly a politics of exclusion of the lower castes. Even the measures of positive discrimination had been reduced to selective patronage for loyal acquiescence to dominant class interests. A strong sense of discontent about the system began to emerge among those who had taken advantage of protective discrimination and also among many from other lower castes who had migrated to the cities in search of work. At the same time the intra–Congress competition of the privileged elites was expanding and was threatening to become uncontrollable.

Recognizing the dual problem of a lack of an established state base within the pluralist system and of the growing discontent about the system among the more conscious elements of the deprived classes, Mrs. Gandhi seems to have decided to confront the managers of Congress pluralism with an alternative strategy. She resorted to populist slogans and symbolic radical gestures such as the nationalization of banks and abolition of the privileges of the princes. She had also inherited some of her father's visibility and admiration among the common people. She decided to put that inheritance to use by means of a nation–wide campaign for support from those who had been ignored and exploited by the privileged classes. One way to demonstrate her commitment to their cause was to encourage their increased participation in state and national legislatures.

The strategy of populism came to Maharashtra in 1972. Its intention was to confront the established structures of pluralist competition. Paradoxically, its main instrument was V.P. Naik, the Chief Minister, who had already become adept at the management of pluralism. Naik wanted to enhance his own political base in Vidarbha and to reduce his dependence on Y.B. Chavan. He was, therefore, willing to cooperate with Mrs. Gandhi to a limited extent. As a member of a settled tribal community (Vanjari) he was also well suited to claim the championship of

Mrs. Gandhi's new constituency. Naik's list of recommended candidates for the election to the state legislature included large numbers of non–Maratha candidates, a major departure from the two previous elections. At the same time both he and Y.B. Chavan made sure that this inclusion would not affect the chances of the Congress party to win a majority. This meant that where the dominant Maratha elites were in control the chosen candidates had to be from or acceptable to the elites of that caste. In 1972, the success of the populist strategy of introducing non–Maratha candidates was restricted, primarily, to the Vidarbha region.

While Chavan was in charge, politics had followed the general pluralist pattern set up by him. Important regional differences in the structure of Maratha domination had remained beneath the surface. Although the proportion of population that claims to be Maratha is roughly the same in the various regions of the state, the articulation of its elite–mass components is somewhat different in social and political history. Chavan had fashioned his factional–alliance strategy on the basis of his experience in western Maharashtra where broad–based alliances between regional (*deshmukh*) and village (*patil*) Maratha elites had become well–established. They and the social reform movements initiated by some of the Maratha elites had helped in the creation of graduated hierarchical structures of pluralist politics. This "civilized" relationship between various levels of Maratha elites had not emerged in Vidarbha or Marathwada prior to their entry into Maharashtra. Whereas the designation *kunbi*, indicating a distinction between village and regional Marathas, had disappeared from western Maharashtra by 1940 it was still commonly used in other regions. Through it the Maratha masses remained conscious of their distinction from the local *patils*. More importantly, it separated regionally dominant *deshmukhs* from *patils* as well as *kunbis*.

In Marathwada, initially, the established regional elites with large landed estates, were extremely reluctant to allow local upstarts into regional politics. They preferred not to share the arenas of power with village elites. In the consequent absence of well–articulated structures of power and pressures, of graduated hierarchy, these politicians were unable to compete effectively for a larger share of the state's resources. Since development would have meant opening a wider access to patronage to the village elite and increased competition from them, backwardness became functional for retaining traditional patterns of power in Marathwada.

This configuration began to change slowly with the introduction of uniform structures of government across the state. A younger generation of local Maratha elites found its way to schools and colleges run by the elites and subsidized by the state. Over a period of twenty years these young Marathas became conscious of the impotence of the existing alliance networks in fighting against the economic backwardness of the region. Drought, inflation and unemployment gave a cutting edge to their dissatisfaction in 1972. Initially their agitation for better employment opportunities gave promise of a common cause with scheduled caste students who were demanding better educational opportunities. The latter had become conscious of their depressed status after attending schools and colleges set up with the inspiration of their leader, Dr. Ambedkar. However, the radical potential of such an alliance was not lost on the older upper caste and Maratha elites. They exploited the student agitation for their own ends by diverting its focus away from specific issues, towards a vague demand for regional development.

In Vidarbha, the four districts of Nagpur, Bhandara, Chanda and Wardha (Nagpur districts) had a distinct political history and a *zamindari* system of land tenure. They are primarily grain growing, dry farming areas, in contrast to the Berar districts (Akola, Amaravati, Buldhana and Yeotmal). In the latter, *ryotwari* was the prevalent land tenure with cotton as the primary crop. In the Nagpur districts both economic and socio–cultural distance between the regional Maratha elite and the *kunbis* (including *patils*) is greater than that in the Berar districts. In both areas Congress leadership had originally rested in the hands of Brahmin landlords, officials and professionals. In the Berar districts it was replaced by a combination of *deshmukhs* and Marwaris. The long–standing kinship ties of Vidarbha *deshmukhs* with other parts of the state were instrumental in their affinity for Maharashtra state and in their subsequent entry into integrated elite Maratha alliances. Beneath the surface calm of *deshmukh*-Marwari domination, basic conflicts between the interests of rich cotton traders and cash crop farmers, smaller grain producers, peasants and laborers remained. The last two groups are socially separated, as *kunbis*, from *deshmukhs*. Thus, on the whole, there exists greater socio–economic distance between Maratha elites and masses in Vidarbha than in western Maharashtra. A similar distance separated the middle castes from elite Marathas and made them potential allies for a struggle against a *deshmukh*-Marwari dominated Congress establishment.

These different socio–economic and political configurations in different regions suggest that there is greater potential for populist appeal against established alliance structures in Vidarbha than in western Maharashtra. In Marathwada, meanwhile, populism has turned poor Marathas and middle castes into elite Maratha allies against the Scheduled Castes. This polarization has been exacerbated by the meagerness of resources channelled into the region, a consequence of its weak bargaining power at the state level. In the Konkan districts, politics either follows the elite Maratha pattern (as in Kolaba) or is influenced by the politics in Bombay city on which lower castes depend heavily for employment (as in Ratnagiri and Thana). In the Khandesh districts (including Nasik), non-Maratha counter-elites have aquired a certain anti-establishment and yet pragmatic consciousness of interests. They have rendered Congress politics much more fluid, thus allowing some but not complete domination by the products of populism.

Despite systematic efforts to weaken the pluralist system through the induction of non-Brahmin, non-Maratha candidates, no serious confrontation between the old and the new had occurred. Even though populism arose out of some of Mrs. Gandhi's personal compulsions, it served a very useful function in Maharashtra. It came at a time when the threat to the pluralist system was serious. Elements which would have otherwise staged frontal attacks on the system from the outside were instead incorporated within. The terms of inclusion were set by the dominant Maratha elite who were still in command between 1971 and 1977. Whereas the governments in Gujarat and Bihar collapsed under such external pressures, Jayaprakash Narayan, who had spearheaded the movement, praised V.P. Naik for his progressive policies. Most of the new entrants to the Congress party who joined under the populist strategy of the early 1970s and some of the members of the older Maratha establishment joined Mrs. Gandhi's new Congress(I) in 1978. Most of the Maratha elite remained with Y.B. Chavan in the original Congress. In the legislative elections of February 1978, Congress(I) won 62 seats, mostly in Vidarbha (as against the Janata Party's 99 and the old Congress Party's 69). The two Congresses chose to form a coalition government in order to prevent the Janata party from ruling the state. As the Congress(I) gained ground nationally, most of the leaders of the older Congress prepared themselves to unite with it and eventually did. However, the division between those who remained loyal to Mrs. Gandhi during her difficult days (the self-styled loyalists) and those who joined later is remembered and often exploited by the loyalists in order to counter the return of Maratha hegemony to the ruling party.

That the loyalists have had little success in countering the influence of the pluralists should be clear from the fact that men like Y.B. Chavan continue to wield substantial power within the state. The regional differences also allowed for the containment of the new element. In Maharashtra, since the days of Y.B. Chavan's total dominance, many elites from the Scheduled Castes and Tribes and from Muslim communities have been more "generously" accommodated within the Congress system than elsewhere. They have developed a vested interest in the maintenance of the system. While they exploit the appeal of populism when it is advantageous, they can also be counted on to moderate possible confrontations. For example, when they are bypassed in candidate selection by ardent loyalist–populists, as more established elites they remain available as rivals on whom pluralists can depend for a counter attack. Their loyalty to the Congress system is based on pragmatic considerations. For example, those from the "other backward castes" (the high and low artisan castes) have realized that without control over land or trade, without a caste–cluster ideology equivalent to that of the Marathas or Mahars, and without spatial concentrations, mobilization against Maratha hegemony or the Congress system cannot yield a lasting alternate system of rewards. Similar pragmatism has characterized the attitudes of elites from among the *dalits* and Muslims of Maharashtra. Consequently, by astute management of this pragmatism and of regional differences, men like Y.B. Chavan and Vasant Dada Patil (Dada) are able to blunt the edge of the populist strategy. Attempts to counter them with the exercise of centralism have so far failed. Of the four Chief Ministers that the state has had since January 1980, three have been elite Marathas, and two of these are ardent pluralists (Pawar and Dada). The other two, Antulay (a Muslim) and Bhosle, belong to the loyalist group.

The current uncertainties and the apparent instability of the party system, reflected by the shifting fortunes of the chief ministers, is an outcome of the presence of a large contingent of loyalist–populist legislators. Because of their record of defections and maneuvers Mrs. Gandhi has been reluctant to trust the loyalists like Vasant Dada Patil even though she is forced to depend on them. Hence in 1980 she placed A.R. Antulay, M.P., in charge of the choice of candidates for the legislative elections. A large number of those selected were without grass–roots support and today are unsure of their future, should the Maratha elite regain total control of the party. They are thus forced to stage many confrontations against the current chief minister. This would not have been possible without the desire of the national leader to keep the situation fluid. Hence, apart from the change in style, involving public display of internal dissensions and dissatisfactions, which the old pluralists have had to adapt to, populists have also produced some new challenges for policy formation. The significant old structures of elite competition, especially the cooperatives, but also *zilla parishads* and educational institutions, still remain, by and large, under the control of the pluralists. They are still the mainstay of the rural Congress system. Lasting structures of voter support – factions and alliances – are built on their potential for patronage. The state has had to create alternative channels of patronage for the newcomers, those who must stand outside the old bastions of Maratha hegemony. The objective context of the origin of the Sanjay Gandhi Niradhar Anudan Yojana and the Sanjay Gandhi Swavalamban Yojana (which provided pensions for destitutes and loans for artisans), launched and later made famous by Antulay, can be traced to this compulsion of populism. After winning the 1980 elections, Mrs. Gandhi inducted A.R. Antulay into the cabinet as the Chief Minister, even though he had not been allowed earlier to contest the elections. This move was unexpected by and against the wishes of the Maratha elite. Antulay saw his major task as that of helping his proteges secure lasting support in their constituencies. He managed to secure massive donations for his programs and trusts from many of the privileged entrepreneurs and corporations (including the Maratha–dominated cooperative sugar mills) which are heavily dependent on state patronage. Non–official committees set up to handle the allotment of loans, pensions and awards became major alternate sources of patronage on which the newly anointed loyalists were expecting to build themselves lasting structures of popular support. For a large number of specially hand–picked loyalists, the loyalist MLAs in the legislature of 1980, this became a lifeline.

A major attack on these potentially threatening alternate structures was led as an attack on Antulay, not surprisingly by an outspoken pluralist, Shalini Patil. Since Dada was an M.P. and a secretary of the national party at the time of the 1980 elections, his wife, Shalini, was asked to contest from his usual legislative constituency. Given the importance of his support for the party, she was also given an important cabinet post in Antulay's ministry. However, she remained a champion of the pluralist cause and Antulay dropped her from the ministry. In January 1981, a judge of the Bombay High Court ruled that Antulay had misused the discretionary powers of the state in allotting cement quotas to those who had given donations to his trusts and programs. Antulay, was forced to resign under pressure from the pluralists led by Shalini. His successor, Bhosle, once a loyal supporter of Antulay was also forced to resign under similar pressure. In the end Mrs. Gandhi reluctantly asked

Dada to take over the post in January 1983, in spite of the strong opposition of the loyalists. As a compromise she insisted on the resurrection of the long abandoned post of Deputy Chief Minister and assigned Ramrao Adik, a loyalist from a Bombay constituency, to that post. One of Dada's early moves as the Chief Minister was to remove many of the loyalists from these committees. He took advantage of the prevailing atmosphere of suspicion and criticism resulting from the various court cases against Antulay in connection with his trusts. The ensuing furor is claimed to have posed a major threat to Dada's position. It is hard to believe that he would not have anticipated the reactions of his rivals. The continuously threatening presence of Antulay, his attitude of defiance towards the national leadership, his "Robin Hood" image among some of the intellectuals, and his boasts that "I cannot forget I enjoyed their affection to the extent very few CLP (Congress Legislative Party) leaders ever did," make sense in the light of the composition of the present legislative assembly and the sense of fear among the loyalists about the pluralists. [13]

A number of policy dilemmas have arisen either directly or indirectly out of the changing trends in the political economy of the state. Issues associated with industrialization and urbanization such as land acquisition for New Bombay, the eviction of pavement dwellers and protection for slum dwellers, have fed the fires of competition both internal and external to the Congress party. That they have claimed many lives, some under police firing, others from slow death under inhuman living conditions, seems to be a matter of only indirect interest. There is no reason to doubt, however, that the system will produce acceptable reactive solutions to each one of these problems by treating them in isolation from each other. This has already been demonstrated by policies such as the Employment Guarantee Scheme (initiated by V.P. Naik in 1972), the Cotton Procurement Scheme, sanctions for profit-making private enterprise in technical education and proposed protective discrimination for "other backward castes." Together, such policies help maintain the necessary state of flux without which competitive arena politics cannot sustain itself. The added element of populism makes the flux far more visible and the competition much more acute but it essentially serves the function of maintaining long term stability. It allows for further incorporation of new and vocal non-hegemonic elites within the Congress system. Attempts by Mrs. Gandhi to tilt the existing balance decisively in favor of the populists, through the imposition of "loyal" chief ministers have failed. This proves, once again, that no matter how arbitrary she may appear, an apex arbitrator in the Congress system can never call all the shots. At best, she has been able to maintain the tension between pluralists and loyalists. Her appointment of Ramrao Adik as Deputy Chief Minister is a case in point. In June, 1984 a detailed account of Adik's drunken misbehavior aboard an Air India international flight was published in most newspapers. Pluralists used the occasion to force Mrs. Gandhi to have him resign his cabinet post.

THE ELECTORAL PROCESS

Given the resilience and continuity of the established social (dominant castes, hegemonic elites) and political (cooperatives, zilla parishads, flexible party units) structures of the Congress system, it is difficult for me to visualize drastic shifts in the associated electoral process. This, it may be argued, is a consequence of my perspective to which the reality is not obliged to conform. This may be so and the proof may not lie too far into the future. As the various contributions to this volume suggest, the current debate among political scientists as to whether the Congress(I) of 1980 is in any way a return to the old Congress system of one-party dominance is also a matter of perspectives. Neither of the sides in the debate seems to take into account the changing objective conditions and the long run significance of the established social and political structures, at least not in the way I do. I suspect, however, that both Weiner[14] and Manor[15] are right. It is just that they are holding on to two different parts of the elephant.

An essential element in the electoral process of the Congress system has been the formal procedure for candidate selection. It has always been understood that in spite of all formal safeguards, "selection committees are essentially the creatures of dominant alliance leaders."[16] Committees work out compromises so as to take out as much guesswork as possible from the actual electoral outcomes. These forecasts about the electability of a candidate were never foolproof. Hence the effectiveness of a compromise was always a function of correspondence in the perceptions of the rivals of the strength of their support structures. The dominant alliance leaders at the state and the Center, acting as final arbitrators, had to adjudicate between the claims of rival aspirants on the basis of less than complete information and make the best possible guess. Disgruntled rejects always had the options of sabotaging the official nominees's chances from within or of running as rebels. Successful ones among the latter were able to return to the party after a brief period of formal disgrace. During the 1972 elections when an element of populism was first introduced into the process, these basic elements were still at work in Maharashtra. Even though Y.B. Chavan's position as the apex arbitrator for Maharashtra was openly challenged by Mrs. Gandhi through attempts to encourage dissidence by men like Y.J. Mohite and S.B. Chavan, in the end she had to settle on V.P. Naik as a matter of compromise with Y.B. Chavan. Thus the latter's role was somewhat diminished but could not be abolished. Although overt competition in arena politics was suspended during the Emergency the various structures of power remained intact and were mostly in the hands of the pluralists. S.B. Chavan had finally become the Chief Minister, displacing Naik, early in 1975. He was at the helm when the Emergency was declared. When the Lok Sabha elections were announced in 1977, all the Maratha alliance leaders returned to competitive politics with a vengeance. Most of them had to be accommodated. In the election that followed, the only real loser was S.B. Chavan. All but one of his hand-picked nominees were defeated in his native Marathwada. The rebellious Congressmen who accomplished this task all belonged to the "old order." It seems S.B. Chavan had taken his role as the agent of populism far too seriously. He either forgot or failed to use the Emergency as an opportunity to build for himself a lasting support structure in his region.

This pattern of Lok Sabha elections was repeated in the assembly elections of 1978. There were two major differences. First, a patchwork of opposition parties had come to power at the Center under the title of Janata Party. In Maharashtra it had three major components: the socialists, the Congress dissidents and the Jana Sangh. Second, there were now two Congress parties instead of one (Congress and Congress(I)). The first held together most of the eminent pluralists including Dada, Y.B. Chavan, V.P. Naik and Sharad Pawar. The other was led and inhabited by loyal supporters of Indira Gandhi's populism and included men like Adik, Antulay, Bhosle and Tirpude. The contest between pluralism and populism was thus clearly articulated. The outcome generally conformed to the regional variations described earlier. The Janata Party, mainly as a result of straight contests, won ninety-nine seats. Its influence was concentrated mostly in Bombay, several district towns and in part of the Konkan region. Pluralists won sixty-nine seats, mostly in western Maharashtra and the populists sixty-two, mostly in Vidarbha. Immediately after the elections, the contest between the two Congresses gave way to an uneasy alliance in order to form the government. Dada became the Chief Minister with Tirpude, the architect and orchestrator of Vidarbha populism, as his Deputy.

In 1978, soon after the formation of the Congress–Congress(I) coalition government, many pluralists had begun to desire the emergence of a united Congress party. Y.B. Chavan and Sharad Pawar, who had only reluctantly agreed to the coalition, continued to oppose unification at this stage. Consequently, they, along with their allies, became more and more isolated from the other pluralists. Pawar, fearful of slow decimation of their support structure, finally resigned from Dada's cabinet in July 1978 to form his new "parallel Congress" and a coalition government with the Janata party as a major ally. This was done, at least overtly, against the opposition of Y.B. Chavan who was still the major leader of the old Congress, which became Congress(Urs) in 1979 at the national level. Thus the two main Congresses found themselves in opposition to Pawar's coalition. This produced even greater pressures towards unity and Y.B. Chavan's increased isolation from his old allies. In August 1979 most of the pluralists from Congress(Urs) in Maharashtra joined Congress(I). They ensured the spectacular success of Congress(I) in the parliamentary elections of January 1980. Pawar and Chavan, whose alliance had become overt after the return of the pluralists, fielded 24 candidates but Chavan alone was elected from his traditionally safe seat in Satara district. Finally, in March 1980, Pawar's ministry was dissolved and fresh elections were held. In spite of the loss of direct access to patronage and the clear emergence of Congress(I) as the real Congress, the Pawar–Chavan alliance displayed a surprising strength in the state elections. It became abundantly clear to both Pawar and Chavan, however, that attempts to gain or retain power from outside the Congress system bound to fail in Maharashtra.[17] It had also become obvious that the pluralists could not be dismissed or ignored by Mrs. Gandhi; at best, they could be held in check by means of a coalition. She was called upon to repeat her 1978 performance in February 1983 when she had to accept Dada as the Chief Minister. This was after two of her attempts (Antulay and Bhosle) to tilt the balance against the pluralists had completely failed. In September 1983 some informants claimed that Ramrao Adik's concern for the symbols of power and his relationship with the Chief Minister reminded them of Tirpude. One could not help but wonder whether Adik also pondered (among other things) the denouncement of Tirpude's short regime in 1979. As it turned out, Adik was also displeased in June 1984.

Unlike in 1978, Dada and Adik were both in the same Congress Party. Theirs was an uneasy but intra–party alliance. Y.B. Chavan also returned to the same Congress party after his much maligned "home coming" in May 1981. Pawar has not returned, at least not yet. Indications are that just before the parliamentary elections of 1980, he would have liked to, but it was Y.B. Chavan who had persuaded him not to return to Congress(I). By that time Congress(I) had become the dominant alliance within the Congress system of Maharashtra. The main pluralists such as Dada and Y.J. Mohite had already returned to its fold. Chavan had urged Pawar to count on the logical preference of the rejected alliance leaders (from Congress(I)) for the nearest "Congress alternative." The strategy had worked amazingly well, primarily in western Maharashtra and Marathwada. Y.B. Chavan's subsequent return to the Congress(I), his declaration of friendship with once-alienated Dada, and the latter's elevation to the Chief Ministership with the support of Y.B. Chavan's followers are indications of the resilience, sophistication and flexibility of the Congress system. Ethical denunciations of Chavan's changing strategies by self-defined upholders of integrity and principles in politics have often been interpreted as indications of his declining support structure. They not only display ignorance of the basic structure of Maharashtra politics but also a misunderstanding about the intelligentsia's own share in maintaining the Congress system and in deriving unprecedented benefits from it.

The reluctance of the loyalists towards Y.B. Chavan's reentry and their rejection of that of Pawar are based on fully justified fears of consequences. Rumors that there exists a secret alliance between Dada, Y.B. Chavan and Sharad Pawar, who is currently the leader of the opposition in the State Assembly, are routinely floated by the loyalists. That the three share an understanding of western Maharashtra's political reality cannot be denied. They also share the basic structures of power and compete with each other only on the basis of shared norms. The potential that they, as pluralists, have for containing and perhaps even decimating populism in Maharashtra has been repeatedly demonstrated throughout the 1971-1983 period. The effect of that electoral strategy was most recently felt in two by-elections to the Lok Sabha and the legislative assembly. In the former, Shalini Patil, Dada's wife, was a candidate for the seat vacated by him. Her election with a reduced margin may have been largely a result of known dislike for her even among loyal supporters of Dada. It was very effectively used by the pluralists to accuse the loyalists of sabotage. In return, when a party-rejected nominee of Dada and Y.B. Chavan won as a rebel candidate from Patan constituency, the loyalists launched a concerted attack, accusing the pluralists of sabotage, perhaps not without reason. All this is reminiscent of the old days. One may find in it a confirmation of the Weiner thesis that the Congress system has returned to normal. My problem is that I cannot identify the point at which it could be said to have departed from normality in the first place. A former Congress MLA, now being wooed by both Congress(I) and Pawar's Congress(S) said to me in September 1983, "I cannot accept nomination from either of them. My rival will automatically become the nominee of the other party. If, on the other hand, I run as an independent and win, no matter which party forms the government my economic and political interests will be well protected." Such men keep the Congress system alive in Maharashtra.

How do loyalists without independent support bases manage to win elections? The radical image of their leaders, appeals to anti–establishment sentiments, and some actual improvements — however marginal — in the unbearable living conditions of the disadvantaged groups (e.g., housing sites, water and sewage systems) provide only partial answers. Elections in India are just as expensive as they are in the rest of the democratic world. An unofficial estimate from Ahmednagar district put the cost for each assembly candidate at between ten and twenty lakhs of rupees.[18] In the absence of an established support structure funds must come from the coffers of the party. In these cases the party must reward the loyalty of these candidates with more than just nominations. It must finance their campaigns. In order to be able to do that, party coffers also have to be filled, somehow. The price of democracy is paid in somewhat different currencies in different parts of the world but everywhere it has to be paid by those who benefit from it and can, therefore, afford it. The question of increasing corruption in the electoral process, it seems to me, is certainly a matter of perspective. Ethical denunciations in this matter come easily to us because even though we live off the system we are spared the unpleasantness of getting our hands dirty.

MAHARASHTRA AND THE CENTER

Now I come to the most difficult part of this paper. The thrust of my argument so far has been that the Congress system is alive and well in Maharashtra. It is of course possible to speculate about emerging scenarios based on projecting contingencies about electoral outcomes in parliamentary and various state elections and the possible initiatives from Mrs. Gandhi, in anticipation of or subsequent to them. At one stage some analysts were hooked on a debate about the "presidential alternative" advocated among others, by barrister Antulay. Since it looked like a plausible way by which a national leader could immunize herself against the structurally constituted uncertainties of parliamentary democracy, many believed that it had the support of Mrs. Gandhi. Whether basic differences among classes, communities, regions and interests will always cancel out in such a way that a specific presidential candidate could ensure her success is, of course, a moot point. It is not surprising that the issue has not been brought forth in recent months. I intend to refrain from indulging in that or other similar speculations about Mrs. Gandhi's intentions and restrict myself to arguing only from the vantage point provided by my analysis of Maharashtra.

It should be legitimate to ask, in that context, whether the populist strategy has not already peaked in Maharashtra. The necessary widening of the arenas, a consequence of the earlier encirclement and a functional necessity arising out of the changing political economy, has already been accompolished. For example, in response to angry and fearful outbursts of loyalists over the plans to replace them on the various "Sanjay committees" Dada accepted the "seventy percent" solution in the old spirit of pluralist compromise.[19] When the loyalists demanded a very large share in the membership of the MPCC(I), he was able to get the central leadership to agreeably nullify their impact by expanding it to the ridiculous size of ninety-eight. The withdrawal of support for a bill in the legislature that would have helped Antulay save his skin in court is another indication of Mrs. Gandhi's willingness to come to live with pluralism.

Soon after Dada came to power the issue of regional disparities in development was brought to the fore by his detractors. With his rapidly expanding empire of cooperative sugar and ancillary industries in Sangli the poignancy of that critique could not have been lost on him. His reactive response came in the form of a committee to investigate the matter. There have been similar investigations before. What has not been fully understood or accepted by the elites from regions other than western Maharashtra is that they must match the organizational skills of the pluralists from the latter if they wish to reap greater benefits from the Congress system. It has to be recognized that maintaining a level of underdevelopment may in fact be in the interest of many established elites, as seems to have been the case with Marathwada. Unless the anti-establishment orientation of the non-Maratha caste-clusters of Vidarbha finds an effective, organized expression leading to an articulation of clear policy options, its radicalism is in danger of dissipation. It may continue to ensure the electoral success of some of the loyalists but cannot produce stability equivalent to that of the competitive structures of western Maharashtra. Elite Marathas from Dada's region have played the politics of the cooperatives from the beginning of the twentieth century.

The message from these elite Marathas for the rest of Maharashtra is that development, in the sense of access to productive public resources, requires a sense for controlled competition. Pluralism has become their favored strategy because they have discovered that nothing else works for them as well as democracy does. It must be becoming increasingly clear to Mrs. Gandhi that an electoral strategy, based on an appeal to the loyalty of dispersed backward classes and castes and buttressed by encouragement for political participation and symbolic policies for marginal improvement in living conditions, does not produce lasting structures. Such structures are necessary if further improvements in living conditions are to be attempted. The capabilities of these groups for autonomous political economic development can be enhanced only through such structures. If not out of these considerations, at least out of pragmatic consideration of electoral success an ambivalence towards populism seems to be emerging. The reluctance on the part of Mrs. Gandhi and her associates to accept, wholeheartedly, the recommendations of the Mandal Commission seems to suggest this.[20]

In Vidarbha, in the past, resentment against the domination of western Maharashtra and the resultant neglect and underdevelopment of its potential has expressed itself in the language of separatism. When Y.B. Chavan took on the task of bringing Vidarbha into Maharashtra in 1960, he was keenly aware of the threat of separation and the fear of hegemonic domination by alliances of Marathas from Vidarbha and western Maharashtra. He made repeated exhortations to the elites of western Maharashtra to think of Nagpur, Chanda and Bhandara and not only of Kolhapur and Satara.[21] His choice of Naik as his successor was at least in part an attempt to establish effective structures of pluralist competition while taking into account the peculiarities of the social context of Vidarbha. After Naik, Vidarbha has not produced an acceptable arbitrator of his status. Instead, populists have often used separatism as a slogan to rally support for Congress(I) candidates. It is not inconceivable that the separation of Vidarbha may be considered as a possible option in order to strengthen the hold on its polity and to undercut the strength of the pluralists in other regions. However, since this will still not resolve the question of structural alternatives for Vidarbha's development, such an option, if opted for, will simply be an indication of desperation.

Unless the political elites in India are willing to contemplate real and basic structural changes, a prospect that was only remotely evident even in the Nehru era, the pluralist alternative seems to be the only viable way of moderating competition among hegemonic elites in a manner that ensures stability and growth. Populism has shown further tendencies of becoming a tool of repression in the hands of hegemonic elites when confronted with demands that exceed their own terms of accommodation. This was demonstrated vividly by the riots in Marathwada in August, 1978. Populism can be effectively used to unite hegemonic Marathas with their deprived caste fellows for demolishing the resistance of *dalits* and tribals. On the other hand, attempts by urbanized *dalit* elites to arouse the anger of their rural followers, usually in the name of causes that have little more than symbolic significance, prove disastrous for the latter who are usually left behind to bear the brunt of *savarna* retaliation. If centralism includes the use of coercive state power to protect privilege, then the hegemonic rural elites of Maharashtra need no lessons from the Center.

From the broader national perspective also, centralism seems to have been counterproductive for the maintenance of central control over the states. It is often suggested that the rise of regional consciousness in Andhra Pradesh and Karnataka may be attributed, in part, to the ineptitude shown by the central Congress leadership in its treatment of state leaders. In Maharashtra my informants claim that similar attacks by Pawar on the Center strike a sympathetic chord among the rural youth who are said to be flocking to Pawar's side in large numbers. If the emergence of film stars as political heroes is also to be understood as populism then it also may have backfired in the south. Ineptitude as an explanation is viable only if one assumes a level of inflexibility about perspectives among advisors and supporters of Indira Gandhi. Despite many apparently persuasive arguments to the contrary, I have found it possible to understand and explain most of Mrs. Gandhi's actions in terms of rational choices from available and perceived alternatives. Mrs. Gandhi has discovered, in Tamil Nadu, for example, that the predominance of a regional party in a state is not necessarily detrimental to the interests of a strong central Congress Party. Given the structural peculiarities of the various states, especially those in the south, it may in fact be more desirable for her to work with the leaders of regional parties in power than to face the awkwardness and uncertainties of internal competition in her own state parties as parties in power. As a prerequisite of such a strategy she must maintain a large enough assured core of loyal members of parliament. To gain that critical minimum, direct control of state politics in the so-called Hindi heartland may be necessary. It will also be far more manageable. The rest of the seats can be then secured by means of effective bargaining with leaders of the various local parties. This could include even the leftist governments in some of the states. Where would Maharashtra fit in this scenario?

Some of my informants argue that Mrs. Gandhi's current support for Dada shows a realization on her part that he is essential for success in parliamentary elections in western Maharashtra. Once she secures a substantial majority in the parliament she may be ready to come to terms with Pawar either by accepting him back in the party or by letting him form a coalition government with the help of opposition parties. In fact, the latter alternative may fit her plans much more comfortably. His return to the party is currently seen as a threat because of his relative youth and his obvious aspirations for a role at the national level. Past experience has also taught Mrs. Gandhi that given the opportunity or necessity, today's mutual enemies will readily unite in self–interest tomorrow and walk away with the prize. Pawar as the leader of a successful regional party in coalition with several opposition parties may, therefore, be far more acceptable to her. This may not be the preferred option, as far as Pawar is concerned. His current electoral strategy is a continuation of the old Chavan–Pawar plan that has proved its value in every election since 1972. Disgruntled Congressmen, rejected by the official selection committees, will want and have another Congress to go to. Mrs. Gandhi and her current allies in the state would like to somehow disarm that possibility. They will try to insist that the path of honorable return for the victorious rebels will not be open and that Pawar's Congress is no Congress at all. (Although Congress(S), with Pawar as its president, has national pretensions, it is essentially a regional party with its support base primarily in Maharashtra. Hence, in this discussion, I have treated it as such. It is, in terms of its dynamics and strategies, like any other intra–Congress alliance). Decades of contrary experience will tend to frustrate that expectation. The loyalists are already suggesting that in the end Pawar, Dada and Chavan will come together and take away whatever little power base the loyalists may have been successful in creating for themselves. Pawar's extraordinary deference to Dada in his campaign speeches and his avoidance of any criticism of Chavan are already being interpreted as overtures for a future alliance. They are in fact serious messages to both his own party members who are yearning for a united Congress and to his current rivals who may tomorrow have to become once again his allies in opposition to Mrs. Gandhi.

The only effective political idiom in Maharashtra today is still the Congress idiom. The one–party dominance of the Congress is still very much alive. Does it then really matter whether the Congress we are referring to is an "institutionally weak governing party" or just a temporary member of "the fragmented opposition?"[22]

NOTES

1. This paper is dedicated to the memory of Professor A.R. Kamat. He once guided me towards the need for a sound historical analysis of Maharashtra's political economy. I have drawn heavily on his excellent historical analysis in my summary of the political economy. See A.R. Kamat, *Essays on Social Change in India* (Pune: Indian Insitute of Education, 1983). Kamat's departure has left a major gap in the tradition of sober objective analysis of India's problems and prospects.

2. The name most frequently mentioned as Mrs. Gandhi's likely choice for a successor is that of S.B. Chavan. This will please neither the current Chief Minister's supporters nor most of his detractors. Following the Punjab tragedy when Mrs. Gandhi shifted the controversial Home Minister P.C. Sethi, she gave him Chavan's Planning Ministry. Chavan, as a minister without a portfolio, is thus available for dispatch to Maharashtra. This may have temporarily dampened the enthusiam of the rebelling Congressmen but it has also increased the sense of uncertainty in state politics by several degrees. See *The Times of India*, (Bombay), 20 July, 1984.

3. *India Today*, 15 November, 1983.

4. *India Today*, 31 July, 1983.

5. *Economic and Political Weekly* (10 October, 1981).

6. *Economic Political Weekly* (12 July, 1980).

7. D.B. Rosenthal, *The Expansive Elite: District Politics and State Policy-Making in India* (Berkeley, University of California Press, 1977).

8. *India Today*, 15 August, 1983.

9. *Economic Political Weekly* (19–26 May, 1984), pp. 826–830 and *The Times of India*, 20 July, 1984.

10. Jayant Lele, *Elite Pluralism and Class Rule: Political Development in Maharashtra, India* (Toronto: University of Toronto Press, 1981).

11. *Ibid.*, p. 92.

12. *Ibid.*, chapter 1 and Paul M. Sweezy, "Galbraith's Utopia," in *The New York Review of Books*, 20:18 (November 1973).

13. *India Today*, 15 January 1983.

14. Myron Weiner, *India at the Polls, 1980: A Study of the Parliamentary Election* (Washington: American Enterprises Institute, 1983).

15. "Party Decay and Political Crisis in India," *The Washington Quarterly* 4: 3 (Summer 1981).

16. Lele, *Elite Pluralism and Class Rule*, p. 143.

17. For a detailed analysis of these events, see *ibid*, pp. xi–xxxvi.

18. *Sakal*, (Pune), 6 June, 1980. p. 4.

19. The two main bargaining points the loyalists have are their current majority in the State Assembly and Mrs. Gandhi's fears about the pluralists. The loyalists also depend on the new sources of patronage created by Antulay. When Dada threatened to take these away they were able to use their two vantage points to get an assurance that seventy percent of the new appointments on the various committees would be given to loyalists. Since pluralists still control all the old and more substantial sources of patronage, Dada's compromise offer can hardly be seen as a major defeat for the pluralists. For details, see *Sakal*, 12 February, 1984.

20. In 1978 the Janata government in New Delhi appointed a commission to investigate and report on the problems of the so-called "socially and educationally backward classes" under the chairmanship of B.P. Mandal. The focus of inquiry was on those dispersed caste-class groups, other than the ones covered under the Scheduled Castes (SC) and Scheduled Tribes (ST) provisions of various protective discrimination policies. The commission submitted its report to the Congress(I) government in December, 1980. It recommended additional reservation of employment and educational opportunities for the "other backward castes." The government has yet to state its position on the report. See, Government of India, *Report of the Backward Classes Commission*, 1980.

21. Jayant Lele, "Chavan and the Political Integration of Maharashtra" in *Contemporary India*, eds. N.R. Inamdar, et al. (Poona: Continental Prakashan, 1982).

22. Weiner, *India at the Polls, 1980*, p. 41.

8
Congress Restored?
The "Kham" Strategy and
Congress(I) Recruitment in Gujarat

John R. Wood

"[T]he elections of 1980 restored the Congress party to the preeminent position it has held since independence . . . . With the disintegration of Janata, Indian politics has returned to normal."[1]

In 1980, when the Congress(Indira) defeated the remnants of the Janata coalition that had ruled India since 1977, a debate, still to be resolved, arose as to whether India would return to the "norm" of predominant party politics.[2] There were no illusions of a reversion to the Congress of Nehru and Shastri, but it was widely expected that, chastened by its defeat in 1977, the Congress of the 1980s would again become a "catch-all" party of national consensus.[3] The expectation seemed especially valid when, subsequent to the national poll, Congress(I) swept eight of nine state elections. According to Myron Weiner, "the 1980 general election was a reinstating election. The older electoral coalition was reassembled by the Congress party. Congress rule, both at the center and in most of the states, was restored."[4]

Other analysts were doubtful that such a restoration had occurred: Lloyd and Susanne Rudolph pointed to significant changes in Congress' electoral base, both regionally and in terms of the traditional support of minority blocs.[5] Some argued that institutional decay was so advanced in Congress party organization that one could hardly talk of a "predominant party" at all; moreover, what operated as the Congress(I) in the various states was so divergent that it could no longer be said to represent a national consensus.[6]

In this paper I will argue that in Gujarat, a state where Congress(I) won convincingly in 1980, the fundamental underpinnings of one–party dominance, located in the political recruitment of Congress(I) legislators, have changed quite drastically from those associated with the older model. The evidence is found in the "KHAM" strategy — the acronym standing for *K*shatriyas, *H*arijans, *A*divasis, and *M*uslims, and symbolizing a preference for candidates from these and other disadvantaged groups — a new party–building and vote–wooing strategy developed by the Congress(I) in Gujarat between 1975 and 1980. Most of what follows is an attempt to explain the development of the KHAM strategy and to assess the departure it represents from earlier recruitment practice. In addition, the results of the new strategy will be presented in a comparison of the composite profiles of the Members of the Legislative Assembly (MLAs) elected in Gujarat in 1967 and 1980. The consequences of the KHAM strategy, not only for one–party dominance, but for Gujarat state politics in general, will be the ultimate concern of the investigation.

POLITICAL RECRUITMENT: THE CONGRESS "NORM"

Studies of political recruitment in India are currently out of vogue, for at least two reasons. The first is that the concept is associated with structural–functional analysis and rejected for its mechanistic, apolitical, and status quo implications. The second reason is that a plethora of recruitment studies in the 1960s seemed to say all that could be said on the subject. The writings of W.H. Morris–Jones and of Ramashray Roy, among others, established a conventional wisdom about the informal procedures which determined recruitment outcomes.[7] Morris–Jones' contribution, based on data collected during the 1967 election, consisted of enlarging the meaning of the term "political recruitment," which had hitherto referred to the army–associated activity of finding and enlisting people for specific political roles, particularly those of electoral candidates.[8] Whereas political recruitment had previously been understood as "a matter of deliberate manipulation and control to be determined from the top," Morris–Jones argued that a two–way process was involved. Neither formal procedures nor selectors' preferences alone determined the outcome, but, in addition, the career routes, aspiration patterns, and catchment areas of those seeking political power had to be considered.[9]

In his effort "to find out more about the demand side of the relation," Morris–Jones drew attention away from those who controlled access to recruitment and towards those who wanted it and were most likely to get it. This was appropriate in an era when the Congress Party employed relatively open, merit–oriented recruitment procedures, albeit increasingly basing each selection decision on one concern: the candidate's ability to *win*. It was also understandable in a time–context (1952–1967) in which the locus of selection decision–making kept shifting between district, state and central committees.[10] In the presence of changing lines of control from above, it was natural to focus on the characteristics of the would–be candidates from below.

Ramashray Roy's analysis of Congress candidate selection in Rajasthan and Bihar added understanding in two ways.[11] First, it focussed on the power–struggles preceding recruitment decisions and hence on the role of factionalism in the process. The power–struggles took place, first, on a vertical axis, between higher and lower party units, with the former favoring candidates who would "contribute significantly to the party image, the unity of the organization, or the working of parliamentary institutions," and the latter being interested in "putting up a candidate who is a vote–getter."[12] On the horizontal axis, at all levels, the competition was manifested in factional struggles: "the rival factions strenuously strive to prevent their opponents from acquiring a majority position in the legislature. Consequently, each faction seeks to take maximum advantage of the selection process in order to be able to have a preponderant voice in the making of the government."[13]

Secondly, Roy emphasized the fact that at the district and state levels, factional cleavages usually coincided with social cleavages. Since party organization was "directly exposed to the influences of the social structure," it was "natural for the local activists to take into consideration the caste and communal composition of a particular constituency."[14] In 1967, Roy wrote that socio–demographic considerations, including caste, made the Congress Party broadly representative of Indian society: "the dominance of the upper castes in the Congress is a reflection of their dominance in society . . . Thus the relationship between the Congress and its environment is consistent; that is, no serious gap exists between the composition of the society and the composition of the Congress Party."[15] At the same time, Roy noted that political recruitment modified as well as reflected social stratification: "the virtual monopoly of the upper castes over political resources has ended, and the operation of democratic politics has endowed the underprivileged lower castes with two attributes of political influence: numbers and organization. The recruitment patterns in the Congress Party, therefore, can be taken to indicate a shift in the distribution of power, notwithstanding the fact that the political scene in

Bihar is still dominated by the upper castes."[16]

The original Congress recruitment norm, then, may be characterized as one in which the predominant party pursued a "catch–all" policy designed to attract votes from all strata and groups in Indian society with the ultimate purpose of winning legislative majorities. A two–way process was involved in which Congress election committees sought electable candidates and would–be candidates mobilized whatever resources they had to press their case for nomination. A Congress candidate was expected to have a record of social and party service and to subscribe to a vague set of Gandhian–Nehruvian values. There was a sense of merit being more important than ascription, but party factional alignments, ordinarily based on social cleavages, frequently determined who got the Congress "ticket." Up to the 1960s, higher castes tended to dominate the party and to be disproportionately recruited. Minorities and women were given at least token representation and the participation of scheduled castes and tribes was cultivated in order to ensure maximum Congress gain in the seats reserved for these groups. Such disadvantaged groups and other lower castes tended to play subordinate and dependent roles in the party, as they did in the society. However, as Roy indicated, Congress recruitment was flexible enough to allow for gradual restratification, so that middle–peasant and lower castes, depending on their numbers and organizing capability, might aspire to increasing recruitment and control of party machinery.

All "norms" in Indian politics, including those affecting Congress Party recruitment, were fundamentally shaken by the Congress split of 1969 and its subsequent ramifications: the departure of the Congress(O) organizational wing into opposition, the centralization and personalization of control over party decision–making in Indira Gandhi's Congress(R), her party's electoral sweeps in 1971 and 1972, its faltering as a governing party in the face of the Gujarat and Bihar upsurges in 1974, and the declaration of Emergency Rule in June 1975.[17] According to several observers, however, despite these events the recruitment norms described by Morris–Jones and Roy for the 1960s did not change markedly in the Congress of the 1970s insofar as outcomes were concerned. In effect, despite party organizational change and the pursuit of a rejuvenated and radical image, Congress(R) recruitment and party composition remained largely the same. The Congress(R), as Kochanek noted, was still an open, mass party in a highly segmented society: "even Mrs. Gandhi could not bypass local caste, regional, communal, and factional alignments . . . . Congress dominance at the center and in the states was restored by selecting candidates who could win. This . . . tended to make the new Congress look very much like the old."[18]

Kochanek's analysis was published in 1976 during the Emergency; since that time we have only scattered evidence regarding continuity or change in Congress (since 1978 Congress (I)) recruitment practice. Students of India's party system have concentrated instead on the fragmentation and decay of parties as institutions. With regard to Congress (I), most of the blame for its de-institutionalization has been attributed to Mrs. Gandhi: "she has been steadfast in her tendency to centralize power not just at the apex of the political system, but in her own hands."[19] Until his death in 1980, "her" hands included those of her son Sanjay, who was given the task of screening Congress candidates. Before the 1977 parliamentary election it was anticipated that members of Sanjay's Youth Congress would receive as many as 150–200 tickets out of the 542 available. Fearing widespread defection by incumbents, however, the Central Election Committee, presumably with Mrs. Gandhi's concurrence, allocated only 20 to YC members.[20] Instead, it was state level leaders, through the Pradesh Election Committees, who maximized control over the distribution of tickets. As Manor has pointed out, this meant that the Congress organization in different states – where it survived at all after the 1977 defeat – had begun to go separate ways.[21] In the run-up to the 1980 elections Mrs. Gandhi and her son apparently wielded greater control over ticket allocation, but pursuant to the Congress split of 1978 and the increasing de-institutionalization of the Congress(I) at all levels, central control over state units and their recruitment practices varied greatly. The case of Gujarat suggests that while giving lipservice to Mrs. Gandhi's and Sanjay's preferences, state Congress(I) leaders were able to exert almost total control over ticket allocation.

GUJARAT: THE DEMISE OF THE OLD CONGRESS

Gujarat was created in 1960 with the breakup of "bigger bilingual" Bombay State into its Gujarati- and Marathi-speaking components. Despite its historical fragmentation into five British districts and hundreds of princely states and estates, Gujarat, once it was territorially unified, enjoyed a number of advantages: linguistic homogeneity, relatively advanced levels of urbanization, literacy, and education, and especially, impressive economic productivity in industry, commercial enterprise, and cash-crop agriculture.[22] The home of Mahatma Gandhi and Sardar Vallabhbhai Patel, Gujarat and its politics were profoundly influenced by intensive participation in the nationalist movement and the development of a pragmatic, disciplined, and social work-oriented Congress Party organization. By the late 1960s Gujarat had become a Congress bastion shaped and controlled by the proteges of Morarji Desai, Gujarat's *"Sarvocch Neta"* ("Supreme Leader") and India's Deputy Prime Minister.[23]

All of this changed dramatically in 1969 with the Congress split, Morarji Desai's removal from Indira Gandhi's cabinet, and the alignment of almost all of Gujarat's Congress parliamentarians, state legislators, and organizational committees with the Congress(O). A trickle of dissidents, most with personal scores to settle with Morarji, moved to Indira's Congress(R). Soon after the Congress(R)'s sweep of the 1971 general election, however, the trickle became a flood. The Congress(O) government of Hitendra Desai was toppled on May 13, 1971. After ten months of President's Rule, a state election in March 1972 resulted in a resounding Congress(R) victory in 96 out of 140 seats based on 50.9% of the popular vote. Morarji's Congress(O) was a distant runner-up with 16 seats and 23.5%.

Caste had always been an important factor in Gujarat politics, affecting voter support, the composition of political parties, the allocation of cabinet positions, and recruitment practice.[24] During Morarji Desai's ascendancy, high castes, in particular the Brahmins and Banias, despite numerical inferiority held sway in the Congress organization and legislative party. In addition to Morarji (a Brahmin), Gujarat's Chief Ministers had all been Banias (Jivraj Mehta, 1960–63, Balwantrai Mehta, 1963–65) or Brahmins (Hitendra Desai, 1965–71). Gujarat's largest middle-peasant castes, the Patidars of the mainland and the Kanbis of the Saurashtrian peninsula, who had formed the backbone of the Congress under their patron Sardar Patel's leadership and controlled many district Congress institutions, waited impatiently to exert their political strength at the state level.[25] Meanwhile, the increasingly mobilized Kshatriyas, a loosely defined collection of castes ranging from the prestigious Rajputs to lower castes of the cluster formerly known as Kolis, were also waiting for power commensurate with their numerical strength.[26] During the 1960s, some of the richer Patidars and many of the poorer Kshatriyas had aligned in the Swatantra Party in an attempt to defeat the Congress but broke apart in 1970 under contradictory economic pressures.

The caste composition of Gujarat is difficult to ascertain precisely as we have only the 1931 census figures to go by. Roughly, however, the

Table 8:1

Caste Distribution in Gujarat

High Castes	Brahmin	4.1
	Bania	3.0
	Rajput	4.9
	Other high	1.1
		13.1
Middle Castes	Patidar/Kanbi	12.2
	Other middle	0.1
		12.3
Lower Castes	Koli	24.2
	Artisan castes	6.1
	"Other Backward"	10.0
		40.3
Scheduled Castes		7.2
Scheduled Tribes		17.7
		24.9
Non-Hindus	Muslims	8.5
	Other Non-Hindus	1.0
		9.5
		100.1

Source: Adapted from 1931 Census table in Ghanshyam Shah, *Caste Association and Political Process in Gujarat: A Study of Gujarat Kshatriya Sabha* (Bombay: Popular Prakashan, 1975), p. 9.

proportions of high, middle, lower, and scheduled groups, and of non-Hindus, can be found in Table 8:1. Not only are the percentages approximate, but the assignment of "high," "middle," or "lower" caste is to some extent arbitrary. Moreover, each of the entries is a general classification which may contain many endogamous groups (*jatis*) and there may be great variance in the levels of socio-economic prosperity among their members. I have lumped Patidars and Kanbis together as middle-peasant castes, even though the former inhabit mainland Gujarat and the latter the Saurashtrian peninsula and comprise separate *jati* clusters. I have ranked Rajputs as "high" although the British labelled them "intermediate." Despite their ritual prestige many of them have suffered economically since Independence and the loss of princely privilege. Politically too, Rajputs in Gujarat have been disadvantaged in that they were underrepresented in the nationalist movement and in the Congress after Independence. Subsequently, in a well-known instance of caste "federation," they created the Gujarat Kshatriya Sabha and encouraged Kshatriya identification among lower castes for purposes of electoral gain.[27] Thus "Kshatriyas" include about 30 percent of the population or more, depending on the responses of individual castes.

At the bottom of the social ladder, the Scheduled Castes (Harijans, or ex-untouchables) and Scheduled Tribes (Adivasis) made up approximately 7% and 17% of the population.[28] The Muslim minority accounted for another 8%. By 1972 the demands from "other backward" groups for preferential treatment in education and government jobs equivalent to that given to the Scheduled Castes and Tribes, resulted in the appointment of the Bakshi Commission which identified and recommended for reservation benefits an additional 82 groups labelled "socially and educationally backward."[29] The Congress from Independence onwards strove to bring these deprived groups, especially the Scheduled Castes and Tribes, under its patronage through the reservation policy and extensive networks of Gandhian *sarvodaya* (social welfare) institutions. By the 1970s, however, the patronage links were weakening as a new generation of leaders among the deprived groups began to assert their numerical strength for political gain.

But first it was the turn of the middle peasants. Their frustration was clearly evident in the competition for the Congress(R) chief ministership after the 1972 election. Amidst bitter recrimination regarding who was quickest (or, more opportunistic) in joining Mrs. Gandhi's Congress(R), an ambitious Patidar, Chimanbhai Patel, asserted his claim against those of two Banias, Kantilal Ghia and Ratubhai Adani. Eventually, Mrs. Gandhi picked a less-known Brahmin, Ghanshyambhai Oza, and instructed him to give cabinet posts to the others. The factional war that followed resulted in Oza's overthrow by Patel in 1973, and then in turn the latter's ouster and the dismissal of the entire state assembly in the populist upsurge that rocked Gujarat in 1974.[30]

The debacle of the old Congress in Gujarat was completed in 1975. Threatened by the potential consequences of a fast-unto-death by Morarji Desai, Mrs. Gandhi allowed an interim state election in Gujarat in June. Two parties and one *morcha* ("front") emerged to contest: 1) the

Table 8:2
Gujarat State Assembly Election Results, 1975

Party	Seats	% of Votes
Congress(R)	75	40.7
Janata Morcha:		
Congress(O)	56	23.6
Jana Sangh	18	8.8
Bharatiya Lok Dal	2	1.5
KMLOP	12	11.5
Other parties	3	2.2
Independents	15	11.7
	181*	100.0

Source: *Report on the General Election to the Gujarat Legislative Assembly, June 1975* (Gandhinagar: Chief Electoral Officer, 1975), pp. 34–37.
Note: *One poll countermanded. KMLOP = Kisan Mazdoor Lok Paksh

Congress(R), disgraced and demoralized by the upsurge of 1974; 2) the Kisan Mazdoor Lok Paksh (KMLOP), a new middle–peasant party led by Chimanbhai Patel; and 3) the Janata Morcha, consisting of Morarji Desai's Congress(O), the Bharatiya Jana Sangh, the Bharatiya Lok Dal (mostly ex–Swatantra Party) and some splinter parties and independents. In the event (see Table 8:2), the Congress(R), while emerging as the party with the largest share of seats and votes, was defeated by the Janata Morcha; KMLOP held the balance with 12 seats, but Chimanbhai Patel's personal defeat resulted in KMLOP's cooperation with the Janata governing coalition.[31]

As is well known, the Congress(R) defeat in Gujarat in June 1975 was a significant factor in Mrs. Gandhi's decision to declare an all–India Emergency. For Gujarat politics, however, even more significant were the shifts and splits which now began to take place in caste support for various parties. Generally speaking, Brahmins and Banias who continued to be loyal to Morarji Desai remained with the Congress(O) and thence joined the Janata Morcha; others, often with left–wing ideological leanings, supported Mrs. Gandhi and the Congress(R). The Patidars, who had previously divided their support between the Congress and Swatantra Parties how moved in sizable numbers to the Janata Morcha. Their middle-peasant counterparts in Saurashtra, the Kanbis, divided their support between the Congress(R) and Chimanbhai Patel's KMLOP. Meanwhile, the Kshatriyas, who had earlier been divided in their allegiance to the Congress and the Swatantra Parties, remained divided, but large numbers moved into the vacuum created in Congress(R) by the departure of the Patidars. Many members of Gujarat's deprived communities — the Harijans, the tribals, the Muslims — remained loyal to Mrs. Gandhi's Congress(R), although some observers, in view of the Janata victory, perceived their support to be wavering.[32]

It is difficult to overstate the confusion reigning in the Gujarat Congress(R) both prior to and after the 1975 election. The Gujarat Pradesh Congress Committee (GPCC) had been dissolved along with the Gujarat Assembly in March 1974; an *ad hoc* committee appointed by the Congress High Command in New Delhi struggled for a year to overcome rampant factionalism. Finally, Mrs. Gandhi chose as GPCC(R) President Madhavsinh Solanki, a young Kshatriya who, although loosely associated with the Adani faction, had kept a low profile during the 1974 upsurge. His task was a daunting one: as Pravin Sheth observed, the GPCC(R) had "no party apparatus, no cadre of active members, no party offices in sight in districts for all practical purposes."[33] In office only a few months before the Congress defeat of 1975, Solanki became Leader of the Opposition to the Janata Front government of Babubhai Patel on June 18, 1975. Six days later the President of India issued the Emergency proclamation.

REBUILDING THE CONGRESS PARTY IN GUJARAT, 1975-1980

During the Emergency, the Janata Front government of Babubhai Patel, a Congress(O) stalwart and disciple of Morarji Desai, was initially tolerated by the Center. This was partly because Patel, a pragmatist, concentrated on economic development, efficient administration, and not antagonizing Mrs. Gandhi. But it was also because of the weakness and disarray of the Congress(R). Of the 140 Congress(R) MLAs who had been elected in 1972, only 22 were re-elected as Congress(R) legislators in 1975 and stayed that way once the Assembly was called.

Rebuilding the Congress(R) Party was begun in the summer of 1975 when ex-Chief Minister Hitendra Desai joined and was given the position of GPCC(R) President. There being virtually no organizational wing, however, the real power lay with the Congress(R) legislative wing. Its composition was highly significant: fully two-thirds of the members, most of them new to the Assembly, represented the disadvantaged sections of Gujarati society: lower Kshatriyas, Harijans, tribals, Muslims and "other backward" groups. The Congress(R) had retained its image as the champion of the deprived and vulnerable. This was confirmed in the panchayat elections of November 1975, in which Congress(R) won 2667 seats to Janata's 1719.[34]

Five men exerted influence within the Congress(R) legislative wing, two from outside and three from within. Among the former, Ratubhai Adani from Junagadh, the oldest and most eminent in terms of his record as a nationalist freedom fighter and as a minister since the 1950s in the Saurashtra, the Bombay, and two Gujarat governments, had emerged as the faction leader who defeated Chimanbhai Patel in 1974. Although he still "spoke for Saurashtra" and was widely respected, he had lost much of his following in the 1975 election. The second outsider was Zhinabhai Darji, a long-time Congress activist in Surat District who had built a network of tribal support in south Gujarat and wrested control of that region, Morarji Desai's home base, from Congress(O) and Janata.

Inside the Assembly, Sanat Mehta from Baroda was a talented trade union leader who led the ex-Praja Socialist forces that had entered the Gujarat Congress in the mid-1960s. Another influential was Harihar Khambolja from Kheda District, who had gained fame as a student agitator in the Mahagujarat struggle for an independent state. His main asset was his link to Mrs. Gandhi in New Delhi, forged in the 1950s and 1960s when he worked as a secretary to the All-India Congress Committee.

Adani and Mehta were Banias, Khambolja a Brahmin, and Darji from a "backward" tailoring caste. Although ideologically committed to Mrs. Gandhi, none, save Darji, who was not an MLA, represented the growing strength of the numerically dominant lower caste and minority elements in the Gujarat Congress(R). Thus the most influential figure in the Congress(R) revival was to be Madhavsinh Solanki. He had been a member of four assemblies and had performed well as a Deputy Minister. He was a practising lawyer of the Gujarat High Court and an effective speaker. Although originally from a poor lower Kshatriya family in Broach District, Solanki married the daughter of Ishwarbhai Chavda, a prominent nationalist Kshatriya in Kheda District. Thanks to a scholarship arranged by a Congress district boss, he acquired an education, and, while finishing his law degree in Ahmedabad, became a copy-editor for the *Gujarat Samachar*, and later worked as a publicity officer for the

Ahmedabad Municipality. His Horatio Alger rise coincided with and to some extent was helped by the political rise of the Gujarat Kshatriya Sabha, but whereas the Sabha had supported the Swatantra Party in the 1960s, Solanki had chosen the Congress route. In 1975 he caught Indira Gandhi's eye because he was not identified strongly with any of the factional groupings in the Congress(R) and because his youth and background fitted him well for the leadership of the new Gujarat Congress(R), which was about to make an even stronger bid for the support of the disadvantaged elements of Gujarat society.[35]

By mid–1976, at the Emergency's height, Babubhai Patel's Janata Front government was finally brought down through defections and President's Rule was declared in Gujarat. PR was lifted in December, three months before the Emergency's end, and Madhavsinh Solanki was asked to form a government. The caste composition of his ministry, as compared to that of the Janata ministries which came before and after it, is shown in Table 8:3. Whereas the 1975–76 Janata ministry reflected the dominance of its upper and middle caste support, the Congress(R) ministry gave greater weight to lower caste and more deprived elements. The new Congress(R) ministry had been in place barely three months, however, when the Emergency ended and the Janata Party won the Lok Sabha election of March 1977. Despite a creditable showing by the Gujarat Congress(R) in that election (winning 10 out of 26 seats with 46.9% of the vote, compared to Janata's 16 and 49.5%), Solanki's MLAs were now subject to the same pressure to defect as Patel's had been in 1976. Solanki's government was toppled on April 8, 1977 and Patel's second Janata ministry installed three days later. Its continuing high and middle caste emphasis can again be noted in Table 8:3.

Once more, the Gujarat Congress(R) fell into total disarray, only this time, the party at the national level was in opposition and dividing under the strain of post–Emergency factionalism. The Gujarat Congress(R), riddled with defections, likewise began to experience divisiveness between those who supported Mrs. Gandhi and those who did not. The latter grouped around Kantilal Ghia, who had been named GPCC(R) President prior to the 1977 election, and Hitendra Desai, who had been elevated to the central cabinet in 1976. Ultimately, however, the pro–Indira forces led by Solanki prevailed, just as she did nationally, by intensifying Congress(R) identification with the cause of the poor. This became clear in October 1977 when Mrs. Gandhi, emerging triumphantly from the Janata government's first attempt to jail her, made a tour of south Gujarat and devoted her attention almost exclusively to the

Table 8:3

The Caste Composition of Gujarat's Cabinets, 1975–80

Caste	Janata Morcha Government (Chief Minister: Babubhai J. Patel) June 18, 1975–Mar. 12, 1976 No. of Ministers	Congress(R) Government (Chief Minister: Madhavsinh F. Solanki) Dec. 24, 1976–Apr. 8, 1977 No. of Ministers
Brahmin	4	1
Bania	6	3
Patidar	3	2
Kanbi	1	1
Khatriya	2	4
Harijan	1	2
Adivasi	1	2
Muslim	0	1
OBC*	1	2
Unknown	1	0
	20	18

	Janata Party Government (Chief Minister: Babubhai J. Patel) Apr. 11, 1977–Feb. 17, 1980	Congress(I) Government (Chief Minister: Madhavsinh F. Solanki) Formed June 5, 1980
Brahmin	5	4
Bania	6	1
Patidar	3	1
Kanbi	2	1
Kshatriya	2	5
Harijan	1	2
Adivasi	2	2
Muslim	1	2
OBC*	1	4
	23	22

*OBC = "Other Backward Classes"

scheduled castes and tribes. Decrying Janata "anti-poor" policies, she lunched with Harijan families and visited the location in Bulsar district where Adivasis had, after a long struggle, received at her hand surplus land exactly ten years previously. Escorted by Solanki and Darji through several hundred miles of tribal territory, she spoke everywhere to large crowds; at Surat she addressed a mammoth reception of 200,000 people which the *Times of India* reported "had no parallel in independent India. Old residents recalled the Dandi March as the only comparable occasion."[36]

When Mrs. Gandhi split the Congress(R) in January 1978 and created her own Congress(I) Party, virtually all of the lower caste and minority elements in the Gujarat Congress(R) stayed with her. Significantly, most of the Gujarat Congressmen who decided to support the Congress led by Swaran Singh and Y.B. Chavan were of higher caste. This still left a number of higher caste leaders in the Gujarat Congress(I), such as Adani, Mehta, and Khambolja. But from late 1978 onward, as Mrs. Gandhi made her comeback first in the Chikmagalur by-election and then step by step with the disintegration of the central Janata government, Madhavsinh Solanki and the lower caste/minority elements asserted their influence within the Congress(I) in Gujarat.

Their strength was clearly visible in the general election of 1980 which swept Mrs. Gandhi back to power.[37] In Gujarat, out of 26 available parliamentary seats, Congress(I) took 25; 18 of these were won by lower caste or minority candidates. Madhavsinh Solanki, having regained control of the GPCC(I) presidency and having "delivered Gujarat" in the general election, was now in a position to determine who would be Congress(I) candidates in the sure-to-follow Assembly elections.

THE 1980 ASSEMBLY ELECTION IN GUJARAT: THE "KHAM" STRATEGY

Between the dissolution of the Gujarat Assembly on February 18 and the state election on May 29, 1980, what had already become a reality was given a name. Interestingly, the KHAM strategy was not Madhavsinh Solanki's creation; he has steadfastly maintained that the Congress(I) is "for all the people."[38] Instead, the strategy's authors are generally said to be Zhinabhai Darji, Harihar Khambolja, and Sanat Mehta, the last-mentioned having coined the acronym for "*K*shatriyas, *H*arijans, *A*divasis, and *M*uslims." In Khambolja's words:

"Our thesis was KHAM . . . . We took the results of the '71 [parliamentary], '72 and '75 [assembly] elections, the panchayat elections of '72 and '75, and the '80 [parliamentary] election. We gave these to a professor at Baroda and he did some research. Then we decided the hairsplit of constituencies. After all, before forming a united front, Mao had done a study of the classes in China.

We drew four parallel strips on the map, east to west:
1) from Mt. Abu to Dangs there are Adivasis,
2) next, lower Kshatriyas and backward classes: Vaghris, Rabaris, Thakardas . . .
3) along the railway line and in the big towns: more Kshatriyas, Harijans, Muslims, and a few lower Patels,
4) and, on the coastline, Kharwas, Machimars [fishing communities] and Kolis.

We thought we would give preference to these. We toured twenty days in a month, looking in each constituency for machine leaders, caste leaders, good candidates. In Saurashtra we found more Kshatriyas, backward classes, and lots of dissident Patels opposed to Janata Patels. Everywhere the caste leaders get challenged every five years; we picked up the challengers, the dissidents.[39]

The KHAM strategy, in effect, was an attempt in the best Rikerian tradition to assemble a minimum winning coalition.[40] We should be clear as to its implications for Congress(I) recruitment. First, it did not signify an increase in Harijan or Adivasi nominations, as these were fixed according to the number of reserved seats available. However, a determined attempt was made to find Harijan and Adivasi leaders who would maximize Congress(I) electoral appeal. Secondly, "KHAM" did not refer only to Kshatriyas, Harijans, Adivasis, and Muslims; as Khambolja's account reveals, the acronym was also meant to include representatives of the socially and educationally backward communities named by the Bakshi Commission. Moreover, the strategy did not preclude giving Congress(I) tickets to higher or middle caste candidates: for example, the "dissident Patels" in Saurashtra. But "hairsplitting" implied that wherever close calculation of the caste/communal composition of a constituency indicated that a candidate from one of the

KHAM (or other deprived) groups might attract the minimal votes needed to win, such a candidate would be nominated. This meant that in many cases "recruitment" reverted to the pre–Morris–Jones connotation of selection from above: the Congress(I) went looking for the candidates it wanted. In the end, higher and middle caste aspirants were given tickets in less than two–fifths of the available constituencies. In the eyes of its authors, the KHAM strategy was a practical attempt, via affirmative discrimination, to realize Mrs. Gandhi's goal of uplifting the disadvantaged in Indian society. "We didn't *believe* in caste," said Harihar Khambolja, "we just *used* it."[41]

There are several indications that the Congress(I) state leaders enjoyed a free hand in implementing the KHAM recruitment strategy prior to the 1980 assembly election. The first was that after the Lok Sabha victory of January, the all–India Congress(I) lacked the organizational capacity to screen the "hordes of opportunists" seeking Congress(I) tickets in the nine state elections which followed in May; as a result, the Central Election Committee could exercise only a "perfunctory scrutiny of the thousands of names that [were] being dumped on their desks."[42] Second, although the party high command had declared in March that PCC(I) presidents would not be allowed to contest, an exception was made for Madhavsinh Solanki, who retained the GPCC(I) presidency and contested the election.[43] Yet another indicator that the Center would not interfere in Gujarat was the fact that 51 out of 53 sitting Gujarat Congress(I) MLAs were given tickets.[44]

But what is most noteworthy is the thoroughness with which Congress(I) implemented the KHAM strategy, with regard to both recruitment and getting candidates elected. In 1975 (see Table 8:4) the Congress(R) had run KHAM candidates in 93 out of 182 available seats (51.1%) and got 47, or 50.5% of these candidates elected. In 1980, the Congress(I) ran KHAM candidates in 111 out of 182 available seats (61.0%) and got 96, or 86.5% elected. It should also be noted that non–Congress parties also increased their allocation of tickets to KHAM candidates: in 1975 the leading non–Congress candidate was KHAM in 69 out of 182 available seats (37.9%) and in 1980 the number rose to 78 (42.9%). But this was still far short of the Congress(I) proportion of KHAM candidates, by 13% in 1975 and 18% in 1980. And, whereas non–Congress parties got 31 KHAM candidates elected in 1975 (44.9% of their total), they got only 11 KHAM candidates elected in 1980 (14.1%).

Table 8:4

Developing the "KHAM" Strategy: Congress Versus
Non-Congress Candidates and Victors, 1975 and 1980

Parties	KHAM		NON-KHAM	
	Candidates	Elected	Candidates	Elected
1975				
Congress(R)	93	47	88	28
Non-Congress(R)*	69	31	112	75
	162	78	200	103
1980				
Congress(I)	111	96	70	44
Non-Congress(I)*	78	11	102	30
	189	107	172	74

*Numbers refer to totals of leading non-Congress candidates, i.e. those who
   won the most non-Congress votes in their constituencies.
Source: Adapted from *Report on the General Election to the Gujarat
   Assembly*, 1975 and 1980.

Table 8:5

Gujarat State Assembly Election Results, 1980

Party	Seats	% of Votes
Congress(I)	140	51.1
Janata	21	22.7
Bharatiya Janata	9	14.1
Janata(S)	1	0.6
Other parties	0	1.6
Independents	10	9.9
	181*	100.0

Source: *Report on the General Elections to the Gujarat Legislative Assembly,
   May 1980* (Gandhinagar: Chief Electoral Officer, 1980), pp. 36–39.
Note: *One poll countermanded, and one contested victory for Congress(I)
   Janata(S) = Janata (Secular), led by Charan Singh

As the election results show Congress(I) increased its share of the popular vote by an impressive 10.4% over that won by the Congress(R) in 1975 (see Table 8:2 and 8:5). Much of the explanation of the victory can be found in the breakup of the Janata Morcha combination and the disappearance of KMLOP. The Janata Party rump attracted almost the same proportion of votes in 1980 as the Congress(O) did in 1975 (22.7% and 23.6% respectively). The Bharatiya Janata Party actually increased its share over that won by its predecessor, the Jana Sangh, from 8.8% in 1975 to 14.1% in 1980. But the seat/vote ratio had completely changed. In 1975, 23.6 % of the vote won Congress(O) 56 seats; in 1980, 22.7% won Janata only 21 seats. Similarly, the Jana Sangh had won 18 seats on 8.8% of the vote in 1975 but the Bharatiya Janata Party won only 9 seats on 14.1% in 1980. Meanwhile, whereas 40.7% of the vote in 1975 had won the Congress(R) 75 seats, 51.1 % won Congress(I) 140 seats in 1980. A 10.4% vote share increase, in effect, had brought Congress(I) a 35.7% increase in its seat share in the Assembly. Not only was the opposition divided and weak, but the Congress(I) had implemented a recruitment and electoral strategy which earned it the optimal ratio of seats to votes.

On June 6, 1980, Madhavsinh Solanki's new Congress(I) government was sworn in.[45] Even more than his short-lived first government (see Table 8:3), his second, which incidentally contained only five members with previous ministerial experience, strongly represented the hitherto disadvantaged elements in Gujarati society.

MLA PROFILES: DEPARTURES FROM THE CONGRESS "NORM"

One way of assessing the extent of Congress(I)'s departure from the recruitment norm described by Morris-Jones and Roy is to measure changes in the socio-economic profiles of MLAs since the time when the Congress party was undivided. To do so, we narrow our focus to examine candidates who were not only recruited but also successful at the polls.

On two variables, education and age, I have obtained data from the Gujarat Legislative Assembly *Who's Who* handbooks for all MLAs elected in 1967 and 1980, and with help from officials in the legislative secretariat I have added information on a third variable, caste.[46] Other information is taken from a sample survey of Gujarati MLAs elected in 1980 which I carried out in 1982 for purposes of comparison with data collected in 1968 on MLAs elected in 1967.[47] In the tables that follow, I have included data on non-Congress MLAs as a check against hasty

Table 8:6

Caste Distribution Among Gujarat MLAs, 1967–1980

| | 1967 | | | | 1980 | | | |
| | Congress | | Non–Congress | | Congress(I) | | Non–Congress(I) | |
Caste	No.	%	No.	%	No.	%	No.	%
Brahmin	14	15.1	11	14.7	15	10.7	5	11.9
Bania	22	23.7	11	14.7	9	6.4	4	9.5
Patidar/Kanbi	20	21.5	16	21.3	15	10.7	22	52.4
Other High	1	1.1	0	0.0	5	3.6	0	0.0
Kshatriya	10	10.8	21	28.0	33	23.6	5	11.9
Harijan	4	4.3	7	9.3	12	8.6	1	2.4
Adivasi	15	16.1	6	8.0	27	19.3	2	4.8
Muslim	3	3.2	1	1.3	11	7.9	0	0.0
Other Backward	4	4.3	2	2.6	13	9.2	3	7.1
	93	100.1	75	99.9	140	100.0	42	100.0

Source: Government of Gujarat, *Gujarat Legislative Assembly Who's Who* 1967 and 1980, (Gandhinagar: Gujarat Legislative Secretariat).

generalization about trends among Congress MLAs.

Beginning with the caste of MLAs, Table 8:6 in the proportion of KHAM MLAs in the Congress legislative party, from 38.7% of Congress MLAs in 1967 to 68.6% of Congress(I) MLAs in 1980. The move of the Kshatriyas from the non–Congress parties (in 1967 they were a major element in the Swatantra Party) to Congress(I) where in 1980 they formed the largest single caste segment, can be noted. The rise in the numbers and proportions of Harijans, Adivasis, and Muslims is also clear. A drop in the proportion of high caste Congress MLAs is also evident, although it should be noted that Brahmins and Banias have declined in numbers among non–Congress MLAs also. The Banias' overall position has deteriorated drastically; Brahmins, meanwhile, have held their own numerically in the Congress(I) and are stronger in the Congress(I) than in the non–Congress(I) opposition. But it is the change in the proportion of Patidars/Kanbis which is most striking: between 1967 and 1980 their proportion in the Congress dropped by more than half while their numbers have so increased among the non–Congress parties that they make up fully half of all opposition MLAs elected in 1980.

With regard to MLAs' education (Table 8:7) we find mixed results. There has been a clear rise, strikingly in absolute numbers

Table 8:7

Educational Achievement Among Gujarat MLAs, 1967–1980

| | 1967 | | | | 1980 | | | |
| | Congress | | Non-Congress | | Congress(I) | | Non-Congress(I) | |
Education	No.	%	No.	%	No.	%	No.	%
Non–Matric	39	41.9	31	41.3	69	49.3	20	47.6
Matric	9	9.7	10	13.3	12	8.6	9	21.4
Some College	12	12.9	12	16.0	10	7.1	0	0.0
B.A.	10	10.8	8	10.7	18	12.7	5	11.9
M.A.	3	3.2	1	1.3	3	2.1	1	2.4
LLB	18	19.4	10	13.3	24	17.1	4	9.5
Other Prof'l	2	2.2	3	4.3	4	2.8	3	7.1
	93	100.1	75	99.9	140	99.7	42	99.9

Source: Government of Gujarat, *Gujarat Legislative Assembly Who's Who*, 1967 and 1980. (Gandhinagar: Gujarat Legislative Secretariat).

although less so proportionately, in less–educated Congress MLAs, that is, those with less than high–school matriculation. Nearly half the Congress(I) legislative party elected in 1980 consists of these less–educated MLAs and my impression while interviewing my sample of them was that many have only primary school education. Meanwhile, the proportion of Congress MLAs with graduate or post–graduate degrees has declined only slightly (from 35.6% in 1967 to 34.7% in 1980); the more educated MLAs still remain a sizable minority. (The more educated/less educated proportions among non–Congress MLAs are similar and have also remained relatively constant.) The net effect within the Congress(I) legislative party today is educational polarization, between a minority of MLAs with university degrees and a majority whose formal education is fairly limited. The impression gained during interviews was that the former were more knowledgeable and articulate about state–wide and national issues; the less–educated MLAs were much more parochial, albeit well–versed in the problems of their own constituencies.

When we turn to MLAs' occupations (see Table 8:8), we face a lacuna in *Who's Who* data; in 1967, MLAs' occupations were not listed. According to my sample survey, in 1967 only 36.4% of Congress MLAs and 16.0% of non–Congress MLAs had agricultural occupations; these proportions shot up to 51.1% and 64.3%, respectively, in 1980.[48] This

Table 8:8

Occupation of Gujarat MLAs, 1967–1980

Occupation	1967 Congress		Non–Congress		1980 Congress(I)		Non–Congress(I)	
	No.	%	No.	%	No.	%	No.	%
Agriculture	12	36.4	4	16.0	23	51.1	9	64.3
L.'Lord/Prince	1	3.0	6	24.0	1	2.2	0	0.0
Business	5	15.2	6	24.0	5	11.1	3	21.4
Lawyer	4	12.1	3	12.0	6	13.3	0	0.0
Other Prof'l	2	6.0	3	12.0	3	6.7	1	7.1
Public Work	9	27.3	3	12.0	7	15.6	1	7.1
	33	100.0	25	100.0	45	100.0	14	99.9

Source: Survey of MLAs from 5 disrticts (see note 47).
Note: 1967 n = 58, 1980 n = 59.

marked increase reflects a ruralizing trend in all parties' recruitment; it is more dramatic among non–Congress MLAs because of the Patidar/Kanbi strength among the latter. It should be noted that among Congress(I) MLAs the proportion of urban occupations (business, lawyers, other professional) has only slightly declined (from 33.3% to 31.1%); thus, as with education, there appears to be a polarization, this time between non–agricultural and agricultural occupations in Congress(I). Part of the explanation lies in the sharp drop in MLAs reporting "public work" as their occupation, that is, those who devote themselves to running charitable organizations or Gandhian constructive work, which might be rural or urban.

As regards age, the average age of Congress MLAs in 1980 was 47 (compared to 46 for non–Congress MLAs), exactly the same as the average Congress MLA age in 1967 (non–Congress 45). This suggests that Congress(I), in Gujarat at least, is not as "rejuvenated" a party as Mrs. Gandhi intended. The passage of thirteen years, however, has made for profound changes in political socialization. Whereas the average Congress MLA thirteen years ago was 27 years old when India got its independence, the average Congress(I) MLA today was only 14 in 1947. Over half of the Congress MLAs elected in 1967 had participated in the nationalist movement; among today's MLAs only one in five can claim such participation. In fact, whereas the average year of entry into politics

Table 8:9

Family Structure and Marriage Type of Gujarat MLAs, 1967–1980

	1967				1980			
	Congress		Non–Congress		Congress(I)		Non–Congress(I)	
Structure/Type	No.	%	No.	%	No.	%	No.	%
			Original Family Structure					
Joint	29	80.6	18	90.0	41	87.2	11	91.7
Nuclear	7	19.4	2	10.0	6	12.8	1	8.3
	36	100.0	20	100.0	47	100.0	12	100.0
			Family Structure When Interviewed					
Joint	13	36.1	10	50.0	24	51.1	8	66.7
Nuclear	23	63.9	10	50.0	23	48.9	4	33.3
	36	100.0	20	100.0	47	100.0	12	100.0
			Marriage Type					
Arranged	32	88.9	17	94.4	43	91.5	12	100.0
Choice	2	11.1	1	5.6	4	8.5	0	0.0
	36	100.0	18	100.0	47	100.0	12	100.0

Source: Survey of MLAs from 5 districts (see note 47).

Note: Family Structure: 1967 n=56; 1980 n=59

Marriage type: 1967 n=54; 1980 n=59

(defined as the year in which they first contested any election) for 1967 MLAs was 1947 (non–Congress, 1953), for the 1980 MLAs it was 1965 (non–Congress, 1963). Thus today's Gujarat Congress(I) contains a new generation of MLAs who know little of the fight for independence, or even of the struggle for a separate Gujarat state.

Despite the presence of a new generation, however, there is a surprising lack of change towards more "modern" social backgrounds. As Table 8:9 indicates, whereas among Congress MLAs elected in 1967 80.6% were born in but only 36.1% lived in a joint family at the time I interviewed them, among Congress(I) MLAs elected in 1980 87.2% were born in but 51.1%, when interviewed, lived in a joint family. To put it another way, the earlier trend towards nuclear families has been reversed.

Similarly, whereas among Congress MLAs elected in 1967 88.9% had had arranged marriages, among those elected in 1980, the proportion increased to 91.5%. These limited indicators suggest that today's Congress(I) MLAs may be more "traditional" in their social background than those elected thirteen years ago. In conjunction with the other changes I have noted in caste composition, education, and occupation, they confirm the emphasis on recruitment within a social stratum whose political presence was only weakly felt in 1967.

THE "KHAM" BEFORE THE STORM? SOME IMPLICATIONS OF THE CONGRESS(I) STRATEGY IN GUJARAT

> "In virtually all "new states" political recruitment patterns since independence have been shifting substantially, in terms of class and educational levels and in terms of urban–rural and center–hinterland derivations. Always the shifts have been downward and out, that is, in the directions that broaden and diversify the pool of aspirants."[49]

The development of the KHAM strategy in the Gujarat Congress(I) provides a good illustration of Dwaine Marvick's conclusion, the same one mentioned earlier by Ramashray Roy. The KHAM strategy and its outcome can be seen as logical consequences of democratization and restratification in the Indian political system, deriving from processes of socio–economic change which prompt lower caste and marginal peoples to participate politically in order to get their share of rewards. One result is a legislative party more broadly representative of the society: the 1967–1980 trend in the profile of Gujarat Congress MLAs is clearly in the direction of lower social groups, somewhat less education, increasing agricultural occupations, and overall, more traditional, parochial backgrounds. Surprisingly, then, the new "norm" in Congress recruitment seems to be more "catch–all" than the old.[50] But in order to achieve a greater representativeness of society the Gujarat Congress(I)'s recruitment has become more preferential and exclusive. It reflects the fact that the KHAM elements are no longer prepared to play subordinate or dependent roles in the party. Moreover, just as the KHAM phenomenon is an *effect* of social restratification in Gujarat, we may expect that it in turn will become a *cause* of further restratification as its beneficiaries gain control over political recruitment.

To many this is social justice in action, a form of affirmative discrimination which rights ancient wrongs. To many among the high and middle caste elements in Gujarati society, accustomed to political power commensurate with their socio–economic status, it is a disastrously retrograde development. The KHAM strategy, for them, represents the worst of casteism and the corruption that comes when advancement by merit gives way to advancement by ascription. Moreover, they argue that the KHAM strategy was developed not so much as a response to pressure from below but as a political ploy conceived and manipulated from above by a section of the elite and of the better–off members of the deprived non–elite for their own political gain. Worst of all, the critics complain, the authors of the KHAM strategy have unleashed, right down to the village level, social antagonisms that aggregate into a form of class warfare causing needless bloodshed, the destruction of property, and the undoing of the very social progress they aim to promote.

How much truth is there in these allegations? As an outside observer, one cannot help being impressed by unprecedented levels of alienation from and cynicism towards the Solanki regime in Gujarat. Outsiders, of course, tend to get their information from the intelligentsia, who are generally of higher caste. Apart from their disaffection, however, within the Gujarat Congress(I) itself factional strife has plagued Solanki's government since 1981, leading to the splitting away in late 1982 of a group under Ratubhai Adani's leadership, including eight MLAs and four MPs, to form the Rashtriya Congress.[51] Within the Solanki cabinet, too, according to continual press reports, the dissidence extends to key ministers like Sanat Mehta and the ex–prince of Rajkot, Manoharsinhji Jadeja. Even Zhinabhai Darji, Chairman of the State Twenty Point Programme Implementation Committee, has come out in favour of removing Solanki from office. Such dissidence may simply represent normal Rikerian coalition narrowing; it would be naive to expect total or permanent KHAM solidarity. However, the intra–party quarrelling leaves the Solanki government in a state of constant uncertainty.[52]

The more serious consequence of the KHAM strategy can be found almost daily in press reports of increasing caste and communal tension and violence. The most shocking of these occurred in early 1981 in Ahmedabad and its environs when an agitation by medical students against the Solanki government's implementation of the policy of reserving post–graduate university seats for Scheduled Castes, Scheduled Tribes and the deprived groups named by the Bakshi Commission, escalated into riots in which some forty people, mostly Scheduled Caste, were killed.[53] Elsewhere in the rural mainland, Patidar/Kshatriya animosity has frequently erupted in vendettas in which thugs are hired to destroy property and cut down crops; in south Gujarat, tribal versus non–tribal tension is similarly high. In Saurashtra, the new strength of Kshatriyas in the Congress(I) government has prompted the reassertion of *girasdar* (Rajput landlord) power and increasing dacoity against Kanbis. In a few towns, communal tension has resurfaced as mobilizers of the Vishwa Hindu Parishad react to Muslim political gains alleged to have been bought with Persian Gulf money.

At times, it does appear that the Gujarat Congress(I) has provoked what amounts to class warfare in Gujarat. The KHAM strategy, after all, seems to lump together Gujarat's have–not communities and set them against the haves. The haves, possessing social and economic power but excluded from access to political power in the Congress(I), appear to have nowhere to turn except to the hopelessly weak and divided opposition parties, or to lawless behavior.

A class analysis of Gujarat politics, however, fails to embrace the complexity of what the KHAM strategy has produced. First of all, the Solanki government, despite general public adherence to all–India Congress(I) "socialist" policy, has no revolutionary predisposition. The KHAM strategy is a system–affirming, not a system–attacking strategy; the Solanki government may represent the disadvantaged, but it is a government whose programme is suffused with the Bania ethic. Thanks to industrial spin–offs from oil production in the Gulf of Cambay, the return of Gujarati money from Africa and elsewhere, and the Solanki government's cooperative approach to capitalist enterprise in general, Gujarat, "The Japan of South Asia," is currently riding an economic boom unmatched in the subcontinent.[54] With the resolution of the dispute with Madhya Pradesh over allocation of the Narmada River's waters and the prospect of its irrigation and power benefits, the future looks even brighter. One is led to conclude that it is Gujarat's prosperity, stimulated by the Solanki government's economic pragmatism, which allows the KHAM strategy to continue; in a less affluent state the higher caste backlash would be much more severe.

The second weakness of a class analysis of the KHAM phenomenon is that it misses divisions within the have/have–not groupings which undermine concerted political action by either. The divisiveness of the "haves" is based on inter– and intra–caste rivalry and is exhibited in the fragmentation of Gujarat's opposition parties. But more significantly, the KHAM strategy has exacerbated divisions within each of Congress(I)'s Kshatriya, Harijan, Adivasi, and Muslim constituencies — splitting each, in effect, into a better-off "in" group whose leaders are closely linked to the Solanki government, versus a worse-off "out" group, who are not. For example, among the Harijans, the relatively prosperous Vankar (weaver) *jati* is regarded jealously by the Chamars (leatherworkers), and similar antagonism can be found between landed and non-landed Adivasis. Among the Kshatriyas and Muslims too the more prosperous have close ties to the Congress(I); the worse-off "out" group may turn to opposition parties or strive to displace the "in" group in local Congress(I) organization.

All of this tension and the instability it brings suggests fundamental change in the politics of Gujarat, once described as "gentle."[55] In Gujarat at least, the "norm" of one-party dominance featuring an open, consensual approach to representation and government has been replaced by one which is more restrictive and confrontational. The "older electoral coalition" based on higher and middle caste support and their patronage of lower castes and minorities has disintegrated and dispersed. The new Congress(I) coalition, produced by a recruitment strategy reaching further "downward and out" into Gujarati society than ever before, is not only heavily composed of representatives of disadvantaged groups but, to a unprecedented extent, is controlled by them. Their new hold on political power has been made possible partly by social changes which have eroded, particularly in rural Gujarat, the patron-client ties on which the old Congress was based. More directly, it was the events pursuant to the Congress split of 1969 and the movement of the middle castes to the Janata Morcha which created the opportunity for the KHAM elements to become established in the Congress(I). The implementation of a recruitment and electoral strategy that would strengthen their grip and keep the middle castes in opposition was the next logical step.

The one-party dominance produced by the KHAM strategy, even though based on a "minimum winning coalition," is precarious. This is true not only because of the incongruence of the KHAM coalition's political as opposed to socio-economic power, but also because of the level of de-institutionalization in the all-India Congress(I) and the unpredictability of Mrs. Gandhi in center-state relations. Mrs. Gandhi has so far seen fit not to remove Madhavsinh Solanki as she has done several other chief ministers, but the threat is always there. Several times she has received delegations of Congress(I) dissidents with complaints of corruption and mismanagement against Solanki, but so far, these occasions have been used by Mrs. Gandhi to prevent complacency and evoke demonstrations of loyalty. The Prime Minister must be mindful of the costs of displacing Solanki: in terms of both parliamentary and assembly strength, Gujarat is one of her party's strongholds. Madhavsinh Solanki has the backing of impressive numbers; to sack him would invite even greater factional disorder in the Gujarat Congress(I) and much more damaging political instability in a state which is crucial to India's economic well-being. The KHAM strategy has produced a government which is loyal to Mrs. Gandhi personally, which falls in line with her ideologically, and which is representative of the "weaker sections" that she herself has championed. With more difficult troublespots in mind and with an eye to the elections of 1985, Mrs. Gandhi is likely to let the experiment in "affirmative discrimination" continue in her westernmost state.

NOTES

* The research upon which this paper is based was carried out in Gujarat in 1968-1969, 1973-1975, and 1981-1982, thanks to fellowship support from the Southern Asian Institute, Columbia University, the Shastri Indo-Canadian Institute and the Social Sciences and Humanities Research Council of Canada. The assistance of Pamela Fletcher in preparation of the MLA data is gratefully appreciated. Roderick Church, Atul Kohli, and Ghanshyam Shah were helpful with critical comments on an earlier draft.

1. Myron Weiner, "Congress Restored: Continuities and Discontinuities in Indian Politics," *Asian Survey* 12: 4 (April 1982), pp. 339, 347.

2. For the opening statement, see Girilal Jain's "One Party Dominance Again," *Times of India*, 9 January, 1980.

3. For the original model, see Rajni Kothari, "The Congress 'System' in India," Centre for the Study of Developing Societies, *Party System and Election Studies* (Bombay: Allied Publishers, 1967), pp. 1-18.

4. Myron Weiner, *India At The Polls, 1980: A Study of the Parliamentary Elections* (Washington: American Enterprise Institute, 1983), p. 140.

5. Lloyd I. Rudolph and Susanne Hoeber Rudolph, "Transformation of Congress Party: Why 1980 Was Not a Restoration," *Economic and Political Weekly* 16: 18 (2 May, 1981), pp. 811-818.

6. See, for example, James Manor, "Indira and After: The Decay of Party Organization in India," *The Round Table* 272 (October 1978), pp. 315-324; and "Party Decay and Political Crisis in India," *The Washington*

Quarterly 4: 3 (Summer 1981), pp. 25–40; and Paul R. Brass, "Pluralism, Regionalism and Decentralizing Tendencies in Contemporary Indian Politics," in *The States of South Asia: Problems of National Integration*, eds. A. Jeyaratnam Wilson and Dennis Dalton (Honolulu: The University Press of Hawaii, 1982), pp. 223–264.

7. There are many other useful studies which describe political recruitment or its consequence for the composition of legislatures in the 1960s. See, for example, Ratna Dutta, "The Party Representatives in the Fourth Lok Sabha," *Economic and Political Weekly* 4:1 & 2 (Annual Number, January 1969), pp. 179–189; Duncan B. Forrester, "State Legislators in Madras," *Journal of Commonwealth Political Studies* VII: I (March 1969), pp. 36–57; Stanley A. Kochanek, *The Congress Party of India: The Dynamics of One-Party Democracy* (Princeton N.J.: Princeton University Press, 1968), pp. 267–298, 342–404; and "Political Recruitment in the Indian National Congress: The Fourth General Election," *Asian Survey* 7:5 (May 1967), pp. 292–304; and Richard Sisson and Lawrence L. Shrader, *Legislative Recruitment and Political Integration: Patterns of Political Linkage in an Indian State* (Berkeley: University of California, 1972).

8. W.H. Morris–Jones' most representative work on recruitment is in "Political Recruitment and Political Development," in *Politics and Change in Developing Countries: Studies in the Theory and Practice of Development*, ed. Colin Leys (London: Cambridge University Press, 1969), pp. 113–134, and "Candidate Selection: The Ordeal of the Congress, 1966–1967," in *Studies in Politics: National and International*, ed. M.S. Rajan (Delhi: Vikas Publications, 1971), pp. 33–54, and *The Making of Politicians: Studies From Africa and Asia* (London: The Athlone Press, 1976).

9. Morris–Jones, "Political Recruitment," pp. 113–121.

10. Morris–Jones, "Candidate Selection," pp. 36–37.

11. Ramashray Roy, "Selection of Congress Candidates," Parts I–V, *Economic and Political Weekly* I (31 December, 1966), II (7 January, 1967), III (14 January, 1967), IV (11 February, 1967), and V (18 February, 1967).

12. Roy, II, 7 January, 1967, pp. 21–22.

13. Roy, III, 14 January, 1967, p. 62.

14. Roy, II, 7 January, 1967, p. 22.

15. Roy, IV, 11 February, 1967, p. 376.

16. Roy, "Caste and Political Recruitment in Bihar," in *Caste in Indian Politics*, ed. Rajni Kothari (New Delhi: Orient Longmans Ltd., 1973, reprint), p. 241.

17. See my "Extra–Parliamentary Opposition in India: An

Analysis of Populist Agitations in Gujarat and Bihar," *Pacific Affairs* 48:3 (Fall 1975), pp. 313–334.

18. Stanley A. Kochanek, "Mrs. Gandhi's Pyramid: The New Congress," in *Indira Gandhi's India: A Political System Reappraised*, ed. Henry C. Hart (Boulder: Westview Press, 1976), pp. 105–107. See also Robert L. Hardgrave, Jr., *India: Government and Politics in a Developing Nation* (New York: Harcourt Brace Jovanovich, Inc., 1980, 3rd edition), p. 214.

19. James Manor, "Party Decay and Political Crisis in India," p. 31. See also Paul Wallace, "Centralization and Depoliticization in South Asia," *Journal of Commonwealth and Comparative Politics* 16:1(March 1978), pp. 3–21.

20. Myron Weiner, *India at the Polls: The Parliamentary Elections of 1977* (Washington, D.C.: American Enterprise Institute, 1978), p. 15.

21. Manor, "Where Congress Survived: Five States in the Indian General Election of 1977," *Asian Survey* 18:8 (August 1978), pp. 785–803.

22. See my "British versus Princely Legacies and the Political Integration of Gujarat," *Journal of Asian Studies* (forthcoming).

23. For background on Gujarat politics, see D.N. Pathak, M.G. Parekh and K.D. Desai, *Three General Elections in Gujarat: Development of a Decade, 1952–1962* (Ahmedabad: Gujarat University, 1966); Howard L. Erdman, *Political Attitudes of Indian Industry: A Case Study of the Baroda Business Elite* (London: The Athlone Press, 1971); and *Politics and Economic Development in India* (Delhi: D.K. Publishing, 1973); Thomas Pantham, *Political Parties and Democratic Consensus* (Delhi: MacMillan, 1976); Pravin N. Sheth, *Patterns of Political Behaviour in Gujarat* (Ahmedabad: Sahitya Mudranalaya, 1976); and A.H. Somjee, *Democracy and Political Change in Village India* (New Delhi: Orient Longman, 1971), and *The Democratic Process in a Developing Society* (New York: St. Martin's Press, 1979).

24. On Gujarati caste, see A.M. Schroff and R.G. Schroff, "The Vahivanca Barots of Gujarat: A Caste of Genealogists and Mythographers," in *Traditional India: Structure and Change*, ed. Milton Singer (Philadelphia: American Folklore Series, 1959), pp. 40–70; David F. Pocock, *Kanbi and Patidar: A Study of the Patidar Community of Gujarat* (Oxford: Clarendon Press, 1972); Jan Breman, *Patronage and Exploitation: Changing Agrarian Relations in South Gujarat, India* (New Delhi: Manohar Publications, 1979, reprint); and I.P. Desai, *Untouchability in Rural Gujarat* (Bombay: Popular Prakashan, 1976).

25. On the role of the Patidars in Congress, see Anil Bhatt, "Caste and Political Mobilization in a Gujarat District," in *Caste in Indian*

Politics, ed. Rajni Kothari (New Delhi: Orient Longmans Ltd., 1973, reprint), pp. 299–339, and Myron Weiner, *Party-Building in a New Nation: The Indian National Congress* (Chicago: University of Chicago Press, 1967), pp. 69–91.

26. Ghanshyam Shah, *Caste Association and Political Process in Gujarat: A Study of Gujarat Kshatriya Sabha* (Bombay: Popular Prakashan, 1975).

27. See *ibid.*, and Rajni Kothari and Rushikesh Maru, "Federating for Political Interests: The Kshatriyas of Gujarat," in *Caste in Indian Politics*, ed. Rajni Kothari (New Delhi: Orient Longmans Ltd., 1973, reprint), pp. 70–101.

28. See Ghanshyam Shah, *Politics of Scheduled Castes and Tribes: Adivasi and Harijan Leaders of Gujarat* (Bombay: Vora, 1975).

29. *Report of the Socially and Educationally Backward Class Commission* (A.R. Bakshi, Chairman), Vols. I and II (Gandhi Nagar: Government of Gujarat, 1976).

30. See Dawn E. and Rodney W. Jones, "Urban Upheaval in India: The 1974 Nav Nirman Riots in Gujarat," *Asian Survey* 16:11 (November 1976), pp. 1012–1033, and Ghanshyam Shah, *Protest Movements in Two Indian States* (Delhi: Ajanta Publications, 1977).

31. Ghanshyam Shah, "The 1975 Gujarat Assembly Elections in India," *Asian Survey* 6:3 (March 1976), pp. 270–282.

32. *Ibid.*, pp. 273, 279–282.

33. Sheth, *Patterns of Political Behaviour in Gujarat*, p. 135.

34. However, the Janata was able to win a majority of seats in municipal elections in the same year. *Ibid.*, p. 140.

35. Interviews with Solanki, 12 December, 1968, 19 February, 1969, and 24 February, 1982.

36. *Times of India*, 6–9 October,1977.

37. For the parliamentary results in Gujarat, see Weiner, *India At The Polls, 1980*, pp. 93–94. .

38. Interview with Solanki, 24 February, 1982. See also *Times of India* (Ahmedabad), 28 December, 1982.

39. Interview with Khambolja, 16 July, 1981.

40. William H. Riker, *The Theory of Political Coalitions* (New Haven and London: Yale University Press, 1967), pp. 32–76. It was more than "minimum" if one reckons the KHAM plus other backward castes to comprise about 70 percent of the Gujarat population. But not all members of KHAM castes would vote Congress(I) and non–Congress parties would also run KHAM candidates (see Tables 8:1 and 8:4).

41. Interview with Khambolja, 16 July, 1981.

42. Inder Malhotra, "State Assembly Polls: Much Heat and

Dust," *Times of India,* 24 April, 1980.

43. *Times of India,* 24 April, 1980.

44. *Times of India,* 1 May, 1980.

45. *Times of India,* 7 June, 1980.

46. Government of Gujarat, *Gujarat Legislative Assembly Who's Who (as on 1st December, 1967)* (Ahmedabad: Gujarat Legislature Secretariat, 1968), and Government of Gujarat, *Sixth Gujarat Legislative Assembly (1980–1985) Who's Who,* (Gandhinagar: Gujarat Legislature Secretariat, June 1981).

47. The sample consisted of all the MLAs from five of Gujarat's nineteen districts: Bhavnagar and Rajkot in Saurashtra, Kheda and Surat in the central–south mainland, and Mehsana in north Gujarat. In 1967 it comprised 58 MLAs out of the assembly total of 168 and in 1980 64 MLAs out of 182. Tests of the sample against *Who's Who* data for all MLAs indicate a high degree of representativeness.

48. Although numerous MLAs reported their occupation as "agriculture" in 1980, my impression was that while agriculture provided their principal source of income, few actually tilled their land.

49. Dwaine Marvick, "Political Recruitment and Careers," in *International Encyclopedia of the Social Sciences,* ed. David L. Sills, Vol. 12 (New York: MacMillan Company and The Free Press, 1968), pp. 275.

50. The non–Congress parties may also be following this trend in recruitment, although not as avidly and not with the same electoral effect.

51. *Times of India* (Ahmedabad), 27 December, 1982.

52. "Solanki Gov't Weathers the Storm," *Times of India* (Ahmedabad), 7 February, 1983, and "Solanki's Dilemma," *The Week* (Cochin), 9–15 October, 1983, p. 38.

53. See I.P. Desai, "Anti–Reservation Agitation and Structure of Gujarat Society," *Economic and Political Weekly* 16:18 (2 May, 1981), pp. 811–818, and Devavrat N. Pathak, "Reservation: The Real Issues," *AmdaVadmA* (Ahmedabad), 10 (June, 1981), pp. 15–19.

54. See "Special Report: Industrialization in Gujarat," *Business India* 74 (5–18, January 1981), pp. 49–57; "The Gujarat Blueprint," *Business World* 1:11 (17–30 August, 1981), pp. 26–39; and Madhavsinh Solanki, "A Japan in South Asia," *Indian Express* (Ahmedabad), 14th Anniversary Special Supplement, 25 February, 1982.

55. Myron Weiner, "India: Two Political Cultures," in *Political Culture and Political Development,* eds. Lucian W. Pye and Sidney Verba (Princeton, N.J.: Princeton University Press, 1965), p. 200.

9
Conclusion: The Pattern of State Politics in Indira Gandhi's India

Roderick Church

The previous chapters tell us a great deal about what has been happening in seven Indian states since Indira Gandhi first came to power in 1966. They testify to the wonderful diversity for which India is so famous. The question which remains is whether they do anything more than this. Do they suggest any general pattern to the development of state politics in Indira Gandhi's India?

Although I think they do, readers can answer this question for themselves. One advantage of the previous chapters is that they do not share a common framework. This rewards us with studies which reflect the particular circumstances of individual states and enlarge our view of Indian politics. They also alert us to the ways in which our conclusions will depend on our historical and theoretical perspectives. As Manor points out for Karnataka, our views about political continuity and change in just one state will depend on the times we compare (he suggests three turning points) and on our definition of political "normality" (he offers five options). Other authors offer still more possibilities. As a result, the previous chapters raise more questions than they answer and they leave comparative interpretation open in a way that studies within a single framework could never do.

I say this by way of warning. What follows is not a summary, nor is it the only way to compare the seven states. In fitting the individual states into a larger picture, I try to stand back from personalities and the twists and turns of political life — not because I think these things are unimportant, but because case studies can easily make too much of them. Comparative analysis requires us to overlook much of what makes situations unique. This is its cost. As compensation, it allows us to examine the importance of broader socio–economic and institutional influences and to see whether the conclusions about one state have wider application.

To begin, I want to point to two crises, two turning points which have given rise to instability and confusion in Indian politics. Both crises run throughout the period since Indira Gandhi came to power and both are central concerns in most of the previous chapters. The more fundamental of these is a participation crisis. The more visible one is a crisis in the party system.

THE PARTICIPATION CRISIS

The current participation crisis is simply the latest stage in a long process in Indian politics. Over the last century, group after group has become politicized and forced the equations of political power to be recalculated. For many, especially the Muslims and the Scheduled Castes and Tribes, this struggle for recognition is far from over. Even the middle castes in north India have yet to receive what they consider their due. All these groups continue to be an important part of the current crisis. Yet what is new in recent years, and what gives the current situation much of its distinctive character, is the focus of the participation crisis among the lower castes.

Since there is some inconsistency and ambiguity in the previous chapters regarding caste terminology, I want to be clear about the meaning of "lower" castes, especially to avoid confusion with terms like "backward" castes.[1] In the following pages I will distinguish four caste categories. The "upper" castes, the "high" castes, or the "twice–born" castes are the Brahmins, Kshatriyas and Banias. They have long dominated society and politics as landlords in the countryside and as businessmen and professionals in the city. The "middle" castes are the principal farming castes (Jats, Yadavs and Kurmis in the north, for example; Marathas in Maharashtra, and so on). According to caste tradition they are Sudras, the term for all those below the twice born and above the untouchables, but they have special status and importance because of their numbers and land. Typically they are *kisans* (farmers, or middle peasants). At the bottom of the traditional status hierarchy are the "scheduled" castes, the ex–untouchables who now have special constitutional protection and privileges. They are primarily agricultural laborers.

The "lower" castes form an economic and social stratum which is sandwiched between the middle castes above them and the Scheduled Castes below. It is composed of marginal farmers, sharecroppers, and landless laborers from low status agricultural castes together with the traditional service and artisan castes — barbers, boatmen, blacksmiths, carpenters, fishermen, grain–parchers, oil–pressers, and so on. The proportion of people in this stratum varies from region to region, but it is usually about a third of the population (see Table 9:1).[2] Because individual castes are usually small and widely dispersed, as well as poor, the lower castes find it difficult to develop a common sense of identity or to assert much political power on their own.

The lower castes are the last stratum to be brought into politics — a point which deserves some comment. It is a common observation about Indian politics and politics generally that political participation has been expanding downwards to include ever lower social strata. But India does not follow this pattern exactly, primarily because the Scheduled Castes and Tribes, the poorest and most oppressed segments of the India population, received special recognition and privileges at Independence. For the rest of the population, participation has spread in the expected way, from upper castes in the city, to upper castes in the countryside, to the middle castes. By the 1960s, the only people systematically excluded from a share of political representation and policy benefits were the castes below the middle castes and above the Scheduled Castes. And they wanted a larger share of state power and its rewards. Not surprisingly, dominant groups have tried to resist, redirect, and exploit this potential shift in political power. This is evident in new levels of violence and corruption, in populist appeals to the "poor," in calls for law and order, in the emergence of regionalism, in struggles over reservations for the "backward classes," and in the efforts of political parties to recruit representatives from the lower castes.

Because the lower castes have both economic and status interests, they can be mobilized for political purposes in several ways. One is a straightforward appeal to their economic interests. This means getting them to see themselves as "the poor" and to recognize their affinity with the Scheduled Castes and Tribes who have a somewhat similar economic position but who are below them in the traditional status hierarchy. This is easier said than done. The traditional "feudal" ties between the lower castes and the middle and upper castes and the natural desire of people to

Table 9:1

Caste and Community in Seven States

	U.P.	Bihar	W.B.	Kerala	Karnataka	Maharashtra	Gujarat
Caste Hindus							
Upper	19	13	11	5	5	5	13
Middle	12	18	9	13	32	40	12
Lower	31	30	32	31	34	23	44
Scheduled Castes	22	15	20	9	15	6	8
Scheduled Tribes	–	9	6	1	1	8	14
Muslims	15	13	20	20	11	8	8
Other Religions	1	3	1	21	3	10	1

Source: Figures for Scheduled Castes and Tribes and for religious minorities are based on data from the 1971 Census. Figures for the different categories of caste Hindus are estimates only. For further details on sources and the construction of this table, see discussion and notes 1 and 2 below.

Note: Figures are percentages. Totals may not equal 100 because of rounding.

identify with those who have more status work against class consciousness and populist mobilization of the lower castes.

Other ways of mobilizing the lower castes rely on recognizing their status aspirations as well as their economic interests. One way is for a hard–pressed upper caste group to recruit their support by offering them upper caste status. The Kshatriya movement in Gujarat is an example of this rare phenomenon. More common is the attempt to establish a link between the middle castes and lower castes as fellow members of the "backward classes" or "backward castes" in opposition to the upper castes. Although the presumption of shared economic interests is an important part of the appeal of the "backward" label, so is the willingness of the middle castes to acknowledge a shared status with the lower castes — something they have not always been ready to do. A third possibility is to emphasize the regional community. When upper and middle castes appeal to the lower castes and say that we are all Telegus or Bengalis and that we must be united in our fight against New Delhi, they grant the lower castes an equality of status which they have not traditionally had. If this call to share a broader community identification can be coupled with arguments which blame outsiders for the economic difficulties of a region and the poor, it will be particularly appealing to lower castes.

The basic problem with any of these attempts to unite the lower castes with the castes above them is that the coalition will contain real differences in economic interests, and the lower castes may soon find that others are reaping most of the rewards. Since the lower castes cannot in most cases easily mobilize on their own behalf, they must find other leadership. They can respond to the populist appeals and more concrete enticements of Indira Gandhi's Congress, but they can also be drawn to more radical alternatives, as well as to the regional parties. The net effect is to make political coalitions more fluid and to add a new element of uncertainty to party politics. This brings us to the crisis in the Congress, a party which celebrates its centenary in 1985 and which must provide the focal point for any discussion of change in the party system and the way Indian politics works.

THE CRISIS IN THE CONGRESS

The Congress has been in almost continual crisis since Indira Gandhi came to power. The party has twice done badly in elections (1967 and 1977) and followed this both times by splitting in two (1969 and 1978).

Following the splits, again in both cases, Indira Gandhi and her Congress confounded the experts by winning stunning victories in national elections (1971 and 1980) and recapturing power in nearly all the states. As new general elections approach, there are signs (reminiscent of the mid-1970s) that Indira Gandhi and the Congress are losing authority once more. So striking is the parallel that many people speculate about another Emergency or major constitutional changes to forestall defeat.

To understand some of the changes in the party system and the Congress under Indira Gandhi, we need a baseline for comparison. The obvious one is the middle 1960s, just as Indira Gandhi was coming to power within the "Congress system." Most analysts of the Congress state parties in this period agreed that the Congress was controlled by elite social and economic interests. This came in several guises. In the north (most clearly in Bihar and Uttar Pradesh, but also in Gujarat and West Bengal) the upper castes dominated, with the middle castes in a secondary role, and the Muslims and Scheduled Castes in a still more subordinate position. Only the lower castes were excluded almost entirely. In the Deccan (Maharashtra and Karnataka in this book) the pattern was different. Here large landlords were less common, the proportion of upper castes was lower, and anti-Brahmin movements had already forced Brahmins to the sidelines. This left the Congress in the control of the middle castes — or, more accurately, in the hands of elite segments of these castes. As in the north, only the lower castes were systematically shut out of politics.

Politicking over scarce resources still flourished under these patterns of domination, but the situation is well described by Lele's phrase "elite pluralism and class rule."[3] The openness and competitiveness of the political arena worked primarily to ensure that different segments of the elite could get a share of state resources and build their patronage networks. Policies to benefit the poor were usually stillborn or administered in such a completely biased way that they helped the rich as much or more than the poor.

Despite much academic discussion during the mid-1960s about the "Congress system" and the self-perpetuating features of India's model of dominant party politics, the Congress was already in crisis when Indira Gandhi came to power. It is important to remember this if one is inclined to blame her for later destroying a strong and well-functioning party. The party was increasingly out of touch with society. Voter support had dropped in 1962 and in later by-elections. In 1967 the Congress captured only 41 percent of the national vote and only 54 percent of the seats in parliament. In the states, it lost power in the far south (Tamil Nadu and Kerala) and throughout the north. Clearly, the Congress system did not work, and it did not work in part because the existing patterns of domination were being challenged by those who appealed to the lower castes and the poor.

One way to see what has happened to the Congress since 1967 — and to link it to the participation crisis — is to focus on Indira Gandhi's bold attempt to remake the party in a more progressive or populist mold. This began in late 1969 when she split the Congress, identified herself with the poor and the minorities, and championed such causes as bank nationalization and the abolition of privileges for princes. The process of change accelerated when she won a sweeping victory in the 1971 national elections with the slogan "abolish poverty." This victory was a personal triumph for her and her populism, not for party organization. Her Congress(R) did as well or better in states in which most of the old Congress had aligned against her (Gujarat, Karnataka) as it did in states in which much of the existing Congress organization had rallied to her cause. In March 1972, after the Bangladesh war, the Congress(R) won sweeping victories in most of the states.

These electoral victories, and her obvious personal popularity, put Indira Gandhi in a position to select chief ministers and to begin to remake the character of the state Congresses. "Socializing" the party was one term for the changes. She made it clear she wanted more policies which appealed to the poor and more representation in the party from the minorities, the Scheduled Castes and the lower castes. Whether she realized all the implications of what she was doing or not, Indira Gandhi and her populism were both accelerating and adapting to the new political importance of the lower castes.

If she had succeeded, Indira Gandhi would have moved Indian politics slightly to the left, won the support of the poor and lower castes and ensured herself a secure political future. Of course, she had not succeeded, at least not completely. As the previous chapters make clear, state Congresses have gone very different ways — sometimes supporting progressive social and economic change, sometimes supporting the status quo and repression — and the future of the Congress is hardly secure anywhere. Why should this be so? Why had Indira Gandhi's strategy of the early 1970s failed?

Before proceeding, however, I want briefly to consider the usefulness of assuming, as I do in the following pages, that Indira Gandhi set out to remake the Congress in a more progressive mold and that she has continued to do so where circumstances have permitted. This does not mean I assume that a more progressive Congress was her only goal. Like most politicians, Indira Gandhi's first concern is to remain in power. Nonetheless, I am inclined to accept her commitment to a more progressive Congress in 1969 and the following years. As it turned out, a progressive image proved to be good politics. But this was not obvious at the time, and it seems unfair to reduce her populism to political opportunism. A progressive image fitted her better than it fitted most other Congress leaders. And there can be no doubt that she did try to move the Congress in a new and more progressive direction in the early 1970s.

But what about more recently? Even if one accepts her populist commitment in the early 1970s, one can argue that this was soon dissipated with the ascendancy of Sanjay Gandhi or in the years out of power in the late 1970s. And it is true that in recent years the Congress has come to rely more and more on traditional structures of local power and on Indira Gandhi as a symbol of "mother India." Still, I think it obscures our understanding to argue that the current crisis of the Congress is simply the result of Indira Gandhi's perversity, or changes in her motivations or her centralization of power. For one thing, the populist impulse is not dead. Wood shows that the Gujarat Congress — with Indira Gandhi's support — is still a progressive force. Lele also relates how Indira Gandhi made continuing efforts in the early 1980s to bolster populist politicians in the Maharashtra Congress. This suggests to me that for purposes of analysis we can assume some consistency in what Indira Gandhi would prefer to achieve if she could. The advantage of this assumption is that it invites us to look beyond Indira Gandhi and to examine the circumstances in different states if we want to understand what has happened to the Congress.

CONTINUITY AND CHANGE IN THE STATES

If we review the previous chapters in terms of the two crises, we can, I think, make two general distinctions. First, there are those states in which lower castes have achieved positions of power in the legislature and government and where government policy to some extent addresses the concerns of the poor. These include West Bengal, Gujarat, Karnataka,

Kerala and (perhaps to a lesser extent) Maharashtra. Uttar Pradesh and Bihar remain states where the lower castes have made little progress. Second, among states in which the lower castes have made the most progress, there are those in which the Congress has taken the initiative in recruiting the lower castes and bringing change. These include Karnataka, Gujarat and Maharashtra. These distinctions result in three groups:

Bihar	Gujarat	Kerala
Uttar Pradesh	Karnataka	West Bengal
	Maharashtra	

Although these groupings will not cause much surprise among students of Indian politics, it is worth considering them in a little more detail.

Bihar and Uttar Pradesh. India's two largest states, lying side-by-side on the north Indian plain, share many social and economic characteristics. In the 1980s they are also similar in the way that upper castes continue to dominate politics and the Congress, just as they have always done. This does not mean the middle castes are excluded from power. For example, in Bihar by the early 1960s, middle castes had about 20 percent of the legislative seats and cabinet positions, or slightly more than their proportion of the population. The problem was that the upper castes had almost half of these positions – three or four times their proportion of the population.[4] The story of politics in these two states in recent decades is not about the incorporation of the lower castes into the structure of power. The lower castes continue to be excluded. The story is about the struggle of the middle castes to win greater recognition, to get more attention to their interests as *kisans,* and to expand into non-agricultural occupations now dominated by the upper castes.

Brass focuses on this story in U.P., and in particular on Charan Singh and his following of Jats and other middle castes. According to Brass, Charan Singh's decision to leave the Congress in 1967 changed the style of U.P. politics by bringing certain policy debates into the open. It did less to change the substance of policy, because the various governments which involved Charan Singh's followers necessarily contained representatives of other interests. Although Singh sought to speak for all "backward" castes, Brass shows how the clear differences of interest between the middle and lower castes made this difficult. Yet the Congress, with its traditional bases of support among the upper castes, Scheduled Castes and Muslims, was not able (or willing?) to mobilize the lower castes either. When the U.P. Congress, like Congresses elsewhere, did promote some populist programs during the 1970s, the upper castes apparently made little effort to draw the lower castes into the party and the adminstration. At most this was a populism of noblesse oblige which left the upper castes firmly in control.

The Bihar story, despite differences in detail, produced remarkably similar results. For example, the middle castes did not leave the Congress as they did in U.P., but in 1970 when the upper castes in the U.P. Congress were undermining a coalition government headed by Charan Singh, the upper castes in the Bihar Congress were doing much the same thing to the middle castes and a middle caste chief minister in their own party. As in U.P., the upper castes made sure they retained control of the Congress. Even though Bihar has produced a popular lower caste leader, this has not made much difference. As Blair shows, the attempts of Karpoori Thakur to promote the "backwards" during the Janata regime were effectively checked by upper castes within the Janata as well as the Congress. With the return of the Congress to power, there is no question about upper caste dominance. The caste composition of the Bihar cabinet under Jagannath Mishra in 1980 was, for example, almost identical to that under K.B. Sahay in the middle 1960s.[5]

Karnataka, Gujarat and Maharashtra. Although these states share a common parent in the old state of Bombay, it is a bit unusual to link the three of them together. The reason for doing so here is that they are states where the lower castes and the interests of the poor achieved some political recognition and where the state Congresses have assisted this process and remade themselves in a more progressive image. In short, as far as Indira Gandhi's goal of the early 1970s is concerned, these states come closest to being success stories. That they are no more than partial successes shows just how difficult it can be for politicians to build new and stable bases of support.

According to Manor, the changes in Karnataka's politics came quickly in the early 1970s under the leadership of Devaraj Urs. Urs remade the Congress by recruiting minorities and the lower castes, thereby reducing the political domination of the middle castes. He also incorporated lower caste people into the civil service and effectively pursued some policies which benefitted poorer sections of the population. If Urs had stayed with Indira Gandhi in 1979, this pattern may have been consolidated further. As it turned out, Manor argues, Urs miscalculated on her chances of survival, and since 1980 Karnataka has been thrown into a period of "confusion" in which parties are less distinct in their bases of support and where the incompetent administration of Gundu Rao resulted in the defeat of the Congress in the 1983 state election. However — and this is important — the inclusion of the lower castes and more progressive governmental policies may be here to stay. Both the Congress and the Janata Party, Manor says, now appeal to the lower castes, and the Janata regime has continued some of the progressive policies of the Urs years.

The transformation of Gujarat politics began in a more confused fashion in the early 1970s when the Congress was unable to achieve internal unity and eventually lost power. Even at this time, however, the Congress was moving towards a new constituency based on minorities and the lower castes. In the late 1970s, as Wood shows, this became known as the KHAM strategy, and it has become the basis for a thoroughly remade Congress party under Madhavsinh Solanki. It is not clear whether this remade Congress has been effective in redistributing the rewards of politics in Gujarat, but the increasing violence in the countryside and the objections to reverse discrimination suggest that it has. In this sense the transformation of Gujarat politics has proceeded less smoothly than in Karnataka, and Wood has real doubts about the ability of the Congress to manage the process of change within the traditions of civility which characterize Gujarati politics. Yet, as in Karnataka, there is also evidence that some of the changes in Gujarat are here to stay. Although the Congress is the leading edge of change, Wood's data show that the opposition is also appealing to the KHAM communities. No matter who wins in future, the lower castes are likely to be better represented in Gujarat politics than they were in the past.

Maharashtra has changed less than Gujarat or Karnataka since Indira Gandhi came to power, but Lele shows that it has changed. Because most of the Maharashtra Congress sided with her in 1969, Indira Gandhi tried to alter the party by encouraging lieutenants of Y.B. Chavan to strike out on their own. V.P. Naik, the Chief Minister and a tribal, obliged and was successful in recruiting lower castes into the legislative party and in pursuing some progressive policies. In 1980 the attempt to remake the Congress was carried forward by A.R. Antulay, a Muslim. Again he had some success in reducing the hold of the Marathas, but Lele argues that the established elites of the Maratha caste (the pluralists) were able to accommodate the dissidents and the lower caste newcomers (the populists) without even seriously disrupting the system. Just how far this accommodation has gone remains an open question. The pluralists have maintained their structures of local power and frustrated attempts by the populists to build new ones. Populism, Lele suggests, may have "peaked" short of any significant change, and Indira Gandhi now appears reconciled, at least until the next election, to "live with pluralism." Still, the Congress includes some lower caste people, and government policy addresses some of the specific problems of the poor.

Kerala and West Bengal. These two states are often linked in discussions of Indian politics because they have elected communist governments. The additional reason for linking them here is that the lower castes are now heavily involved in politics through the Communist Party (Marxist). Kerala and West Bengal are also the two most densely populated states, and both have a high proportion of religious minorities and Scheduled Castes and Tribes. Yet there are very real differences in their politics. Caste and communal loyalties are relatively unimportant in West Bengal; in Kerala they are a central feature of political life.

What has happened to state politics since the late 1960s is also strikingly different. Politics in Kerala has changed scarcely at all. As Varkey notes, it was and remains a matter of coalitions. Both the Congress and the Communists attempt to rule by winning the support of several minor parties which are based on caste, religion and ideology. The situation in the 1980s is almost exactly what it was in the 1950s. In West Bengal, on the other hand, politics has changed as much or more than it has anywhere else in the country. The Congress has lost its position of dominance and politics has become polarized between the Congress and the CPM, which has now won two successive elections (1977 and 1982).

This difference between continuity in Kerala and change in West Bengal can be explained in part by the different initial positions of the lower castes and poor in politics. In Kerala — and in this the state is unique among the states considered in this book — the lower castes and the poor were already mobilized by the late 1950s. This helped to set the pattern of politics at that time and it left little room for the Congress to develop new bases of support in the 1970s. The CPM already had the support of the lower Hindu castes and the Congress was caught in its role as a middle class and predominantly Christian party.

In West Bengal, the initial situation was much like that in north India. The Congress was a marriage of urban commercial interests and rural landlords and rich peasants who could still control the poor beneath them. The CPM, as Kohli stresses, was essentially a party of the intelligentsia and the urban areas. Then, in the late 1960s and the early 1970s, the Congress failed to move beyond its traditional bases of support.

The CPM did not make this mistake. From its urban base it reached out to the countryside and the lower middle and lower classes. Although the CPM won the 1977 elections for many of the same reasons that non–Congress parties won everywhere in north India, it continued to establish itself with exactly that group which Indira Gandhi had hoped to mobilize — the lower classes and castes of the countryside. This, plus moderate and effective government, enabled it to withstand the national momentum back to Indira Gandhi in 1980.

UNDERSTANDING LOWER CASTE PARTICIPATION

The political arrival of the lower castes can come in many ways — through the Congress, through the CPM or through other political parties. This suggests that the processes at work in the political mobilization of the lower castes go well beyond the cut and thrust of partisan battles for power. With this in mind we can consider lower caste participation in politics as something to be explained in its own right, irrespective of the ways it gets represented in the party system. There are two major questions to ask. The first concerns the general rate of change. Why have the lower castes and the interests of the poor been incorporated more quickly into the politics of some states than others? The second concerns the ease with which this transformation takes place. Why does it proceed more smoothly, with less violence and turmoil, in some places than others?

Probably the most important answer to both questions is economics — the inherited structure of inequalities and the general level of development and prosperity. It is no accident that Gujarat, Karnataka, Kerala, Maharashtra and West Bengal are among India's more econom- ically developed and socially advanced states, while Uttar Pradesh and Bihar lag at the opposite end of the continuum (see Table 9:2). For the poor, development leads to new hardships, new expectations and new opportunities for change. It accelerates the rate at which they become politicized. At the same time, general economic growth and prosperity eliminate the need for the bitterness of zero–sum politics. It makes it possible to meet new demands without having to harm the existing positions of anyone else. In Gujarat, for example, Wood suggests that the general prosperity of "the Japan of South Asia" has prevented a more serious backlash against the rapid political rise of the lower castes. By contrast, U.P. (especially the eastern half) and Bihar are poor with slow rates of growth. Blair documents this well for Bihar. With a history of large landlords, and in the absence of development, repression and

Table 9:2

Literacy, Urbanization and Income in Seven States, 1971

	Literates per 1000	Urbanites per 1000	SDP in Rs. per capita
Maharashtra	392	312	809
Gujarat	358	281	829
West Bengal	332	249	735
Karnataka	315	243	685
Kerala	604	162	564
INDIA	295	199	638
Uttar Pradesh	217	140	486
Bihar	199	99	402

Source: Literacy and urbanization figures are based on the 1971 Census.
SDP (State Domestic Product) figures are for 1970–71 and are from
the *Reserve Bank of India Bulletin,* 35:9 (September 1981), p. 821.

"feudal" relationships continue to give upper castes a claim on lower caste
loyalties and votes.

The caste system and traditions of caste exclusiveness also
combine with economic factors to influence lower caste mobilization. In
explaining the success of the CPM in penetrating the countryside and
mobilizing the poor and lower castes, Kohli emphasizes the relative
weakness of caste domination in West Bengal. He attributes this to both
the general weakness of caste in the state and the practice of absentee
landlordism which make it difficult to maintain "feudal" relationships.
Kohli's implicit contrast is with states like U.P. and Bihar, where there is a
somewhat larger proportion of upper castes, a strong correspondence
between caste and class, and a weak reform tradition within Hinduism.

The interesting thing about the weakness of the caste system as an
explanation for lower caste mobilization is that it can be extended to the
other states where the lower castes have been successful in moving into
politics. For example, Kerala is a special situation as far as the lower
castes are concerned. First, there is a large Christian and Muslim
population and a smaller proportion of upper and middle caste Hindus.
Second, most of the lower castes are from a single caste (the Ezhavas) and

they are concentrated in certain areas. The first factor weakens the structures of domination, the second facilitates organization.

In Karnataka, Maharashtra and Gujarat, the relatively ready acceptance of the lower castes in politics may be due to a less rigid caste system and a more ambiguous division between middle and lower castes. This comes about in different ways in the three states, but compared with the situation in north India, these states are more alike than different. This is clearest in Karnataka and Maharashtra where the proportion of high castes is small and where political power in the first decades of independence already rested with the large middle castes who led anti-Brahmin movements. The anti-Brahmin movements had the effect of uniting the middle and lower castes in a common cause. The middle castes themselves have also been relatively open. The Lingayats (more a sect than a caste) in Karnataka and the Marathas in Maharashtra are both large and rather elastic identifications which have important internal divisions. In Gujarat the Kshatriya movement has produced a somewhat similar situation. By linking upper caste Rajputs and lower castes together in a quest for political power, it has blurred the status differences between upper and lower, and united many lower castes by giving them a common identity. Gujarat is also like Kerala in the sense that there is one very large lower caste (the Kolis) and this facilitates political mobilization.

If economics and the caste system give us a better understanding of why lower caste participation occurs when and where it does, this is not to deny the importance of politics. In their quest for support and power, leaders and parties can encourage or oppose the lower castes and their demands. And politics can be crucial in managing change. It determines how the interests of the poor will be articulated (through the Congress or an opposition party, for example) and it can help to determine whether the change will come peacefully or violently. In short, politics helps to determine whether change comes within the existing institutions and conventions of political life, or whether it produces a crisis in public order and the party system.

UNDERSTANDING THE CONGRESS DILEMMA

If Indira Gandhi had had her way in the years following 1969, she would have used her populism to harness lower caste support to the traditional support of Muslims and Scheduled Castes and thereby build herself a new base of political power. Although she succeeded in some .

places and at some times, the general lesson of state politics since 1972 is that this strategy can go awry in many ways. State Congresses can be resilient to change (U.P. and Bihar) or they can lose lower caste support to the CPM (Kerala and West Bengal). Even where the Congress is successful in initiating change or adapting to the new importance of the lower castes (Karnataka, Gujarat and Maharashtra) this is no guarantee of long–term success.

To understand how the partisan pressures of politics have played a role in what has happened, we can begin with U.P. and Bihar, two states where the lower castes have not made a political breakthrough. Why has Indira Gandhi not pushed harder for changes in these states — as she did in Maharashtra, for example? One answer, already suggested, is that these states were not really ready for change. But this cannot be the whole explanation, especially since it was the troubles of the Congress in places like U.P. and Bihar in the late 1960s which helped lead to the split in the Congress and to Indira Gandhi's populism. Another part of the answer may be the precarious position of the Congress. Ever since she became Prime Minister, the Congress has been weak in Bihar and U.P., and it continues to be weak (see Table 9:3). In the early 1970s the Congress(R) had slim majorities in the U.P. and Bihar assemblies. This gave Indira Gandhi and her proteges very little room to maneuver and it helps to explain why it was so difficult to remake the Congress in these states. In the 1980 state elections, the Congress won a comfortable majority in U.P., but its majority remained slim in Bihar, and the percentage of the vote in both states remained low. Again, there was little room to maneuver.

The irony, of course, is that without a new base of support the Congress in U.P. and Bihar remains vulnerable. It continues to rely on traditional structures of local power.[6] In the short run only the lack of unity among the opposition keeps Congress in power. In the long run, as the lower castes become more important politically, the Congress may well find that it has lost its opportunity to remake itself.

Karnataka, Maharashtra and Gujarat presented very different structures of opportunity for Indira Gandhi. These states were Congress strongholds in the 1960s and they responded well to Indira Gandhi's call in the 1971 election to "abolish poverty." The Congress(R) votes in Karnataka and Maharashtra in 1971 were by far the highest of all the fifteen major states, and even in Morarji Desai's Gujarat the Congress(R) did well. The public response to the new populism indicated that these states were ready for change and it made state politicians eager to follow

Table 9:3

Congress Electoral Success in Seven States

Election	U.P.	Bihar	W.B.	Kerala	Karnataka	Maharashtra	Gujarat
1962 National	38	44	47	34	53	53	53
1962 State	36	41	47	–	50	51	51
1967 National	33	35	40	36	49	49	47
1967 State	32	33	41	35	49	47	46
1971 National	49	40	28	20	71	63	45
1971–72 State	–	33	49	–	52	56	51
1974–75 State	32	–	–	–	–	–	41
1977 National	25	23	29	29	57	47	47
1977 State	32	24	23	20	–	–	–
1978 State	–	–	–	–	44	18	–
1980 National	37	36	37	26	56	53	55
1980 State	38	34	–	18	–	45	51
1982–83 State	–	–	na	12	40	–	–

Sources: Most figures are from the reports of the Election Commission. Figures for the 1974–75 state elections, the 1980 national election and the 1982–83 state elections are from various other sources, including the previous chapters in this book.

Notes: Figures are percentages. "–" means no election. Figures for the years from 1971 to 1977 are for the Congress(R); from 1978 onwards they are for the Congress(I).

Indira Gandhi's directions to remake the party.

If Karnataka and Gujarat ultimately took more readily and completely to Indira Gandhi's populist strategy than Maharashtra did, this may have an additional "political" explanation. In Maharashtra most of the Congress sided with Indira Gandhi at the time of the party split in 1969. By contrast, in Karnataka and Gujarat the state Congresses sided almost completely with the Congress(O). In 1971 they were the only states in India with Congress(O) governments. After her 1971 victory, this gave Indira Gandhi and her followers a relatively free rein to build a new base for the Congress(R) in these two states. The spectacular support for Indira Gandhi in Karnataka and the success of Devaraj Urs in excluding "defectors" from getting tickets in the 1972 elections may even help explain why rebuilding the Congress(R) on a new basis proceeded more quickly in Karnataka than Gujarat.

In any case, the state elections in 1972 produced massive legislative majorities for the Congress(R) in Karnataka (76 percent), Gujarat (84 percent) and Maharashtra (81 percent). This left Indira Gandhi and her followers freer to push for more change. There was no danger that a small faction could obstruct change with the threat to bring down the government. The high levels of support for the Congress in later elections (even in 1977!) provided continuing support for Indira Gandhi's populist direction in these states. They may also provide some confirmation of its success. There are many explanations for the marked difference between north and south India in support for the Congress in the 1977 elections, but another one which deserves consideration is the Congress' success in establishing itself among the lower castes in the south.

For Indira Gandhi, Karnataka and Gujarat teach an important lesson about political performance. Even when the Congress is successful in establishing itself as a progressive party with the support of the lower castes, the advantage can be temporary. The pressures of poor harvests and internal quarrels brought an embarrassing (if temporary) end to Congress rule in Gujarat in 1974. In Karnataka a chief minister of dubious competence produced a similarly embarrassing defeat in 1983. Several chapters of this book agree that voters are sophisticated enough to demand some performance along with the rhetoric of populism.

Karnataka also demonstrates the most fundamental weaknesses of a populist strategy directed at the lower castes. If there is a general willingness to accommodate the lower castes, others can play the same game as the Congress, and sometimes with extra advantages. In explaining what he calls the "confusion" in the social bases of Karnataka parties after 1983, Manor may place too much emphasis on Devaraj Urs' decision to break with Indira Gandhi. Manor assumes that a rational party cannot hope to please everyone, and that normally it must restrict its social base. Yet, under certain circumstances, competitive party politics can lead to widespread recruitment and catch–all coalitions. Gujarat suggests this possibility. There the opposition has attempted to match the Congress in recruiting support from the lower castes. Even if Urs had stayed with Indira Gandhi, the opposition may have attempted to recruit its own supporters among the lower castes. Regionalism – which is on the increase in Karnataka – can be an especially potent force for doing this.

The importance of regionalism is well illustrated in Andhra Pradesh, where a film star, N.T. Rama Rao, and his new regional party, the Telegu Desam, defeated the Congress in 1983. In many ways developments in Andhra in the 1970s and early 1980s paralleled developments in neighboring Karnataka and Maharashtra, and for many of the same reasons. The sudden success of the Telegu Desam came in part from its ability to attract lower caste support and beat the Congress at its own game.[7] It did this by combining populism with a fresh (less corrupt) image and a strong appeal to regionalism. Because regionalism appeals to the status interests of the lower castes as well as to their economic concerns, the combination with populism is particularly potent. All Indira Gandhi and the Congress can do in reply is to supplement populism with cries of "India in danger" and use central powers to undermine the state government.

Kerala and West Bengal suggest that attempts to remake the Congress along more progressive lines had little chance of success in competition with a strong leftist party like the CPM. Either the CPM already had the support of the lower classes and castes (Kerala) or it was in a better position to mobilize them (West Bengal). In other states Indira Gandhi's Congress could legitimately claim to be more progressive than its most serious rivals. In Kerala and West Bengal this was not the case, and the CPM had the advantage of a disciplined organization with which to extend its base.

Stated this way, the conclusion is undoubtedly too simple. The Congress can compete with the CPM. For example, in Kerala the Congress ruled in a coalition with the CPI in the 1970s, and it was able to broaden its base and establish its progressive credentials. Then, in 1978, the newer and more progressive elements in the party sided against Indira Gandhi. This group, the Congress(S) associated with A.K. Antony, eventually joined with the CPM and CPI in the 1980 elections and helped form the Left Democratic Front government. As Varkey explains, when the CPM provoked a confrontation on behalf of the poor, Antony rejoined forces with the Congress(I) in defence of law and order. Although the result demonstrates the inherent limitations in Congress' commitment to the poor and the lower castes, there is no reason why the Congress has to represent reaction when it is locked in a duel with the CPM. In the 1982 election, the Congress in Kerala argued with some success that it represented the poor as well as law and order. If the Congress can make good this claim, if it can achieve some mildly progressive changes while maintaining political order, it has a future in states like Kerala.

Unfortunately for the Congress, it cannot monopolize the theme of orderly progress. As Kohli shows, in the process of consolidating its position and running a government in West Bengal, the CPM has lost its revolutionary edge. It accepts the constraints of the capitalist economy and it promotes policies which are mildly progressive rather than radical. In some ways it has become the sort of party which Indira Gandhi said she wanted to build. The difference is that the CPM has a strong party apparatus with collective leadership and a disciplined cadre. This makes it much more cohesive and much less subject to capture by conservative forces than any Congress(I) organization can hope to be. It also makes it more capable of bringing about orderly change — so much so that urban commercial interests in West Bengal can conclude that a CPM in power may be better than a CPM out of power. This points to a real dilemma for the Congress.

CONCLUSION

At this time there is no way to tell when the crises in participation and the party system will resolve themselves. Both crises are long-term ones. They have been going on since Indira Gandhi came to power and they are far from over.

The general outcome of the participation crisis is perhaps the easier to predict — in the long run at least. The lower castes will receive a modest place in the structures of power, and state governments will pay somewhat more attention to the poor than they have done in the past. This shift has already taken place in several states. It may be delayed and eventually come with more difficulty in states like U.P. and Bihar, but time is on the side of the economic and political forces which are driving the participation crisis forward. This does not mean that we should expect any basic changes in India's political economy. Representatives of the lower castes will be as much co–opted by existing elites as they will challenge them. Even where there seems to be the most potential for radical change, in states like West Bengal and Kerala, the constraints of Indian capitalism and democratic politics limit the possibilities for change.

The outcome of the continuing crisis in the Congress and the party system is very unclear. Indira Gandhi deserves credit for accelerating the incorporation of the lower castes into politics and moving politics in a more progressive direction in many parts of the country. But she has been unable to use populism to remake the Congress and provide herself with a reliable base of support. In Bihar and U.P. the Congress continues largely unchanged in character and its position remains weak. In other areas the Congress has seen its populist claim on the lower castes challenged successfully by those on the left, especially the CPM, and by parties which can offer their own combination of populism and regionalism. This had led the Congress to stress law and order (against the left) and nationalism (against the regionalists) in addition to populism. Whether this will be enough to ensure the political survival of Indira Gandhi and the Congress remains to be seen.

NOTES
1. The most troublesome distinction is between the middle and lower castes. The distinction I make between the two is consistent with the discussions by Brass (Uttar Pradesh), Lele (Maharashtra) and Manor (Karnataka). It is also very close to the categories which Blair (Bihar) and Wood (Gujarat) use. Blair usually uses the broad term "backwards," but he sometimes recognizes the distinction between the middle and lower castes within this category. He does so explicitly in his 1980 article (see note 4 below) where he distinguishes "upper backward" (what I call "middle") and "lower backward" castes. For Gujarat, Wood uses the term "Kshatriya" to cover both a few upper caste Rajputs and many lower castes, but he also uses the general distinction between middle and lower castes. For Kerala and West Bengal there is greater ambiguity. Varkey divides Hindus in Kerala into high, middle and low. His "high" category consists of what I would call upper (mostly Brahmin) and middle (Nair) castes, his "middle" corresponds to my "lower" category and his "low" to the "scheduled" category. Kohli makes little use of caste in his discussion,

and it is true that the distinction between middle and lower castes is more problematic in West Bengal than in other states.

2. Since the 1931 census was the last to include caste, there are many problems in determining the proportion of lower castes in the population, quite apart from the difficulty of deciding the ranking of particular castes. In general, I proceeded by elimination. First, using 1971 Census data, I calculated the proportion of religious minorities and Scheduled Castes and Tribes. The remainder, I assumed, constituted the proportion of caste Hindus. I then divided them, using various sources, according to their proportion of the population in the 1931 Census. I determined the proportions of upper castes (Brahmin, Kshatriya, Bania, Kayastha) and middle castes. The remainder, I assumed, was the proportion of lower castes. The middle castes used in these calculations are as follows: Uttar Pradesh (Jat, Yadav, Kurmi), Bihar (Yadav, Kurmi, Koiri), West Bengal (Mahisya), Kerala (Nair), Karnataka (Lingayat, Vokkaliga), Maharashtra (Maratha), and Gujarat (Patidar, Kanbi). In addition to the papers in this volume, I have consulted: 1931 Census data for Uttar Pradesh; Myron Weiner, ed., *State Politics in India* (Princeton, N.J.: Princeton University Press, 1968), especially the chapter by Marcus Franda on West Bengal; Iqbal Narain, ed., *State Politics in India* (Meerut: Meenakshi Prakashan, 1967), especially the chapter on Kerala by D.B. Mathur and others and the chapter on Maharashtra by V.M. Sirsikar; Ghanshyam Shah, *Caste Association and Political Process in Gujarat* (Bombay: Popular Prakashan, 1975), and Harry Blair's 1980 article (see note 4).

3. Jayant Lele, *Elite Pluralism and Class Rule: Political Development in Maharashtra, India* (Toronto: University of Toronto Press, 1981).

4. Harry W. Blair, "Rising Kulaks and Backward Classes in Bihar: Social Change in the Late 1970s," *Economic and Political Weekly* 15:2 (12 January, 1980), pp. 64–74.

5. Haridwar Rai and Jawahar Lal Pandey, "State Politics in Bihar: A Crisis of Political Institutionalization," *The Indian Journal of Political Science*, 41:3 (July–September 1981).

6. Paul R. Brass, "National Power and Local Politics in India: A Twenty–year Perspective," *Modern Asian Studies*, 18:1 (February 1984), pp. 89–118.

7. M. Shatrughna and G. Narayana, "Social Background of Telegu Desam Legislators," *Economic and Political Weekly*, 18:52–3 (24–31 December, 1983), pp. 2204–5.

Index

Abdullah, Farooq, 5–6

Abdullah, Sheikh Mohammed, 5

Adani, Ratubhai, 204, 206–207, 220

Adik, Ramrao, 185–188

Adivasis, *see* Scheduled Tribes

agriculture, in Bihar, 53–62; Karnataka, 147–148, 159–160; Kerala, 15; Maharashtra, 172–173, 179, 181; Uttar Pradesh, 24–30, 33–35, 37–38, 40–46; in West Bengal, 94–96. *See also* Green Revolution, irrigation, landholding, landless laborers

Akali Dal, 3–4

All-Assam Students' Union, 4–5

All India Muslim League, 106, 108, 112, 127–128

Andhra Pradesh, 15, 18, 54, 58, 165, 193, 247

Antony, A.K., 110–111, 113–115, 121, 248

Antulay, A.R., 169, 183–185, 187–188, 190–191, 239

Anushilan group, 87–88

Assam, 3–5

backward classes, 14, 196, 230–233, 235–238, 249–250; in Bihar, 64–71; Gujarat, 204–206, 211, 215, 220; Karnataka, 150–153, 155–156, 158–160; Kerala, 122; Maharashtra, 175, 180, 183, 185, 192, 196; Uttar Pradesh, 24, 27–28, 39, 42–43, 46, 47; West Bengal, 81, 86, 89

Bahuguna, H.N., 24, 36

Bakshi Commission, 204, 211, 220

Bangarappa, S., 151–157

Banias, 23, 202, 204–205, 207, 215, 221, 230

bhadralok, 82–85, 87

Bharatiya Janata Party (BJP), 13; in Gujarat, 214; Karnataka, 151–152; Kerala, 125–127, 131, 137. *See also* Jana Sangh

Bharatiya Kranti Dal (BKD), 21–24, 34–41, 46–49, 51

Bharatiya Lok Dal (BLD), 46–47, 205

Bhindranwale, Sant Jarnail Singh, 4

Bhosle, Babasaheb, 169, 183–184, 187–188

Bhumihars, 6, 26, 62–63, 165

Bihar, 10, 12, 14, 53–79, 230, 232, 235–236, 239–240, 242–243, 247; agriculture in, 54–62; atrocities against Harijans, 68–69; caste and politics, 62–71; Green Revolution in, 55–62; landholding in, 57–60; rise of backward castes, 64–68; state domestic product 53–54

Bommai, S.R., 152–155

Bose, Subhash, 84

Brahmins, 230, 234, 243; in Bihar, 62–63, 66; Gujarat, 202–203, 205, 215; Karnata-

251